Truth is my country

Truth is my country

Portraits of Eight
New England Authors

HILDA WHITE

DOUBLEDAY & COMPANY, INC.
GARDEN CITY, NEW YORK

Designed by Wilma Robin

Grateful acknowledgment is made for the use of the following copyrighted material:

Excerpts from *Ancestors' Brocades: The Literary Debut of Emily Dickinson* by Millicent Todd Bingham. Reprinted courtesy of Harper & Row, Publishers.

Excerpts from *The Portable Thoreau*, edited by Carl Bode. Published by the Viking Press, Inc.

"The Figure a Poem Makes" from *Selected Prose of Robert Frost*, edited by Hyde Cox and Edward Connery Lathem. Copyright 1939, © 1967 by Holt, Rinehart and Winston, Inc.

Excerpts from *A Swinger of Birches* by Sidney Cox. Copyright © 1957 by New York University Press, Inc. Reprinted by permission of New York University Press, Inc.

Excerpts from *Edwin Arlington Robinson, A Biography* by Hermann Hagedorn. Published by Macmillan, 1938. Reprinted by permission.

Excerpts from *The Correspondence of Henry David Thoreau*, edited by Walter Harding and Carl Bode, © 1958 by New York University Press. Reprinted by permission of New York University Press.

Excerpts from poems ⚡797, ⚡657, ⚡754 copyright 1929, © 1957 by Mary L. Hampson, poems ⚡674, ⚡1705 copyright 1914, 1942 by Martha Dickinson from *The Complete Poems of Emily Dickinson*, edited by Thomas H. Johnson. Reprinted by permission of Little, Brown and Company.

Excerpts from *The Letters of Emily Dickinson* by Thomas H. Johnson, editor. Reprinted by permission of the publishers, Cambridge, Mass.: Harvard University Press, 1958.

Excerpts from poems ⚡313, ⚡613, ⚡783, ⚡1129, ⚡1331, ⚡1498, ⚡1535 from *The Poems of Emily Dickinson*, edited by Thomas H. Johnson. Copyright 1951, 1955 by The President of Fellows of Harvard

Inc. Reprinted by permission of Holt, Rinehart and Winston, Inc.

Excerpts from *Walden and Other Writings* by Henry David Thoreau. Courtesy of Random House, Inc.

Excerpts from *A Week on the Concord and Merrimack Rivers* by Henry David Thoreau. Courtesy of publisher Houghton Mifflin Company.

FOR JEAN
*my sister, whose gift to me on my
tenth birthday of Longfellow's
Collected Poems started a never-
ending journey.*

To all who have helped this project along the way, the author wishes to express her appreciation. I am indebted to Norma Millay for her generosity in granting permission to quote from copyrighted poems and letters, and for reading the Millay chapter and offering helpful comments; also to Mrs. Harold W. Holt, niece of Edwin Arlington Robinson, whose warm hospitality opened for me at Head Tide, Maine, the childhood home of the poet. To Mrs. Helen Purdy and Mrs. Eleanor Weirman of the Hart Memorial Library, Shrub Oak, New York, a special thanks for their patience in helping in the collection of research materials; to David Walker, who was our student guide through Bowdoin College during a literary tour of New England, I also express appreciation. To Dr. Annette Rubinstein for loan of materials and for her constant encouragement when the going seemed rough; to Barbara Greenman and George Shively for editorial guidance; to Sybil Kaufman who aided in the research and collection of photographs; to Dorothy McKittrick and Bernice Berkowitz for assistance in obtaining permission to use copyrighted material I am deeply grateful.

Last, but far from least, I give thanks to my daughter, Julie, who though busy with college assignments voluntarily proofread my entire manuscript for technical errors. Her unflagging enthusiasm and belief in this project through three long years strongly contributed to its fruition.

HILDA WHITE

CONTENTS

Nathaniel Hawthorne
page 1

Ralph Waldo Emerson
page 29

Henry David Thoreau
page 63

Harriet Beecher Stowe
page 99

Emily Dickinson
page 131

Edwin Arlington Robinson
page 177

Edna St. Vincent Millay
page 207

Robert Frost
page 237

Bibliography
page 275

Index
page 279

ILLUSTRATIONS

FOLLOWING PAGE 76

Nathaniel Hawthorne
"The Old Manse," Concord, Massachusetts

Ralph Waldo Emerson
Concord, Massachusetts, in Emerson's boyhood
Concord Bridge

Henry David Thoreau
Thoreau's home, Concord, Massachusetts
Concord River

Harriet Beecher Stowe
Violence in the 1840s
Civil Disobedience in 1851

FOLLOWING PAGE 196

Emily Dickinson
The Dickinson house, Amherst, Massachusetts

Edwin Arlington Robinson, 1888
Edwin Arlington Robinson, 1916

Edna St. Vincent Millay
Camden, Maine
Edna St. Vincent Millay, being escorted to prison

Robert Frost
Robert Frost at Franconia, New Hampshire
The farmer-poet in Vermont

Country . . . a shape of each man's mind . . .
An inward vision

JAMES RUSSELL LOWELL
from "Under the Old Elm."

And I believed the poets; it is they
Who utter wisdom from the central deep,
And listening to the inner flow of things
Speak to the age out of eternity.

JAMES RUSSELL LOWELL
from "Columbus."

Truth is my country

Nathaniel Hawthorne
(1804–1864)

"I, a Watchman."

One day in the year 1825 a slender, dark-haired young man freshly graduated from Maine's Bowdoin College boarded the stagecoach in Brunswick which was to take him home to his mother's house in Salem, Massachusetts. As the coach got underway his feelings were strangely mixed. Although he was relieved to have at last completed the four years of higher education urged upon him and paid for by a generous uncle, he was not looking forward to confronting this uncle or any other member of his family with the news that under no circumstances would he now pursue any further studies leading to such respectable professions as medicine or law. Indeed, he had made up his mind to try his luck in a field barely considered a profession at all.

More than one relative and teacher had warned him that writers in America dared not depend upon the pen alone: Washington Irving and William Cullen Bryant both had taken up law before venturing into the literary world. Even James Fenimore Cooper, son of a well-to-do squire, served two years in the Navy, then struggled at farming his own land to make his finances secure before becoming a novelist. It was unthinkable, people said, that any healthy, well-educated young man should spend his time only at writing, especially if the welfare of others was his responsibility. But, nursing a stubborn streak of ambition, twenty-one-year-old Nathaniel Hawthorne determined not to heed such talk—he was going home now to dare the unthinkable.

No bells welcomed him to Salem. No voices other than that of his two spinster sisters. A brief walk took him into the shadows of the starkly plain house where his recluse mother, enveloped in black, sat waiting for him in her upstairs room. In this house, built by his grandfather in the seventeenth century, shut in with these companions, he would remain for as long or as short a time as it would take to prove not only his talent, but the dignity of writing as a profession. That day would come, young Hawthorne vowed, when his labors would make the bells of Salem ring, and perhaps—he often dreamed of it—the bells of all America.

Salem today is a busy, crowded, thriving industrial town not dependent upon its harbor. In its early history all roads led to the sea. The windows of the town looked out upon the harbor. Children hung about the wharf watching sturdy little merchant ships unload their wealth of cinnamon and sugar. Women watched for the return of husbands, brothers, or sons who had sailed off to the West Indies or the Mediterranean. Men not away at sea were for the most part prosperous shipowners and merchants. In those days it was talk of sea weather, return of vessels from distant lands, talk of life at sea or death at sea that made for conversation.

Every Salem schoolboy could recite the glorious tales of his village. The first American ship for Calcutta and China had sailed from Salem. Salem ships had opened American trade with New Holland and the South Seas. During Revolutionary times, ships, often four tiers deep, crowded into port, their captains having made the name of Salem famous by their exploits against the British. But its sea history was not Salem's only source of pride. The village boasted America's first millionaire, Elias H. Derby, "King Derby" as the newspapers called him. The Crowninshields, the Grays, the Peabodys, whose Salem mansions visitors viewed with awe, were families influential far beyond New England borders. Indeed, as a writer in *Harper's New Monthly Magazine* later commented, prosperity had made these Salem merchants so giddy in their sense of power that they, even more than the southern slaveholders, firmly believed they constituted the nation.

When Nathaniel Hawthorne was born on the auspicious date, July 4, 1804, young boys were still being brought up on Guthrie's *Geographical Grammar*, taking their lessons aboard ship before they were in their teens, some rising to captain before they were twenty. There seemed every likelihood that this newest arrival into the Hawthorne family would follow in the footsteps of grandfather, uncles, and father, all seamen. The boy's mother, eighteen-year-old Elizabeth Clarke Manning, watched as did other Salem wives for her husband's ship to return; and she, like many another, knew at last what it meant to wait in vain. In 1808, when

Nathaniel was barely four years old, news came that the beloved husband and father who in good health had sailed for Surinam had died there of yellow fever.

Stunned with grief, young Mrs. Hawthorne locked herself away into her room from which she was seldom to emerge throughout the forty years she lived thereafter. It was an act destined to have a profound effect upon her three young children, Elizabeth, Louisa, and Nathaniel. With one blow they had, in effect, lost both parents. They were also destitute, for the dead sea captain had left little property. Mrs. Hawthorne's family, the Mannings, owners of a prospering stagecoach business, offered assistance which the young mother was forced to accept. But the blow to her pride for doing so did not help to ease her suffering. Her retreat began to take on aspects of martyrdom, the folly of which her son would later dwell upon as one of the tragic consequences of Puritan heritage.

At the moment, however, he was merely an observant, somewhat self-willed little boy overseen by doting aunts and uncles. As his father's death had left him the last of the male Hawthornes, lessening the likelihood that he would be apprenticed for the sea, the women of the family were much relieved. But the boy knew how to use the sea as a weapon. "I'll run away to sea and never return!" he would threaten whenever he wanted to have his own way.

But the tragedy did not altogether mar Nathaniel's happiness. "All through our childhood," his sister Elizabeth said in later years, "we were indulged in all convenient ways and were under very little control except that of circumstance." The "very little control" was exactly the way of life pleasing to Nathaniel who passionately cherished personal freedom. Without the constant supervision of his mother, and with a boy's talent for getting around his aunts, he was often free to wander along the wharf where, among the sights and sounds of the port, he picked up exciting tales with which to entertain his sisters at the meals they took alone, for their mother did not join them even then.

The boy's flair for telling stories was almost as great as his passion for listening to them. Especially did he like to hear old family legends. Consciousness of himself as an indigenous American began very early in Hawthorne's life. Time and again he heard from his elders that the name Hawthorne had always been one to reckon with in Salem.

Big, blustery William Hathorne (the earlier spelling of the family name) had been the first to arrive, sailing from England in 1630 with

Winthrop on the fair ship *Arbella*. When William wasn't fighting off
Indians or, as magistrate, making treaties with them, he was dealing out
justice as he and his God-fearing colonial townsmen understood the meaning of the word. Salem annals record Magistrate Hathorne causing one
Ann Coleman to be lashed at the tail of a horse; John Flint to be hung
for murdering an Indian; and numerous unnamed citizens sent to the
stocks for violations of the Puritan code. In due time William's son,
John, also became a magistrate, sitting in judgment in 1692 over accused
"witches," one of whom, Rebekah Nurse, reputedly put him under a
curse, shouting as she was being taken to her doom, "I am no more
witch than you are wizard. If you take away my life, God will give you
blood to drink." The curse had hung heavy over Hawthorne heads ever
since, such ills as financial loss, bad health, sudden death inevitably
being attributed to it.

Often in his wanderings when he would hear the wind off the sea
make the naked trees creak up on Gallows Hill, Nathaniel would look
in awe to that piece of American earth where an ancestor of his had
helped send nineteen persons to their death. He felt somehow personally
responsible for the ghosts of Gallows Hill, the gnawing at his conscience
seeming to him *his* share of the witch's curse.

It has been said of Hawthorne that he had a private key to tradition.
Coming by it early in his childhood, he knew its value and never
consciously lost it. With this key he was to find himself as a man; with
it, through his art, unlock the meaning of his family history as a symbol
of the entire New England experience. But to those who knew him best
as a young boy, such depth of awareness was far from apparent. He seemed
entirely fun-loving, spoiled, bent only upon selfish activities, doing his
utmost to avoid all responsibility, all chores and organized study.

At eight years of age he was confined to his room for months by a
minor foot injury, having malingered long past recovery, as he himself
later admitted, so as to be free from work and school. No one was
happier than he when his mother's financial difficulties forced her to
abandon her house in Salem and take up residence in an old farmhouse
owned by the Mannings in Raymond, Maine, for now not even the
aunts would be close by to hover over him. In Raymond he was free to
roam at will, no one there apparently even remembering that he was
supposed to go to school.

This state of affairs the boy hoped fervently would go on forever.
Behind the farmhouse lay deep woods through which, gun in hand, he

could follow bear tracks. Closer by meandered a stream bordered by an overhanging rock (afterward known as "Nat's Rock") from which he could fish to his heart's content. For skating in winter there was great Lake Sebago. On inclement days he always found some nook in which to read or daydream. Raymond was a wilderness in which a boy could feast on freedom, a wilderness destined to haunt Hawthorne's memory throughout his life.

> I ran quite wild and, I doubt not, would have willingly run wild till this time, fishing all day long or shooting with an old fowling piece, but reading a good deal too on the rainy days, especially in Shakespeare and the Pilgrim's Progress and any poetry or light books within my reach. Those were delightful days, for that part of the country was wild then, with only scattered clearings and nine-tenths of it primeval woods.

Running wild ended when Uncle Robert Manning, who had been a youth of twenty when Nathaniel was born, came forward to take a hand in his nephew's upbringing. Nathaniel, he said, must begin to take life more seriously, must settle down to studies. "I am sorry you intend to send me to school again," the wily boy wrote to his uncle, "Mother says she can hardly spare me." But this time no charm or trick saved him from the classroom.

First he was sent to a country school in Raymond to make up back work, then returned to Salem where, at age fifteen, he was still not reconciled to organized study. "I have begun to fit for college under Benjamin L. Oliver, Lawyer," he wrote mournfully to his mother who had remained in Raymond. "You are in danger of having one learned man in your family. Shall you want me to be a minister, doctor, or lawyer? A minister I will not be. Oh, how I wish I was again with you with nothing to do but to go a-gunning. But the happiest days of my life are gone."

Grown more reflective in adolescence, he replaced gun with pen, took to "scribbling" poetry and issuing a little newspaper which he called *The Spectator* in imitation of other papers he had read with the same name. He was surprised to discover in himself a knack for writing, became a spectator in earnest, watching and recording, often in wry humor, the antics of himself and his fellow humans. On the demise of his newspaper, he announced editorially that it had folded because "no deaths of importance have taken place except that of the publisher of this paper who died of starvation owing to the slenderness of his patronage."

If ever another edition was printed by him, he declared, it would come out under the title "Miseries of Authors." It looked, for the moment at least, as if he had been cured of this unprofitable ambition.

Bowdoin College, according to the inaugural address given by its first president in 1794, had been founded as one of those institutions "endowed for the common good and not for the private advantage of those who resort to them. It is not that they [the students] may be able to pass through life in any easy or reputable manner, but that their mental powers may be cultivated and improved for the benefit of society." On entering Bowdoin under Uncle Robert Manning's persuasion, Hawthorne had no idea how he could ever benefit society and was inclined to believe that life itself—outside of institutional walls—was the best school for a ne'er-do-well like himself. "I do not know what to do with myself here," he was soon complaining to his mother. "I wish I was but in Raymond and I would be happy." A little later he consoled himself: "I am quite reconciled to going to college since I am to spend the vacations with you. Yet four years of the best part of my life is a great deal to throw away."

Such an attitude, needless to say, did not make for a shining college record. But young Hawthorne was popular with his classmates and in the company of two of them, Horatio Bridge and Franklin Pierce, soon began to sow a few wild oats. His family got wind of it, warned him against the sins of drinking and gambling. He confessed that he had, indeed, *almost* been caught at gambling but intended to be more careful in the future; as for drinking: "I have not drunk any kind of spirits or wine this term and shall not till the last week."

His study habits did not improve even with mild resolutions. With his friends Bridge and Pierce, he "lolled under tall academic pines," or watched the great logs tumbling along the current of the Androscoggin. Often they went shooting pigeons and gray squirrels in the woods or "bat-fowling" in the summer twilight, or, as Hawthorne reminded Horatio Bridge many years later, "catching trout in that shadowy little stream which I suppose is still wandering riverward through the forest though you and I will never cast a line in it again—two idle lads, in short, as we need not fear to acknowledge now, doing a hundred things that the faculty never heard of or else it had been the worse for us."

But Bowdoin was not Raymond no matter how hard Hawthorne tried to relive boyhood memories. Looming over him was the life ahead—a planned career and responsibility. Most of his Bowdoin friends had already settled on their future work according to family expectations. Horatio Bridge planned a career in the Navy; Frank Pierce, whose father had been a hero at Bunker Hill and become prominent in New Hampshire politics thereafter, expected to climb the political ladder; David Shepley, Jeremiah Dummer were heading for the ministry; Henry Wadsworth Longfellow had expressed an ambition to become a writer but yielded to advice from his father, a trustee of Bowdoin College, that poetry was *not* a career—he was heading for a professorship in modern languages.

"Oh, that I were rich enough to live without a profession!" Hawthorne wrote to his mother. "Being a minister is, of course, out of the question. I should not think that even you could desire me to choose so dull a way of life. Oh, no, mother, I was not born to vegetate forever in one place and to live and die as calm and tranquil as . . . a puddle of water. As to lawyers, there are so many of them already that one-half of them (upon moderate calculations) are in a state of actual starvation. I should not like to live by the diseases and infirmities of my fellow creatures. And it would weigh very heavily on my conscience in the course of my practice if I should chance to send any unlucky patient . . . to the realms below." Then, with some trepidation, he put the vital question: "What do you think of my becoming an author and relying for support upon my pen? How proud you would feel to see my works praised by the reviewers as equal to the proudest productions of the scribbling sons of John Bull."

Ringing in his ears at the time was the praise from Bridge, Pierce, and Longfellow for a few short stories he had taken courage to show them. These good friends were encouraging him to do whatever in life he felt inclined toward. "Do what you want. We're behind you," they said. So Hawthorne continued writing stories and, as a result, in grades, stood only at the middle of his class. Growing increasingly impatient with college, especially for the time it detracted from his writing, he would return to school with heavy heart after each brief vacation. "I would not live over my college life again, 'though 'twere to buy a world of happy days," he wrote to his sisters in 1824.

By the time of graduation it was clear that his degree was going to buy him nothing worth envying. His fellow graduates were heading home to security, perhaps a few of them to glory; as for Nathaniel Hawthorne, he was going home only to the "misery of authors."

People in Salem thought the Hawthorne family altogether queer. Mrs. Hawthorne, having returned from Maine, was once again shut in with her two reticent daughters. Now the son had come home and what could one say of him? He came out of the house only after dark. Occasionally he would disappear altogether from Salem and it never became clear where or why he had gone, or how the trip had benefited him. Remembering the carefree boy who had gone off to college four years earlier, neighbors did not recognize this somber young man. In appearance he was more handsome now. Standing five-feet ten and a half inches in height, he was broad shouldered, of light, athletic build, had eyes a striking shade of blue, and thick, dark hair with a long curling wave in it. Why should such a man hide himself away? Why was he not married and out in the world working at a respectable trade? What on earth did he do all day long in that gloomy house on Herbert Street?

Twelve long years were to pass before the people of Salem had their answer—twelve years during which, as they tried to catch a glimpse of him, Hawthorne, in his turn, was trying to get to know them. "On the verge of the harbor is a town and over it am I, a Watchman," he wrote. And what a Watchman he was! Whether from the window on Herbert Street, or on his lonely rambles to Marblehead, Swampscott, North Adams, or the White Mountains, he recorded faithfully all that he heard and witnessed. Nothing was ever lost on him. It was as if he said *out of this and this and this I will make literature.*

The language of an old man to whom he talked in North Adams attracted him and eventually found its way into *Ethan Brand.* A vision of a pretty Swampscott girl catching at her blowing skirt on the beach, he transferred into a scene in *The Village Uncle.* A true story told to him at Crawford Notch in New Hampshire became basis for *The Ambitious Guest.* A quiet, philosophical viewing of "The Old Man of the Mountain," the stone sculpture hanging precipitously above Echo Lake in the White Mountains, produced *The Great Stone Face.* In this story, as in all others, the Watchman's eye was seeing beyond the surface into the heart of humanity.

Hawthorne would sit for hours at a time on the broad porch of the old North Adams House, or in a corner of the barroom, silently smoking, apparently oblivious to his surroundings, yet many of the people he saw there, old and young alike, were sketched into tales. When he was not writing he was reading (four hundred books in seven years, and volumes of magazines and newspapers according to his sister's testimony) concentrating particularly on the subject which now interested him most:

New England history. A folk tale became *Lady Eleanor's Mantle;* old records of the witch trials, or of colonial times, produced such stories as *Alice Doane's Appeal, Endicott of the Red Cross, The Maypole of Merry Mount,* and *Young Goodman Brown.* A newspaper item inspired *Wakefield* just as other actual events, personal or historical, were to inspire in later years his major novels—*The Scarlet Letter, The House of the Seven Gables, The Blithedale Romance,* and *The Marble Faun.*

These long years of apprenticeship were hard, discouraging ones for Hawthorne. *Fanshawe,* his first attempt in print, a novel based on his experiences at Bowdoin, he published anonymously at his own expense. The book failed—as he immediately perceived once he had it in hand— because of its obvious reliance on a Sir Walter Scott style and plot. He saw that he had been unsuccessful in establishing either the characters or motivations he had intended. Despairingly he recalled all copies not yet sold and destroyed them.

The failure of *Fanshawe* prompted Hawthorne to destroy all but seven of the stories he had thus far written. He began over again, knowing now that there was no substitute for originality if one seriously intended to be an artist. Every story he wrote from this point on must have a distinct Hawthorne stamp upon it. Style was to be part of that stamp— the other, theme. Through his readings in regional history he became convinced that the realities of life in the days of his ancestors—all those harsh forces of weather and rocky soil, dangers from Indians and scarcity of supplies—had contributed to the sternness of Puritan Fathers like William and John Hathorne. These duty-oriented men of firm conscience and religious zeal, thought it inconsistent with rigorous struggle to allow leisure, gay apparel, dancing, maypole rituals, or the belief in fairies or other supernatural beings which so many colonists had brought from their homeland. But the fanaticism with which they carried out their governing of the people had put a vise around the spirit and intellect of early New Englanders. That such tight restraint produced greater evils than the "sins" it meant to prevent, Hawthorne set out to demonstrate.

Keeping to his own peculiar style, he tried to make every word count, every scene suggest an idea, idea being paramount to plot. In the new sketches the word "iron" would become a symbolic suggestion of Puritan doctrine. Tones of gray imposed on dress, houses, weather would keep the somber, joyless mood of colonial existence. A mention of roses would contrast with the darker shades to stand for man's natural passions, his native instincts of joy and freedom. A forest at the edge of a village would symbolize precivilization, the temptation of man to break from the rigid patterns of life to find within the secret hiding places of the wilderness a refuge in which to indulge in "sin." Young Goodman Brown would make strange discoveries in the forest. Hester and Dimmesdale would break the code in the forest. An intense light would later shine upon their sin, their guilt, their punishment. Hawthorne had found his method.

The hours of writing and rewriting took a heavy toll on his spirit. Knowing his weaknesses, how easily tempted he had always been to idle pursuits, he became in a sense his own Puritan Father, driving himself mercilessly to work. It was as if he were doing penance for all the wasted years. "For many months together" as he later described this period of his life, "I scarcely held human intercourse outside of my own family . . . I sat down by the wayside of life like a man under enchantment and a shrubbery sprang up around me and the bushes grew to be saplings and the saplings became trees until no exit appeared possible through the entangling depths of my obscurity. . . . I am disposed to thank God for the gloom and chill of my early life in the hope that my share of adversity came then when I bore it alone."

What he feared most was that he would not live to see his dream become reality. This fear became a repeated theme in correspondence with his Bowdoin friends. "It is no use for you to feel blue," Bridge replied to one of his gloomy letters, "I tell you that you will be in a good situation next winter instead of under a sod." Winter came with Hawthorne still plodding on and with still another worry. "I have not lived but only dreamed of living," he wrote to Longfellow, a theme which also crept into his stories. "Sometimes through a peephole I have caught a glimpse of the real world and the two or three articles in which I have portrayed these glimpses please me better than the others." It did not occur to him then that what Henry James was later to call his "cat-like facility for seeing in the dark" gave him deeper vision than most men.

What haunted Hawthorne was a sense of separateness from his fellows. In "Lights From a Steeple" he expressed a wish that the "multitude of chimneys" in Salem could "speak like those of Madrid and betray in smoky whispers the secrets of all who, since their first foundation, have assembled at the hearths within." He thought that the most desirable mode of existence would be that of "a spiritualized Paul Pry, hovering invisible round man and woman, witnessing their deeds, searching into their hearts, borrowing brightness from their felicity and shade from their sorrow, and retaining no emotion peculiar to himself. But none of these things are possible," he said despairingly, "and if I would know the interior of brick walls or the mystery of human bosoms, I can but guess."

He was, of course, the best of Paul Prys, for he himself was New England to the core, and had only to uncover his own heart to have the heart of his townsmen beat in the pages of his work. "I have nothing but thin air to concoct my stories of," he complained to Longfellow. "It is not easy to give a lifelike semblance to such shadowy stuff!" But it was precisely the "shadowy stuff" that was the substance of his art, which had *Hawthorne* stamped into its style, and which would eventually prompt a critic like Herman Melville to find his seemingly simple stories "as deep as Dante." By employing the genius of his imagination to throw many colored textures and lights upon the New England stage, by moving his characters back and forth in time so that we see them wearing masks in public and unmasked when alone, Nathaniel Hawthorne became the first major author to interpret in psychological terms the emerging character of the American. But his underlying theme of guilt, remorse, conscience—was universal: "In the depths of every heart," he said, "there is a tomb and a dungeon, though the lights, the music and revelry above may cause us to forget their existence . . . and the buried ones or prisoners whom they hide. . . . There is a moment just after midnight, with sleep still clinging above the consciousness, when all, despite the darkness, seems astonishingly clear, guilt, remorse, conscience come with disturbing memories. It is a time when the business of life does not intrude; when the passing moment lingers and becomes truly the present."

In 1837 Hawthorne, the author (he was now thirty-three years old) was ready at last to unmask himself. With his two friends Horatio Bridge and Franklin Pierce acting as his financial backers, he published *Twice-Told Tales*, not under a pseudonym this time but boldly under his own signature. The book astonished Hawthorne's neighbors who knew now what he had been up to the past twelve years. Some thought they saw themselves in *The White Old Maid, The Village Uncle, The Gray Champion,* or among the faces at *The Town Pump.* Slowly but surely Salem bells began to ring. "It had the effect," Hawthorne said wryly, "of making me known in my immediate vicinity; I was compelled to come out of my owl's nest and lionize in a small way." The lionizing had a profound effect upon his life; it led him to marry the girl next door.

The Peabodys of Salem were an old and distinguished family. This particular branch had a son who was dying of cancer, and three daughters, Elizabeth, author and lecturer; Mary, shortly to marry Horace Mann; and Sophia, whose paintings and illustrations were praised by the American artist, Washington Allston. For a long time, unknown to Hawthorne, the three talented, brilliant young women had been watching his furtive comings and goings and conspiring together as to how best to get to know him. Elizabeth was deeply involved with some of the leading intellectuals of Boston whose "charmed circle" was watched over by the outspoken young philosopher, Ralph Waldo Emerson. "New ideas are flying high and low," James Freeman Clarke, Unitarian minister, said, "and they are always to be heard at Elizabeth Peabody's bookshop on 19 West Street."

On hearing that their handsome neighbor was none other than the author of *Twice-Told Tales*, Elizabeth determined to draw Hawthorne into the Peabody social net. Before long a note was delivered to the Hawthorne house inviting the sisters and their brother to tea. Somewhat reluctantly Hawthorne put on his best suit and made the journey across the street. Within a matter of weeks he was a constant visitor, especially intrigued by the sharp wit and brilliance of Elizabeth. But it was not with her he fell in love. Upstairs lay an invalid, Sophia, the youngest daughter, who having caught a glimpse of him at the foot of the stairs remarked that he was "handsomer than Lord Byron." Hawthorne was soon climbing those stairs with regularity, finding in Sophia his ideal in beauty and spirit. During the twelve years of his literary apprenticeship when, in his self-imposed confinement, it had often seemed to him as if he were already in the grave, he had once cried out bitterly, "Even a young man's bliss has not been mine. With a thousand vagrant fantasies I have never truly loved and perhaps shall be doomed to loneliness through the eternal future because here on earth my soul has never married itself to the soul of woman." Now he was not only passionately in love but his love was returned, so much so that Sophia's headaches, the alleged cause of her confinement, soon ceased and she was able to accompany Hawthorne on walks and to lectures. Like England's famed poet, Elizabeth Barrett Browning, Sophia had been cured by love.

Sophia quickly agreed to Hawthorne's proposal of an engagement knowing full well that until his finances improved marriage was not possible. Through her many connections in Boston, Elizabeth Peabody quickly managed, in that difficult depression year, 1837, to get Hawthorne a job as weigher and gauger in the Boston Custom House. With this further step out into the world Hawthorne soon found himself far removed from his lonely chamber on Herbert Street, and, for sake of his love, measuring a load of coal on the schooner *Thomas Lowder* ("a little, black, dirty vessel"), going wearily home at night with black streaks of dirt on his handsome face to write down his impressions of his work and his Custom House companions. "Henceforth," he confided to his notebook, "I shall be entitled to call the sons of toil my brethren and shall know how to sympathize with them."

This sentiment helped thrust him into his next adventure, an experiment in communal living with a group of idealistic intellectuals in Boston who had become his friends. It was a time in America when many such socialistic colonies were springing up, and Hawthorne had emerged into the world of Boston when enthusiasm for brotherhood movements were at their height. In Elizabeth Peabody's bookshop he listened to the new ideas and was swept along in the enthusiastic current which began Brook Farm, a community destined to become world famous.

George Ripley, a minister who had resigned his pulpit because of what he felt to be the narrow attitude of the church, began Brook Farm as a place where a thinker could use his hands, a laborer use his brains, inviting an assortment of both groups to come to the farm, invest in it, and prove to the world that men could live amicably together in an atmosphere "harmonious in all its parts." Ripley was a relative of Emerson's, and a follower of the New England brand of *transcendentalism*, the philosophy being promoted by Emerson and Margaret Fuller in their quarterly magazine, the *Dial* (1840–44). Transcendentalism, in Emerson's terms, was a dynamic philosophy stressing "the infinitude of the private man," asserting that man possesses faculties that "transcend" the senses, God being immanent in man thus endowing man with highest creative potential. "Trust thyself; every heart vibrates to that iron string," Emerson preached, a call for self-reliance that quite naturally appealed to Hawthorne. For transcendentalists no formal religion was required, only full expression of the intuitive grasp of nature—a free exercise of soul in the reach for truth-beauty-God.

Hawthorne followed his transcendentalist friends to Ripley's farm which was located in West Roxbury some nine miles from Boston in a beautiful setting of twisting brooks and meadows, and signed up as Chief Ploughman. At the end of six months Brook Farm boasted enough buildings to house ten families as well as a school, all built by the residents themselves. In a burst of defensive pride, Brook Farm's headwaiter, Charles Anderson Dana (later editor of the *New York Sun*) declared: "Our ulterior aim is nothing less than heaven on earth."

The Brook Farm community was spoofed in the press, declared subversive by bigots, looked upon suspiciously by neighbors who kept themselves and their children a safe distance from the "radicals." But many leaders of religious and intellectual thought visited the farm. "There never were such witty potato patches, such sparkling corn fields; the weeds were scratched out of the ground to the music of Tennyson and Browning," wrote George William Curtis who visited as often as possible and became a close friend of Hawthorne's.

The inspirers of this communistic venture, Emerson and Margaret Fuller, did not themselves live at the farm—indeed Emerson thought communal living a distortion of his concept of individualism and privacy—but both he and Miss Fuller came often to teach and to lecture. Hawthorne came to know them intimately, finding Emerson somewhat too optimistic for his taste, and Miss Fuller, brilliant but neurotic. With the latter he went for long walks, observing her closely and listening for hours to her discourses. She lived in a great house in Cambridge where (in the words of Van Wyck Brooks) she thought of herself as a "princess who had been left by mistake on a Cambridge door-step." Surrounded by books, students, and admirers, Margaret held court, counting Nathaniel Hawthorne now as one of her most promising followers. She became the first to publicly praise his work (in the *Dial*) and vigorously pushed sales of *Grandfather's Tales,* a collection of stories written for children, which Elizabeth Peabody had brought out and was featuring in her bookshop.

But Hawthorne soon became disillusioned both with Miss Fuller and with the idyllic atmosphere of Brook Farm. He thought himself out of place among impractical reformers whose zeal for doing good reminded him too much of the passionate fanaticism of his ancestral Puritan elders. Sophia, coming to the farm to bring him shirts and sweaters knitted by her own hands, understood at once that he was not happy. "I could see very clearly thou was't not leading thine ideal life," she wrote after her return to Salem. Behind the gentle mockery of Brook Farm's Quaker atmosphere lay a hope of urging Hawthorne to speed his return to her. He needed no further hint. After a brief nine months of life among congenial thinkers and laborers in which he had done more laboring than thinking, he packed up his belongings suggesting to Sophia that it was time they set up their own heaven on earth.

"I must esteem myself happiest of women whether I wear tow or velvet, whether I live in a log cabin or in a palace," Sophia replied ecstatically. As Hawthorne had sunk most of his savings in the Brook Farm experiment, an investment he was unable to retrieve, it seemed likely that for the moment, anyway, tow and log cabin would be her lot. But Sophia had a firm belief in the genius of this man she was to marry. Already thirty-two years old (spinster age in those times) she declared herself ready to dedicate the balance of her life to giving Hawthorne the calm he needed so that his genius might flourish. But she thought it no sacrifice on her part. "I feel today like a rising Phoenix," she wrote on the eve of her marriage.

The couple were married July 9, 1842, with James Freeman Clarke officiating. They went to live not in a log cabin but, quite to their surprise and joy, in Emerson's former Concord home, The Old Manse. Sitting in the same little west study where Emerson had spent so many hours and been inspired to write *Nature*, Hawthorne hoped, with his new peace of mind, to be able to write *his* masterpieces. He told Sophia, "I never till now had a friend who could give me repose; all have disturbed me, and whether for pleasure or pain, it was still disturbance. But peace overflows from your heart into mine." It was with such peace in the ensuing years, that he did, indeed, write his masterpieces, though not all were destined to be composed at The Old Manse.

Standing near consecrated ground in Concord, the Manse appealed to Hawthorne for more than historical reasons. Two tall gateposts of roughhewn stone guarded the entrance like sentinels, while the house was far enough from the road so that the figures of passing travelers, dimly seen from the study window, did little to disturb his sense of privacy. "My wife," he said, "is in the strictest sense my sole companion, and I need no others; there is no vacancy in my mind any more than in my heart."

Occasionally Emerson came to visit, intruding no more, as Sophia said, "than a sunset or a rich warble." Emerson's young protégé, Henry Thoreau, was more often on the grounds, earning a few pennies by trimming the hedges and generally looking after The Old Manse. In winter the three men often went skating on the frozen river, Sophia looking on in amusement at Thoreau's remarkable but "ugly" leaps, Emerson's numerous sprawls, her husband, of course, appearing to her "like a self-impelled Greek statue, stately and grave," as he swept serenely by wrapped in his dark cloak. Christmas dinners were exchanged between the Emersons at one end of Concord and the Hawthornes at the other, Emerson finding Hawthorne reserved, and Hawthorne preferring to chat with Thoreau who was always invited to dine. "To talk with him," Hawthorne said, "is like hearing the wind among the boughs of a forest tree; and with all this mild freedom there is high and classic cultivation in him, too."

Meanwhile, still in a transport of love, Hawthorne was quietly composing a new collection of stories up in the study which he intended to publish under the title *Mosses from an Old Manse*. He could not believe his luck in Sophia. "I am married to the spring! I am husband to the May," he wrote of her, seeing her below his window gathering columbines. And on another occasion he said: "I used to think I could imagine all passions, all feelings and states of the heart and mind; but little did I know! Indeed we are but shadows; we are not endowed with real life, and all that seems most real about us is but the thinnest substance of a dream till the heart be touched. That touch creates us— then we begin to be—thereby we are beings of reality and inheritors of eternity." In the second year of marriage a daughter, Una, was born to the Hawthornes, bringing Hawthorne more often away from his desk, sometimes even into the kitchen where he hoped to make himself helpful to Sophia. "Imagine him with that magnificent head bent over a cooking stove," Sophia wrote lovingly to her family, "and those star-eyes watching the pot boil."

But new responsibilities as a father brought on additional financial worries which were finally to catch up with the happy young couple. From time to time stories by Hawthorne had appeared in the *Democratic Review* but pay for them was slow in coming. *Twice-Told Tales*, selling slowly, failed to bring in all that Hawthorne had hoped. Expenses at The Old Manse were mounting and the situation began to look desperate. "There is owing to him more than thrice money enough to pay all his debts," Sophia explained to her mother, "and he was confident that when he came to a pinch like this it would not be withheld from him. It is wholly new to him to be in debt, and he cannot 'whistle' for it as Mr. Emerson advised him to do telling him that everybody was in debt and that they were all worse off than he was."

Emerson's view of Hawthorne's character was that he inclined too much toward dark pessimism. Melville, who did not then know Hawthorne personally, saw "darkness" in his stories. All but his most intimate associates thought him humorless. In later years Sophia denied that her husband was a gloomy or morbid person. Admitting that he had the pensiveness and gravity of one who possessed what a friend of his had called "the awful power of insight," she went on to comment that his mood was always cheerful and equal and his mind healthy. "The airy splendor of his wit and humor was the light of his home," she said. Hawthorne himself admitted that "a cloudy veil" stretched over his nature, but that he had no love of secrecy or darkness. "Any mortal capable of full sympathy," he said, "is welcome to know everything there is in my heart. But he must find his own way there. I can neither guide him nor enlighten him." Though he did not readily reveal himself to people, once making a friend (as his daughter Rose was to say of him in her *Memories of Hawthorne*) the relationship was deep and lasting. "No one ever was more faithful to, and consequently ever had more faith in his friends than my father," she wrote.

Horatio Bridge and Franklin Pierce, his former college classmates, both had found their way into Hawthorne's heart. Always when he was in need these two came forward to help him, and he repaid in a gratitude that meant more to them than money. In his present financial crisis, much to Sophia's relief, they pulled political strings in Polk's Cabinet to obtain for Hawthorne another government job, this time as surveyor in the Salem Custom House. When the appointment came through, however, and it came time to leave The Old Manse, the Hawthornes grew uneasy at leaving their paradise in Concord.

> We gathered up our household goods, drank a farewell cup of tea in our pleasant little breakfast room . . . and passed forth between the tall stone gateposts as uncertain as the wandering Arabs where our tent might next be pitched.

But just as Brook Farm would later be captured in *The Blithedale Romance*, The Old Manse, too, survived in *Mosses from an Old Manse* which Hawthorne published in 1846. Besides its memories of Concord and the house in which he had lived, the book contained a collection of new tales. He presented both Emerson and Longfellow with copies and even took courage to send one to Edgar Allan Poe (with whom he was not personally acquainted) saying, "I presume the publishers will have sent you a copy. I confess, however, that I admire you rather as a writer of tales than a critic upon them." Poe had a reputation for being a devastatingly sharp critic and most writers were wary of his opinions.

His review of *Mosses* appeared in *Godey's Lady's Book,* November 1847, citing Hawthorne as *"the* example *par excellence* in this country of the privately admired and publicly unappreciated man of genius." Most critics, said Poe, held back from listing Hawthorne among America's "best authors" because he was neither "a man of wealth nor a quack." But having said this, the rest of the review was a curious mixture of positives and negatives. Poe was not at all partial to Hawthorne's allegorical tales, urged him to "come out of the Old Manse" to "mend his pen," to get a bottle "of visible ink"—examples of Poe's spicy wit.

Poe made good use of this essay on Hawthorne to define the art of the short story, the poem, the allegory, the novel, in phrases which since have become the bible to many teachers and literary critics. In illustration of his principles he relied heavily on Hawthorne's *Twice-Told Tales* which he much preferred to *Mosses.* These tales, he said, "belong to the highest region of Art—an Art subservient to genius of a very lofty order . . . we know of few compositions which the critic can more honestly commend. . . . As Americans we feel proud of the book."

Hawthorne, of course, was pleased despite the attack on *Mosses from an Old Manse.* Not until three years later, after *The Scarlet Letter* was already making him internationally known, did *Mosses* have the kind of comment he had wanted to hear from a critic. On discovering the book, young Herman Melville, author of the popular *Typee* and *Omoo (Moby Dick* was not yet written) ecstatically urged Americans not to give over to future generations the glad duty of acknowledging Hawthorne. "Take that joy to yourself in your own generation," he said, declaring further that *"Mosses from an Old Manse"* should be sold by the hundred thousand and read by the million and admired by everyone who is capable of admiration."

In time, though not for *Mosses,* all of this was to come true for Hawthorne. But in 1847, as surveyor of Salem Custom House, the future did not look promising. The name Hawthorne appeared not on new works of art but, as the Salem surveyor himself so humorously put it, on bags and bales carried to the ends of the earth. He got bogged down in the details of his Custom House job, which dimmed his inspiration to write. "The fault was mine," he later said. "The page of life that was spread out before me was dull and commonplace only because I had not fathomed its deeper import." To offset depression, he busied himself with such activities as acting secretary for the Salem Lyceum in which post he invited Thoreau to lecture, a visit partially responsible for Thoreau's first book, A Week on the Concord and Merrimack Rivers.

There was also another child at home, son Julian having been born in 1846. With his income dependent on politics, Hawthorne was cautiously watching affairs in Washington to see how the next election would affect his security. Numerous candidates were maneuvering to take the surveyor job away from him, and his growing family made it essential that he not be displaced. Politics, to which he was temperamentally unsuited, was destined more than once in his life to cause him bitterness. On June 8, 1849, Sophia wrote a hasty note to her father to announce, "Mr. Hawthorne received news by telegraph to-day that he is turned out of office headlong."

The new President, Zachary Taylor, having said before taking office that he would make no removals except for "dishonesty and unfaithfulness," Hawthorne and his friends were incensed at what seemed a slur on his reputation. The issue became controversial when it was exposed in Salem newspapers, much to Hawthorne's chagrin, for he did not like to be the center of a political squabble. On the one hand Sophia was declaring hotly, "there never has been such a succession of removals of honorable and honest men since we were a nation!" and on the other she was reassuring everyone: "Mr. Hawthorne never liked the office at all and is rather relieved than otherwise that it is taken out of his hands."

With his salary removed, the question of supporting his family once again became Hawthorne's prime concern. Fortunately, his publisher, James T. Fields, arrived in Salem hoping to get a new book out of the author of whom Poe had spoken as having "the purest style, the finest taste, the most delicate humor, the most touching pathos, the most radiant imagination." Fields entered the Hawthorne house to find the author of Mosses from an Old Manse and Twice-Told Tales hovering near a stove to keep warm while Sophia busied herself with little Julian.

"We fell into talk about his future prospects," Fields later said of the visit, "and he was, as I feared I should find him, in a very desponding mood." "Who would risk publishing a book for me, the most unpopular writer in America?" Mr. Fields replied that he not only would take that risk but would start with an edition of two-thousand copies of anything Hawthorne would write.

Early in his position at the Custom House, Hawthorne had found among the dusty debris in his office a scarlet letter A cut out of velvet cloth attached to some faded documents which outlined the crime and punishment of Hester Prynne, a young woman who had lived in colonial New England and had violated the moral code of her village. The details of Hester's story instantly caught his imagination for they contained the very element which had always interested him: man's natural passion in conflict with a strictly structured society. He thought now he might work it into a longer story than he had hitherto tried, one that had for its theme sin, guilt, and fanatical revenge set in the typical New England background. Earlier he had drawn up an outline of the story, but during the course of his duties at the Custom House his inspiration for it had lagged. This outline he showed to Fields, who after reading it, urged him to amplify and finish the work. It was precisely the kind of encouragement Hawthorne needed at that moment.

He worked tirelessly on the new book during the next few months, seeing no one but his wife and children. When at last he copied out the closing sentences, he read them to Sophia. "My voice swelled and heaved as if I were tossed up and down on an ocean as it subsides after a storm," he said of the occasion. "It broke her heart and sent her to bed with a grievous headache which I look upon as a triumphant success."

The Scarlet Letter, published in 1850, was a success far beyond Hawthorne's wildest dreams. It catapulted him to lasting fame. In ten days five thousand copies were sold, praise coming from far and wide to the forty-six-year-old author. Washington Irving wrote "masterly, masterly," while Oliver Wendell Holmes, in an outburst of national pride exclaimed to Hawthorne, "The Yankee mind has for the most part budded and flowered in pots of English earth, but you have fairly raised yours as a seedling in the natural soil." Emerson too was filled with pride, for he had long been calling for just such use of American materials in the art and literature of the time. Quite aside from its theme, as universal as it was regional, Hawthorne had put all of his intensity, sensitivity, and intellect into the work, giving a jewel-like construction to his symbolic novel.

Never again was he to speak of himself as obscure. The next two years produced *The House of the Seven Gables* (1851) and *The Blithedale Romance* (1852). His fame spread abroad. Already in the eyes of his friends and many critics he was assured immortality. Unfortunately his mother was never to know her son's full glory. Just prior to the publication of *The Scarlet Letter*, she emerged from "Castle Dismal" as Sophia called her Salem dwelling, to come to live with her son's family. She seemed for a moment to have miraculously awakened to the pleasures of Una and her new grandchild, Julian. "For the first time since my husband can remember, he dined with his mother!" Sophia told her family. "This is only one of the miracles which the baby is to perform." But the awakening came too late. Mrs. Hawthorne died in 1849 after only a brief time in her new surroundings. While she still lay ill her son had written of her in his journal: "I love my mother, but there has been, ever since boyhood, a sort of coldness of intercourse between us." Perhaps the strained relations between them inspired the passage in *Wakefield* dealing with Wakefield's return home after a long, self-imposed absence: "It is perilous to make a chasm in human affections; not that they gape so long and wide—but so quickly close again . . . by stepping aside for a moment, a man exposes himself to a fearful risk of losing his place forever." By separating herself so long from the world, Mrs. Hawthorne had taken the fearful risk and lost.

Hawthorne wrote *The House of the Seven Gables* during five months in 1850 while living in Lenox, Massachusetts, at Tanglewood. There, also, in a little red house,* his last child, Rose, was born. And here he met for the first time the young man who so glowingly had reviewed *Mosses from an Old Manse*. Herman Melville was living in Pittsfield, a distance of about eight miles, in a small farmhouse he had dubbed "Arrow-Head",† a house with a "huge, corpulent old Henry VIII chimney" where he was hard at work writing *Moby Dick*.

Melville found in Hawthorne what he called an infinite fraternity of feeling. During long talks together the two discussed their individual philosophies of life, discovering many points in common. Symbolism in art, politics, religion, and the nature of sin were subjects that interested them both, and exploring these topics before the fire at Arrow-Head or on walks through the Berkshires undoubtedly proved invaluable to Melville as he proceeded in his work on *Moby Dick*. The theme of this book, like Hawthorne's stories, was symbolic, an allegory of monumental size and significance in which the world, its morals, and manners are dissected as if the earth, floating on the sea, could see itself mirrored as it approached its day of doom.

Overwhelmed with gratitude and affection for Hawthorne's understanding of him, Melville expressed his love for his more reticent friend in almost boyish bursts of enthusiasm: "Your heart beats in my ribs

* The Red House, restored after a fire, may still be seen at Tanglewood.
† Herman Melville's *Arrow-Head* also still standing in Pittsfield.

and mine in yours and both in God's," he replied to a letter from Hawthorne in 1851 in which Hawthorne had praised *Moby Dick*. "When the big hearts strike together, the concussion is a little stunning."

Melville and Hawthorne had met at a turning point in their lives, Hawthorne on the ascendancy to international fame, Melville, despite his masterpiece, soon to sink into Hawthorne's former obscurity. In many ways their lives had points in common: both waited a long time for recognition; both had constantly to be concerned over finances to support their families; both worked in Custom Houses; both knew Salem well, Melville as a seaman, Hawthorne, of course, as a resident. While politically Melville was more articulate and stood more firmly with the forces opposing slavery, both had the artist's insight into their times and used their pens as a medium of comment. Melville unselfishly promoted Hawthorne's cause in his rapturous call to Americans to prize and cherish her writers. "How great the shame if other nations should be before her (America) in crowning her heroes of the pen," he said, ". . . by confessing him (Hawthorne) you confess others; you embrace the whole brotherhood. For genius all over the world stands hand in hand, and one shock of recognition runs the whole circle round."

Hawthorne, if not Melville, was granted that recognition during his lifetime. *The House of the Seven Gables*, with its aura of romance and mystery, its throwback to the Salem Witch Trials, became one of the most widely read, popular books in America. James Russell Lowell (author of *The Biglow Papers*, *The Vision of Sir Launfal*), who like Hawthorne was descended from a long line of illustrious New Englanders, told Hawthorne he thought the book "the most valuable contribution to New England history that has been made." This and other words of praise throughout the nation, set Hawthorne to working at inspired speed on his next book, *The Blithedale Romance*, the seed of which also sprang from Hawthorne's personal background. Brook Farm came to life in this romance which like *The House of the Seven Gables* was also something of a mystery story. In recounting the adventures of his characters at Blithedale, Hawthorne was at the same time explaining his participation at Brook Farm to the world. Although the scheme for "beginning the life of Paradise anew" had exploded, he said, "Whatever else I may repent of . . . let it be reckoned neither among my sins nor follies that I once had faith and force enough to form generous hopes of the world's destiny,—yes!—and to do what in me lay for their accomplishment." He denied that the plot itself had any basis in reality or that his characters resembled any of the real persons involved in the Brook Farm experiment. But certainly Hawthorne himself is revealed as a disillusioned observer.

It is interesting to note Hawthorne's choice of names for characters, how many times, for example he chose names beginning with the letter P for his Puritanical heroines: Pearl (*The Scarlet Letter*); Phoebe, (*The House of the Seven Gables*); Priscilla (*The Blithedale Romance*). Such usage can hardly be accidental. Coverdale, Zenobia, Dimmesdale, Kenyon, all suggest meanings to fit the characters for whom they were invented, as does Blithedale for the paradise in which Hawthorne's "creations of fancy" hoped to find joy and peace.

A *Wonder Book for Boys and Girls* and *The Snow Image and Other Twice-Told Tales* were added to the list of Hawthorne's works in 1852. Now, famous in his own right, Hawthorne came forward to lend intellectual weight to his intimate friend, Franklin Pierce, who was making a bid for the presidency. The writing of Pierce's official campaign biography, published in the fall of 1852, is considered one of the most controversial episodes in Hawthorne's career; yet, if his life and works are carefully studied, his support of Pierce as a friend and as a candidate confirms rather than contradicts Hawthorne's ideas.

Politically Hawthorne was a Democrat. His readings in history had formed in him a horror of excessive zeal in any direction, and his experiences with people had taught him to distrust even those with the best of motives who could not be dispassionate in pursuit of their goals. The hottest issue of his day, of course, was the question of slavery. His abolitionist friends in Boston, his former Brook Farm colleagues counted him as one of them, a man dedicated to the pursuit of justice and the cause of humanity. Hawthorne agreed with them in that. He stood against child labor, was sympathetic to women's rights, was for reform of penal and mental institutions, and the rights of labor. He spoke of "the cottonfields where God's image becomes a beast of burden," in sympathy for the slaves.

Where he differed from his friends, however, was in the methods of putting an end to evil. He, with Pierce, thought the activities of northern abolitionists would bring disaster to the nation, forcing the hand of Southerners, who out of pride would split the nation rather than yield on the question of slavery. "It is a strange thing in human life," he wrote, "that the greatest errors both of men and women often spring from their sweetest and most generous qualities." This theme had been explored by him in many of his tales, and it struck him, as he watched the conflict between North and South that there were good people on both sides racing toward error, toward disaster. He considered his friend Pierce a moderate who might help save the nation, while the abolitionists considered Pierce, and, as it turned out, rightly so, a weak man under the influence of southern land and slaveowners. The quiet man, Hawthorne, had placed himself in the thick of the battle and it was to cause him great suffering. Against the voice of an outraged citizenry demanding the abolition of slavery, Hawthorne was begging for the impossible: "There is no instance in all history," he argued, "of the human will and intellect having perfected any great moral reform by methods which it adapted to that end." In his opinion "divine providence" in its own good time would wipe out evils. "The progress of the world at every step leaves some evil or wrong on the path behind it which the wisest of mankind of their own set purpose could never have found the way to rectify," he said.

Pierce was elected to the presidency with Hawthorne's help but the passions on both sides of the nation mounted at every turn leading to inevitable bloodshed. It was a saddened Hawthorne who having been appointed by Pierce to serve as Consul in Liverpool sailed for England, March 26, 1853. Although many took his appointment to be a reward for his part in Pierce's campaign, the new President was following a long-established policy in appointing a literary man to foreign service. Washington Irving, William Cullen Bryant, James Fenimore Cooper all had served in similar positions under other administrations. But Hawthorne was probably less at ease in this public office than his predecessors. He was away from his homeland at a time of unparalleled crisis and found himself in the position of being part of an Administration unpopular with the most advanced thinkers of the time.

Abroad he met among other distinguished persons, Robert and Elizabeth Browning, Florence Nightingale, and Anthony Trollope who recorded some of Hawthorne's nationalistic statements in defense of America. Hawthorne, as usual, occupied himself by doing his own recording of English manners and morals into notebooks later to be published under the title *Our Old Home*.

At the end of Pierce's administration, Hawthorne—again unemployed—took his family to Italy, living first in Rome, then settling in Florence where he wrote the last of his novels, *Transformation*, or as it was later called in America, *The Marble Faun*. Man's conscience was once again the theme, although with Italy as a background, the psychology of the American is represented through individual characters. This book, like the others before it, has elements of mystery, half fact, half fancy, the characters suggestive and intriguing. The enigmatic Miriam is an extension of earlier Hawthorne heroines, placed in a new setting to show the universality of his theme.

In Florence the Hawthornes lived in a large house standing high on a hill overlooking the city. At one end was a moss green tower haunted by owls and "by the ghost of a monk who was confined there in the thirteenth century previous to being burnt at the stake." "I hire this villa," wrote Hawthorne to a friend, "tower and all, at twenty-eight dollars a month; but I mean to take it away bodily and clap it into a romance which I have in my head ready to be written out." The romance, of course, was *The Marble Faun*, and the Villa Montauto may be found in its pages. Daily observations of life in Italy Hawthorne gathered into his journal, later to be published as the *Italian Notebooks*.

In 1860, on the eve of the Civil War, Hawthorne returned to the United States to live in the only home he ever actually owned—Wayside, bought from Louisa May Alcott's father before the journey to England. The political upheaval that shortly erupted into war greatly depressed him, affecting his health as well as his spirits. Fields kept begging for another book, but though Hawthorne had numerous ideas, began many drafts, he could not bring himself to complete anything more. *Dr. Grimshaw's Secret, Septimius Felton, The Ancestral Footstep*, and *The Dolliver Romance* were all begun and abandoned.

In 1862, Hawthorne went as a member of a Massachusetts delegation to meet with Lincoln in regard to matters concerning the war. The visit did nothing to lift his spirits. "I don't quite understand what we are fighting for," he told Horatio Bridge, quartered in Washington at the time. His total confusion and bitterness were reflected in the further statement to Bridge that "Whatever happens next, I must say that I rejoice that the old Union is smashed. We never were one people and never really had a country since the Constitution was formed."

Shortly after his return from Washington, Hawthorne was made even more gloomy by the death of Thoreau. With Sophia he attended the funeral services where Emerson spoke and Bronson Alcott read from Thoreau's writings. Afterward, with slow gait, he walked from the graveside to the Old Manse to have what proved to be a last look at the house in which he had spent his happiest years. Noting the

frailty of her beloved husband, Sophia wrote in her diary that evening,
"My husband quite ill. Everything seems sad when he is ill."

As if sensing that his own death was imminent, Hawthorne
began to impress upon Sophia that he disliked biographies and wanted
to destroy letters and remembrances he feared would fall into unfriendly
or unwise hands. Sophia pleaded with him to consult Dr. Oliver Wendell
Holmes, advice Hawthorne was slow to follow. When at last he did
consult the famed author-surgeon, Holmes' suggestion pleased him—a
diversion, a complete change of scene. He laid out plans for a tour
of the White Mountains in New Hampshire, Sophia agreeing to let
him go in the care of his old friend Franklin Pierce. In May of
1864 the two men set out on their journey, Sophia little suspecting
that she would never again see her husband alive. Hawthorne died
at Plymouth, New Hampshire, May 19, 1864, only a few days after
the start of the tour.

The gathering at his gravesite at Sleepy Hollow in Concord was
reminiscent of that which had come to say farewell to Thoreau two
years earlier—Emerson, Longfellow, Agassiz, Ellery Channing, Bronson
Alcott, Oliver Wendell Holmes, and many other famous men and
women. James Freeman Clarke, who had officiated at Hawthorne's
wedding, spoke the words of prayer over his grave.

Hawthorne's life had spanned the years between two crucial struggles
in America—the War of 1812 and the Civil War. As a deeply conscious
American he had lived and made heard his voice. However much at
odds with the mainstream of New England thought during the
critical prewar years, he maintained his convictions even under the censure of men and women he most admired. The prefaces of his books
are a mirror reflecting the depth of thought that went into the shaping
of his opinions and each of his major works. What he aimed for, he
said, was the setting of stages "a little removed from the highway of
ordinary travel" where the creatures of his brain might "play their
phantasmagorical antics without exposing them to too close a comparison
with the actual events of real lives." To highlight the *idea*, to reveal the
inner heart—that, said Hawthorne, was his goal.

Most critics agree that Hawthorne was America's first great novelist,
a master of romantic fiction as well as founder of the American
psychological novel. Henry James, while admitting the inexhaustible charm
and mystery of Hawthorne's "Romances" thought his stories suffered
from too much symbolism. D. H. Lawrence saw "hellish" meanings in

his work. Van Wyck Brooks wrote of him as the most "deeply planted" of American writers, one who saw life "as a fable, feeling it as a phantom, not a man." In this regard Brooks linked Hawthorne with Edgar Allan Poe, saying that these two giants of literature had much more in common than the New York or New England of their time.

But while one may read Poe without identifying him with the country of his birth, Hawthorne cannot be separated from the New England soil in which he was reared. He never failed to reflect his land, its origin, its mood, its psychology. Though, as Brooks said, he "modeled in mist as the Greeks modeled in marble," the mist is thin and easily scattered. Underneath we see all too clearly the architecture of Hawthorne's world. It was his genius to understand the nature of his experience and to translate it into terms meaningful to all Americans.

Ralph Waldo Emerson

(1803–1882)

"Nothing is at last sacred but the integrity of
your own mind."

The Reverend William Emerson was a scholarly man with little zeal
for pursuit of worldly goods. He did not relish the thought of leaving
his quiet life in pastoral Harvard Village, but when a call came from
Boston bidding him come live and preach there "because of the alarming
attacks that are made on our holy religion by the larned, the witty,
and the wicked, especially in populous seaport towns," it was too much
of a challenge to his New England conscience. Uprooting himself, his
wife, and two young sons, William, Jr., and John, he soon was making
the rounds to meet his new parishioners while his wife, Ruth, who was
expecting a child, did what she could to make more homelike the First
Church parsonage located on Boston's Summer Street. In the spring
of the year, May 25, 1803, a third son was born to the Emersons
and named, according to family custom, for one of the paternal ancestors.
Who could have foretold the irony that this newborn weakling infant,
Ralph Waldo Emerson, springing from a long line of New England
preachers, one day would be chief among the "larned" in his native
city, causing far greater alarm by his radical pronouncements from the
pulpit than any of those attacks on the holy religion which had prompted
his father to Boston.

Waldo, as he preferred to be called, excited little, if any attention
as a boy. His gait was slow, his habits plodding; he seldom spoke out
of turn, or engaged in fisticuffs with his brothers or classmates. Indeed,
to the casual observer, he seemed somewhat dull, lacking in energy and
imagination. Pushed into an obscure middle place in the family by the
numerous children born after him, obscure he seemed likely to remain.

But the inner life of this boy was developing all the while, perhaps the richer for being let alone. Gentle, brilliant, introspective, Waldo Emerson was merely biding time to give expression to the depth of emotion and poetic imagination that lay beneath his placid exterior.

Life at the Summer Street parsonage was not altogether easy. Poverty dogged Waldo's parents just as it had in Harvard Village. The increased salary promised to the Pastor—a guaranteed fourteen dollars a week and twenty cords of wood annually—did not prove enough, apparently, to offset his constantly growing family and Boston's higher cost of living. But there were certain compensations for the literary-minded William as well as for his sons in living in the heart of this more diverse city. Boston was then a fascinating mixture of rural, urban, and sea sounds. Cows grazed freely on Boston Common; from the houses of rich and poor alike one could hear the back yard din of hens, cattle, and pigs; bells of ships, commerce, and church sang out all hours day and night. Man or boy, left to his own devices, could follow whichever of these suited his fancy. In the crowded streets one could mingle with people of all walks of life, foreign as well as native born, and bring home impressions and experiences that widened horizons. Often it was possible to catch a glimpse of some well-known personality in politics riding by in his carriage to Faneuil Hall or the state-house overlooking the harbor. To an observant boy the city was an education in itself. Though not yet the "hub of the universe" it was later reputed to be by its citizenry, "cultivated" Boston boasted its theater (which introduced *Hamlet* to the public the year Waldo Emerson was born), scores of bookshops, meeting halls, museums, schools, newspaper and publishing houses, and other forms of entertainment to attract the "witty and the wicked."

Only the most high-toned aspect of culture reached into the Emerson parlor where no amount of poverty would ever have permitted a lessening of pride or intellectual aspiration. When not at their books, Waldo, and his brother William, with younger brothers Edward and Charles tagging at their heels, were put to work tending the small kitchen-garden that provided vegetables for their mother's table. Taught early to abstain from idle play—to take their share of manly responsibility, the boys also stacked and carried wood for stove and fireplaces and took care of the barnyard animals. In rare moments of release from such chores, they wandered in the small orchard beyond the barnyard or climbed trees in a neighboring lot to get a glimpse of the sea. Only seldom did they escape to the shore itself where Waldo thought shells far more fascinating than the sailors or ship gear which so excited his brothers. Fortunately, with so little money at home to spare for pleasures or gadgets pleasing to a boy, the things which most intrigued this particular Emerson cost little or nothing at all.

> When a boy I used to go to the wharves & pick up shells out of the sand which vessels had brought as ballast, & also plenty of stones, gypsum, which I discovered would be luminous when I rubbed two bits together in a dark closet to my great wonder—and I do not know *why* luminous to this day. That & the magnetising of my penknife till it would hold a needle . . .

Interest in natural phenomena had stirred as early as his infant years when he had first seen bubbles rising from a small wooden pipe. "What silent wonder is waked in the boy," he was to say in later years recalling and extolling those moments of seemingly idle play which are the beginning of a child's education. To his awed eyes the bubbles, sailing in colorful, transparent circles had seemed to form a temporary universe of moons and disintegrating stars, setting up in him a curiosity never afterward stilled. From stars to things cast from the sea; from rocks to flowering soil; from season to season endless questions about the nature of the universe in which he lived. A "seeker" Emerson would style himself in adulthood. In childhood that was the single description most appropriate for him. A lean, lanky boy stuffed with prayers in his head, stones, leaves, pens, frogs, and whatnot in his pockets, he took it for granted that one day he could know all there was to know if only he collected enough, asked enough, experimented, read, memorized, listened, and watched. He never lost the treasures stuffed in his pockets—they were for his experiments—but he was often careless with treasure his mother put there. One day she gave him a dollar bill with which to buy a pair of shoes for himself at Mr. Baxter's shop. "I lost the bill and remember being sent out by my disappointed mother to look among the fallen leaves under the poplar trees opposite the house . . ." Such mishaps haunted his conscience not alone because money was so hard to come by (one particularly hard winter he and his brother had to share between them a single overcoat) but because in the milieu in which a New England boy was brought up, carelessness or any "slovenly" habit was chalked large upon the mind as sin. Perfection had to be the goal of each individual, a constant self-examination for improvement of habits, attitudes, and spiritual condition in the light of Puritan ethic. One oft-repeated legend about Emerson as a child tells how upon being scolded by his aunt one day for spending six cents to take a novel from the circulating library when he knew the sacrifices family poverty required, he took the book back to the library unread and would not, by his own admission, read it for years afterward—a form of penance presumably.

Reading was a habit early ingrained in him. Almost as soon as he had been able to hold a spoon in infancy, he was handed a book. According to his Aunt Mary (who liked to boast about all her nephews, but none more so than Waldo) he could read well by age three. Enrolled in Boston's Latin School before age six, he learned quickly but apparently so quietly he made no particular impression on Mrs. Whitwell, headmistress. Indeed, like so many others who knew Waldo Emerson in his childhood, it would be a wonder to her in later years that a boy so lacking in "animal spirits" had amounted to anything. According to his own testimony, Waldo was not always the model student. Seemingly bent over his copybook or primer, he often would be reading some forbidden novel kept slyly under the desk, learning more from one or two of these, he said years later, than from his teachers or usual course of studies. He also did more daydreaming than suspected, for throughout his boyhood (and manhood too), he was secretly nursing a variety of romanticized ambitions. "There is almost no walk of the muse," he confessed long after he had become America's foremost philosopher and scholar, "& more, almost no way of life but at some time or other I have caught the romance of it—farmer, stageman, merchant, editor, but far far above all the herb & berry woman."

His vocation, of course, had already been fixed for him by his family, most particularly by Aunt Mary who imparted, not by command but by simply taking it for granted that he and all her other nephews would follow tradition and become churchmen. An off-beat Calvinist, a confirmed spinster, a woman steeped in classical learning, Mary Moody Emerson was a blazing personality of tireless energy, unquestionably the dominant influence in the Summer Street parsonage. She continually was prodding her minister-brother to cure himself of his too arid nature, and his too modest ambition. The Reverend William Emerson, like most Calvinists, believed that a man ought not to push himself— whether out of slavery or poverty—but accept as predetermined by God whatever his fate in life. In his bachelor days when he had confessed to being "poor, wifeless, landless, houseless, and, I am afraid, almost friendless," Mary Moody had first scolded him soundly for lacking "those energies, those keen vibrations of soul which seize pleasure— which immortalize moments and give to life the zest of enjoyment," then set him riding and talking on the subject of matrimony with Miss Ruth Haskins whom she declared to be "virtue's self." This spinster-match-maker, who had a passion for traveling, often declaring she'd never agree to stay too long in any one place, nevertheless did come to live for months at a time in her brother's house after his marriage to Ruth. She was a necessary presence for the most part as it was she who took over family management during her sister-in-law's many confinements. With her own zest for enjoyment and ability to immortalize moments she brought an element that otherwise would have been missing in the life of her nephews, making an impression on Waldo that profoundly influenced his romantic turn of mind. "Immortalizing moments" was to become an essential ingredient in his philosophy when he grew up. Though destined to break away from Aunt Mary's orthodox religion, his debt to her he always freely acknowledged.

> The depth of the religious sentiment which I knew in my Aunt Mary, imbuing all her genius & derived to her from so many godly lives and godly deaths of sainted kindred at Concord, Malden, York, was itself a culture, an education . . . In my childhood Aunt Mary herself wrote the prayers which first my brother William & when he went to college I read aloud morning & evening at the family devotions . . . Religion was her occupation, and when years after I came to write sermons for my own church, I could not find any examples or treasures of piety so high-toned, so profound or promising, such rich influences as my remembrances of her conversation & letters.

Emerson's mother, throughout his childhood, had little time for conversation, even less cause to be always waxing enthusiastic. Seldom had he seen her when she was not either pregnant or in mourning. Indeed on the very day of his birth she had been still in deep bereavement for the loss of her infant daughter Phoebe. In the year that Charles (who was always to be Waldo's favorite brother) was born, young John Emerson died of tuberculosis. Then came Edward who thrived, but the boy Robert, next born, was mentally defective. The grieving mother's troubles were not over. Her little girl, Mary Caroline, healthy at birth in 1811, died unexpectedly a few months later. That same year, with just as little warning, the Reverend William Emerson himself passed away. Only Mary Moody's strong presence during each ensuing crisis helped Ruth Emerson come through so many trials. Daughter of an industrious Boston distiller, Ruth had been at the outset of her marriage, a lively girl, spiritedly rebellious against her husband's fatalistic approach to life, agreeing with Mary Moody that it alone was responsible for their impoverished, lackluster existence. "In things of moment on thyself depend," she once wrote openly in her diary for William to see. But continuing hardship and the tragic loss of one child after another gradually altered and subdued her fighting spirit. In later years one of her sons recalled her "peculiar softness," said that when she came from her room in the morning it was always as if she had come from communion with God.

Waldo was a week short of his eighth birthday when his father died. He remembered him only as "a somewhat social gentleman, but severe to us children, who twice or thrice put me in mortal terror by forcing me into the salt water off some wharf or bathing house, and I recall the fright with which after some of this salt experience, I heard his voice one day (as Adam that of the Lord God in the garden) summoning us to a new bath, and I vainly endeavoring to hide myself. I never heard any sentence or sentiment of his repeated by Mother or Aunt."

Thus passes the good pastor unpraised and unquoted out of the records of his family. Not altogether fairly; the Reverend William Emerson did manage in the latter years of his life to rise beyond obscurity. Appointed chaplain of the Senate of the Commonwealth, he had the honor, from time to time, of dining with the governor. In keeping with this new position, he could be seen walking along Chauncy Street down to the Capitol building in knee breeches, black silk stockings, sporting a gold-headed cane. In the small, but growing literary circle of Boston he was recognized as editor of the *Monthly Anthology* (forerunner of the *North American Review*); in conservative political circles he was recognized as that sound-minded theologian who had expressed the view that social reform was a danger to the country, "talents, honors, wealth having natural sway over the opinions of mankind which ought not to be unbalanced by a rowdy democracy that take the gilt edge off of government." Perhaps it was just as well that Pastor William Emerson did not live long enough to witness Pastor Ralph Waldo Emerson heartily endorsing a "rowdy democracy."

After her husband's death, Mrs. Emerson, being granted a small pension, opened a boarding house in Cambridge as a means of support for herself and her children. Her four boys (she put Robert into the hands of a caretaker) now had to work harder than before, foregoing all the usual sports and play of childhood. In these preadolescent years, with no friends, and remote, even from his brothers, Waldo Emerson developed into a shy, lonely boy whose intellect was far beyond his years. When he reached age thirteen, Aunt Mary began preparing him to enter Harvard College. In the Emerson household, as in most New England families of similar traditions, poverty was no excuse for not striving for the higher life. Industriousness and godliness were the virtues that saw a New England boy through.

Having been equipped by his aunt with knowledge of Plato, Aristotle, Milton, Locke, Coleridge, Lord Byron—Waldo Emerson entered Harvard College in 1817 at age fourteen. His brother William having disappointed Aunt Mary by declaring for law instead of theology, the good lady decided to leave nothing to chance in Waldo's case, and became quite vocal in her determination to see him in the pulpit. She went around Concord boasting to all her friends that Waldo, besides being a practitioner of poetry could correspond with her in Latin and Greek; that of all her nephews none was more suited in temperament and intellect for the clergy than he.

Another influence pushing him in the same direction was his step-grandfather, the Reverend Ezra Ripley, who often invited the Emerson boys to stay with him in Concord at The Old Manse, the homestead in which their father and aunt had been born and brought up. Though Waldo made no effort to resist family aspiration for his future, inwardly he was uncertain whether he was really fit for the chosen profession. At the moment his highest ambition was to become a poet.

Emerson's anticipation of Harvard upon entering was that it would be a kind of laboratory in which in four years he could at least put to the test both his abilities and all the religious ideas hammered into his head since early childhood. But in this and other ways college life proved disappointing. In the beginning it looked as if, for physical reasons alone, he might fail in his studies. Up at dawn, with prayers in a cold hall and the scantiest of breakfasts before going into the lecture room, he usually arrived there in a state of fatigue from having waited on tables in the dining room to help defray cost of his tuition and books. As "president's freshman" he also had to run errands on command, an assignment to which was attached some honor, but did little to bolster energy or time to study. Under pressure of long hours and insufficient rest he shortly began to suffer from what was diagnosed as "weak lungs"—a term bearing the sinister suggestion of tuberculosis. Absence due to illness was so frequent during his first two terms at Harvard that he made a poor showing when grades were posted, and this was even more discouraging to him than his poor health.

Thus, in almost constant physical or mental distress, Emerson spent his crucial adolescent years. Disillusioned at finding the academic world not at all the forum for ideas he had expected, his morale slipped enough at one point to make him equally disappointed in himself. "I find myself often idle, vagrant, stupid, and hollow," he wrote in the journal which, after the custom of the times, he began to keep at age seventeen. "This is somewhat appalling, & if I do not discipline myself with diligent care I shall suffer severely from remorse and the sense of inferiority hereafter. All around me are industrious and will be great. I am indolent & shall be insignificant. Avert it heaven! Avert it virtue! I *need* excitement."

But little glory or excitement befell Emerson as an undergraduate. The verse which he wrote, when shown to his teachers, was passed off by them as being little more than mediocre. His prose, too, did not seem to strike anyone as extraordinary though at least two essays merited him a prize. In the absence of any intellectual peer or soul mate with whom to share illusion and disillusion, he poured all of his thoughts into his journal, testing not only himself as a person, but his ideas against the accepted faiths passed down through the generations.

What is evil? What is Good? What is God? What is Soul? Asking these questions and many more, Waldo Emerson was unafraid in the privacy of his little book, not only to challenge authority, but even his own answers from one day to the next. In a constant juxtaposition of new ideas against old, he vowed never to become like those of his professors who clung to the past as if it were forever holy, unwilling ever to exalt anything new or revolutionary. One day he made a note to himself to keep, throughout life, an open, flexible philosophy, and, above all, to concern himself with *living* history. "It is my own humor to despise pedigree," he wrote, "The dead sleep in their moonless night; my business is with the living."

Had some wise counselor come forward at this moment to advise that church dogma and a flexible philosophy were inconsistent each with the other, Emerson might have been spared much agony in the next number of years. Instead he went on preparing "for the great profession

I have purposed to undertake. I am to give my soul to God and withdraw from sin and the world." As he approached his nineteenth year, he put himself before the most unsparing of mirrors to measure the growth of his intellect and humanity and found much to worry him concerning his future.

> In twelve days I shall be nineteen years old which I count a miserable thing. Has any other educated person lived so many years and lost so many days? Look next from the history of my intellect to the history of my heart. A blank, my lord. I have not the kind affections of a pigeon. Ungenerous & selfish, cautious & cold, I yet wish to be romantic. Have not sufficient feeling to speak a natural hearty welcome to a friend or a stranger. . . . There is not in the whole wide Universe of God (my relations to Himself I do not understand) one being to whom I am attached with warm and entire devotion, not a being to whom I have joined fate for weal or woe, not one whose interests I have heartily & dearly at heart; and this I say at the most susceptible age of man.

At times, however, his head would suddenly go swarming with romantic possibilities even for so awkward a fellow as himself and he would abandon the idea of the pulpit, deciding to plunge into the great world after all. He would see himself as a kind of circuit-riding philosopher-poet like those of early Greek and Roman times, acting as eyes, ears, heart, feeling, and thought for all humanity as he went from town to town seeking and speaking truth as he found it. "Preaching is a pledge," he told himself, "while I wish to say all that I think & feel today with the proviso that tomorrow perhaps I shall contradict it all. Freedom boundless, I wish."

But was freedom possible for him or, for that matter, any young man of his day? Had not everything already been decided for them? What to think, what to wear, how to earn a living, how to act, even, in many cases, whom to marry. For the first time Emerson began to rail out at society as if that were the great monster moving him puppetlike into a fixed fate.

> Who is it that shall control me?
> Why may not I act and speak and write and think with entire freedom. What am I to the Universe or the Universe, what is it to me? Who hath forged the chains of Wrong & Right, of Opinion & Custom? And must I wear them? Is Society my annointed King?

He decided that if he did, indeed, enter the ministry, he would *not* be like all the others, but would bring to that profession something new, a poet's life style, perhaps; certainly a poet's vision of the universe.

As a young man Emerson retained the full force of his childhood enthusiasm for the natural world around him, seeing all of earth's marvelous potential for progress in science, its panorama of beauty, its miracle of rebirth in spring, its varied species of life in a continuity of harmony— above all man with soul and intellect as instruments of originality and creativity. He knew that the only message he could bring to his fellows was one overriding the narrow cant, fear, and pessimism then so dominant in the New England church. Calvinist doctrine demeaned man as less than a worm, earth as less than heaven, placed all its focus on the afterlife rather than the present, putting a damper on the human spirit and blocking, in Emerson's view, motivation for human progress. While walking the fields of New England, mulling over Sunday sermons he had heard which deplored all but literal interpretation of the Bible, he was asking himself: *Is not God in Man and thus Man himself sublime? Is not Now heaven?*

> Is all this beauty to perish? Shall none remake this sun & wind, the skyblue river, the riverblue sky, the yellow meadow spotted with sacks and sheets of cranberry pickers, the red bushes, the irongray houses with just the colour of the granite rock, the paths of the thicket in which the only engineers are the cattle grazing on yonder hill; the straggling wild orchard in which nature has deposited every possible flavour in the apples of different trees.

Offered the position of class poet at commencement after numerous others had turned it down, Emerson grabbed at the opportunity to play the role he treasured above all others. "I am a born poet," he would bravely venture to say some years later to the woman he wanted to marry. But while reciting his carefully worked-over poem before the large assembly gathered for Harvard's graduation exercises in the year 1821, he apparently was still too "cautious and cold" to make any in the audience—except a beaming Aunt Mary—sit up and announce him for genius.

During the following summer and fall his aunt had to keep a fire lit under him to keep him headed straight on to Harvard Divinity School. A "strong imagination and keen relish for the beauties of poetry" were *not* inconsistent with the ministry, she enthusiastically and poetically assured him. Too poor to be at leisure, the not yet twenty-one-year-old Emerson meanwhile was teaching school in Boston and appalled to discover how inadequately he met the challenge of row upon row of young females all surveying him with mocking glances, laughing, and speaking out of turn as if on purpose to vex him. Growing daily more shy and awkward in their presence, he barely managed to maintain discipline. Nor did he do much better with his class of boys. "Oh, sad!" was the strongest reprimand he could summon when his pupils got out of hand. It set him to wondering how on earth his aunt or any one else, including himself, expected him to preach if he showed so spare a talent for teaching.

The dilemma of settling for a profession was a peculiarly sharp one in Emerson's day. Though tradition of following in the footsteps of one's father seemed on the surface to simplify matters, in truth there was a growing discontent among college students, many of whom were beginning to chafe openly both at the burden of pressure to prepare for professional life and at the limited fields open to them. Law (and through law to politics or other forms of government service), medicine, teaching, the ministry—that about summed up the list. Striking out on one's own in youth's restless search for identity, even becoming an ordinary tradesman along the way until able to make a mark in a particular creative field was frowned upon in the genteel circles of New England.

Emerson's inclination now, as in all his earlier fantasies at Harvard, was to defy established practice and do whatever he pleased. But he had younger brothers whom he had to help through college, and there was his aunt whom he despaired of hurting. He could not, at this time, bring himself to outright rebellion. In the spring of 1824 he entered Harvard Divinity School consoling himself that at least as a clergyman he would be following that which was introspective in his nature, would have time to read, write, think, and—when the right moment came—rise in the pulpit to speak truth as he saw it through the eyes of a modern man.

Two years at Divinity School did much to develop Emerson's philosophical mind but little to ease the agony of daily grappling with religious doubts. One day he would be "not certain that God exists" and the next be pondering the thought: "but that he does not is a most bewildering and improbable chimera." As in the past, he had no friend or counselor with whom to share such thoughts, trusting everything to his journal. The entries made during this period indicate his wide range of reading outside the scope of the curriculum and with what maturity he was searching out the riddle of human behavior and human existence. On October 8, 1824, he wrote:

It is a striking feature in our condition that we so hardly arrive at truth. There are very few things of which we can wisely be certain tho' we often let unfounded prejudices grow into bigoted faith. We are immersed in opposite probabilities whenever we turn our thoughts to any of those speculations that are exercise of our understandings. . . .

On January 8, 1826, he jotted down a thought later to become the basis of his great essay, "Compensation."

All things are double one against another, said Solomon. The whole of what we know is a system of Compensations. Every defect in one manner is made up in another. Every suffering is rewarded; every sacrifice is made up; every debt is paid.

He was twenty-three. He thought he was growing old. He had yet had no life to speak of outside of classroom walls and he was restless for the common man's daily experiences. His darkest moments came when recurring illness in his lungs made him suspect he'd die without ever having had a chance to make a showing among his contemporaries, destined not even, as he wrote in the journal, "to get a memory when I am gone." But such moods passed the moment he had an improvement in health. Typical of his lifelong optimism is the journal entry he made July 28, 1826, indicating a turn of mind in religious philosophy directly opposite to that which continued to dominate his father's generation.

Satisfaction with our lot is not consistent with the intentions of God & with our nature. It is our duty to aim at change, at improvement, at perfection. It is our duty to be discontented with the measure we have of knowledge & of virtue, to forget the things behind & press toward those before.

Under the circumstances in which Emerson entered Divinity School, it is hardly to be wondered at that on the very eve of his ordination he still should be vacillating in religious belief. "Satisfy me beyond the possibility of doubt of the certainty of all that is told me concerning the other world and I will fulfill the conditions on which salvation is suspended . . . change that imperfect to perfect evidence & I too will be a Christian. But now it must be admitted I am not certain that any of these things are true." Not many years hence, in his great essay "Circles" he would write: "People wish to be settled; only as far as they are unsettled is there any hope for them." But at the moment, as he took up his duties as junior pastor of the Second Church (Unitarian) in Boston in 1826, he prayed for nothing more than a mind at peace. "Few men have suffered more genuine misery than I have suffered," he wrote in his journal.

Yet, with the inner man in constant battle with the outer, Emerson lasted six years in the pulpit. Telling his parishioners at the outset that he would be original, he dedicated a great deal of time to bringing his ideas into conscious order, wrote sermons that sparkled with innovations in style and thought, and gained, to his surprise, a rather large, liberal-minded following boastful of his intellect and sincerity. Few genuinely understood his revolutionary approach to religion—that the church as an institution meant nothing to him if it survived on form rather than content, on hypocrisy rather than action, if it refused to change as man's knowledge of his physical environment and social needs changed. When the old minister resigned, the congregation enthusiastically elevated its young minister to be senior pastor.

Aunt Mary and his mother were ecstatic at his success, the former even content now to let the younger Charles and Edward Emerson pursue law as their profession. To the members of his family, as to all others who came regularly to listen, Pastor Emerson followed his own rule never to make recitations from the podium but to speak directly to "Mr. A. and Mr. B. and Mr. C." impressing upon them as contemporary men "those arts and objects by which we are surrounded—the printing press and the loom, the phenomenon of steam and gas" (putting such homely fact into the realm of poetry) and thereby arousing pride in them for the genius of Man, the magic of Now. "I would write a sermon upon the text men are made a law unto themselves, to advise them to fear & honor themselves. Don't you see you are the Universe to yourself. You carry your fortune in your own hand."

> Suicidal is this distrust of reason this fear to think, this doctrine that 'tis pious to believe on others' words, impious to trust entirely to yourself. To Think is to receive.

For this "radical" doctrine, orthodox Calvinists came down upon Emerson as a dangerous man preaching an atheistic message. The spread of Unitarianism they saw as a formidable threat to the power of the New England Church. The Reverend Lyman Beecher (Harriet Beecher Stowe's father) was urgently dispatched from Litchfield, Connecticut, to Boston to war against "attacks made on our holy religion." The two great voices—evangelist Beecher and radical Emerson made for a lively time in the populous seaport town. By 1830 evangelists of Beecher's ilk were warning the nation of "materialism" arguing that its preoccupation with technology and science in the industrial age would lead to widespread infidelism; already, they said, every new railroad car and steamboat was bringing in atheists set on undermining God, Church, and State. Emerson, the modern man, had ready his reply: "The religion that is afraid of science dishonours God and commits suicide," he said. "It acknowledges that it is not equal to the whole of truth."

In the more than 160 sermons Emerson preached before finally resigning the pulpit in 1832, he kept hammering away at his central thought: Man is the architect of his own fortune; morality must be based on individual conscience; moral law enters the spirit of man through unity with God and Nature. The *soul* must be elevated, Emerson said, for it, like the heart, refuses to be imprisoned.

> Thus revering the soul . . . man will come to see that the world is the perennial miracle which the soul worketh and be less astonished at particular wonders; he will learn that there is no profane history; that *all* history is sacred; he will learn that . . . the universe is represented in an atom in a moment of time.

It is a mark of the gentle persuasiveness of Emerson's character, and the awe in which his scholarship and poetic oratory was held that his advanced ideas did not affect his respectable standing in the community. Like his father before him he was appointed acting-chaplain for the state senate and became an intimate of the governor. He was a highly respected member of the school board. Thus, his resignation when it was announced in 1832 shocked Boston. "The young minister's gone mad," was the rumor that went around, for who in his right mind would throw up so many honors for "conscience."

Conscience had indeed caught up with Emerson. The surface reason he gave for resigning was that he could no longer perform certain church rituals that were incompatible with his liberal religious ideas. But incompatibility with the church ran deeper than this, and resignation had been brewing for a long time. Particularly did he feel restrained by the hierarchy from speaking out openly on matters other than religion, most especially on the controversial subject of slavery. During a winter trip taken for reasons of health to St. Augustine, Florida, in 1827, he had for the first time come face to face with the reality of human slavery. The town marshal of St. Augustine, who served also as treasurer of the Bible Society, being anxious to keep an eye on all his interests, had arranged a meeting of the society to be held at the same time as a slave auction in an adjoining yard. Emerson was horrified, and wrote in his journal that evening: "One ear therefore heard the glad tidings of great joy whilst the other was regaled with 'Going, gentlemen, going!' and almost without changing our position we might aid in sending the scripture to Africa or bid for 'four children without the mother' kidnapped therefrom."

Organized churchdom of New England turned deaf ears to the appeals of William Lloyd Garrison and others that it take the lead in abolition of slavery. Slavery, said the church, was a political issue and not to be considered within its province. To be free of this institutional tie so as to be able to act as a whole man, answerable to no one except his own conscience, became an imperative for Emerson. To speak out against the shackling of men whether it be their minds, tongues, or bodies—*that* was within the province of the philosopher. "Though the voice of society should demand a defence of slavery from all its organs, that service can never be expected from me," he wrote. "I have not a syllable of all the language I have learned to utter for the planter. If by opposing slavery I go to undermine institutions, I confess I do not wish to live in a nation where slavery exists."

Only his impending marriage to Ellen Louisa Tucker, seventeen-year-old daughter of a well-to-do Boston merchant, had delayed an immediate resignation. The love affair, such as he had dreamed of but never expected would come his way, was momentarily all-consuming, he, for the first time feeling "as happy as it is safe in life to be." All the love and emotion so long held in check he poured into this relationship, his romantic sympathies heightened by the fact that Ellen was so young, so frail (she was suffering from tuberculosis), and so beautiful. "She has the purity and confiding religion of an angel," he wrote blissfully in his diary a few days after she became his "dearest earthly friend"—terminology of the day for partner in marriage. But Ellen was doomed by her illness. She died a short eight months later, leaving Emerson almost numb with grief. Coming away from her funeral, he returned once again a lonely man to a lonely house, with little heart for continuing his own life. But reason, as always with Emerson, prevailed.

> O willingly, my wife, I would lie down in your tomb . . . but will the dead be restored to me? Will the eye that was closed on Tuesday ever beam again in the fullness of love on me? Shall I ever again be able to connect the face of outward nature, the mists of the morn, the star of eve., the flowers & all poetry with the heart and life of an enchanting friend? No. There is one birth and one baptism and one first love.

The death of his wife left Emerson with no further tie holding him either to his post or to Boston. Unruffled by the storm that broke over his head in the wake of his resignation, he set sail out of Boston harbor in January 1833 on a journey to Europe, looking upon it both as a pilgrimage of self-discovery and one to sources of wisdom in the old world that might help him better understand the new. "I want teachers," he told Aunt Mary. The teachers he had in mind were Goethe, the German poet-philosopher (but Goethe died just before Emerson left for Europe); Samuel Coleridge, whose *Aids to Reflection* he had so much admired when it was first published in America in 1829; John Stuart Mill, English Philosopher; Thomas Carlyle, Scottish philosopher; poets William Words- worth and Walter Savage Landor.

The little brig *Jasper*, which besides its five passengers carried a cargo of logwood, mahogany, tobacco, sugar, coffee, beeswax, and cheese, had a stormy voyage. Only occasionally did the sun come out and with it the lanky seasick philosopher Emerson whose wind-whipped face looked almost like that of an Indian—his cheekbones being arched high, his nose eagle sharp under a ponderous brow. Thrown for the first time in close company with men who were not scholars, or of his cultured Boston milieu, he watched in awe and envy the skills of seamen and captain, now far more interesting to him than a beachful of sea-shells.

> Honor evermore aboard ship to the man of action—to the brain in the hand. Here is our stout master worth a thousand philosophers—a man who can strike a porpoise & make oil out of his blubber, and steak out of his meat; who can thump a mutineer into obedience in two minutes; who can bleed his sick sailor, mend the box of his pump, who can ride out the roughest storm on the American coast, & more than all, with the sun & a three-cornered bit of wood, & a chart, can find his way from Boston across 30000 miles of stormy water into a little gut of inland sea 9 miles wide with as much precision as if led by a clue.

He had another lesson too, important to his future. Listening to the uninhibited speech of unlettered Yankee sailors, he found in it an elo- quence all its own, basis for stronger poetry, he thought, than the frilly language so many American poets used in imitation of English verse. It occurred to him that American literature would probably never come fully into its own until it looked homeward and not abroad, until it re- flected with healthy realism the action and language of all its people including these slang-rich seamen. In such company, mid-ocean, detached from civilization he felt almost emboldened enough himself to shed his polite New England skin and shout aloud a damn to all official goodness and hypocrisy. But many years were to pass before, even into the privacy of his journal, Emerson could bring himself to utter a healthy oath.

Most intriguing to Emerson was observation of his own reactions in this new environment. "Wherever we go, whatever we do, self is the sole object we study and learn."

> I bring myself to sea, to Malta, to Italy to find new affinities between me and my fellowmen, to observe narrowly the affections, weaknesses, surprises, hopes, doubts which new dies of the panorama shall call forth in me.

New dies of the panorama awakened in him sensuous, extravagant tastes, revived earlier romantic moods and notions. By diligence, by mule, by foot, by brig during the next few months he went to Syracuse, the peninsula of Ortygia, Mt. Etna, the pillars of the Temple of Jove, the Tomb of Archimedes, the Ear of Dionysius. He heard mass in the ancient temple of Minerva, picked wild flowers near the fountain of Cyane, tasted fragrant Hyblaean honey for breakfast, quails for dinner. Only Italian opera failed to move him. "I am my own comedy and tragedy," he wrote in his journal.

Change of scene, passage of time gradually subdued the nagging grief for Ellen. "Did they tell you that I went away from home a wasted, peevish invalid?" he wrote to assure Aunt Mary. "Well, I have been mending ever since and am now in better health than I remember to have enjoyed since college." Mounting a mule for Messina, the mended Yankee scholar passed through "towns of goats," jogged along roads exposed to sea, watched fishermen drawing nets and stood fascinated by mountains of marble while waiting for a steamboat to Palermo. Sailing between Scylla and Charybdis, he grew so excited "it is hard to keep one's judgment upright." "I want my Virgil and Ovid," he cried, "I want my history and my Plutarch; I want maps and gazeteers. Were I fourteen days earlier here I would sit down in the Capuchin convent and take my chance of begging or buying the right books."

In Paris, "a loud modern New York of a place," it was the *Jardin des Plantes*, the Natural History Museum where "the real is stranger than the imaginary" that excited him.

> Not a form so grotesque, so savage nor so beautiful but is an expression of some property inherent in man the observer . . . I feel the centipede in me—cayman, carp, eagle & fox. I am moved by strange sympathies. I say continually, "I will be a naturalist."

Listening to lectures on evolution at the Sorbonne, Emerson was moved to wish that narrow-minded religionists in America could be prevented from blocking the teaching of this fascinating subject in the colleges. If America were to be a great power, he thought, it could not afford to ignore *any* findings of the scientists. But greatness needed the voice of the philosopher too, to inspire the nation not to lose sight of its soul while reaping the benefit of all that science had to offer. His hope was that one day he himself might be that philosopher.

With this ever-present in his mind, he spent his last weeks in Europe seeking interviews and permanent ties with men whose literary and philosophical works were then profoundly affecting modern thought. For the most part he was disappointed with those he had hoped would be his teachers. In Walter Savage Landor (best known for *Poems* and *Imaginary Conversations*) he found little poetry, no meaningful conversation; his talk with John Stuart Mill dampened his enthusiasm both for the man and his philosophy. At Highgate, home of Samuel Coleridge, he found the poet-critic to be too "old and preoccupied to bend to a new companion and think with him." At Rydal Mount, Wordsworth, "a plain, elderly, white-haired man, not prepossessing, and disfigured by green goggles," offended Emerson's shy nature by reciting one of his own poems "like a schoolboy declaiming" as they strolled through the garden. Saddened that here, too, he'd find no lifetime tie, Emerson went on to Craigenputtock, traveling all day through a driving rain to reach the home of the last of his idols, Thomas Carlyle. "It turned out 'a white day in my years,'" he wrote in his journal, "I found the youth I sought in Scotland."

Living on their isolated farm to which few visitors ever came, Carlyle and his wife, Jane, greeted Emerson warmly, insisted that he send his carriage away and stay overnight. The two philosophers, both of the same age, both seeking in their lives to be what Emerson termed "the genuine man," talked through the night enjoying a heated discussion on religion, politics, literature, America, their talk continuing on at breakfast next morning. Throughout Emerson was certain, no matter how far distant their two lands, he and Carlyle would be united in friendship. Carlyle, though having a fine time talking to a New World Yankee, had no illusion of a prolonged relationship. "I don't know what brought him and we kept him one night and then he left us," he wrote afterward. "I saw him go up the hill; I didn't go with him to see him descend. I preferred to watch him mount and vanish like an angel."

The "angel" refused to vanish. His correspondence with Carlyle over the years fills two volumes. It was Emerson who introduced his friend's *Sartor Resartus* to American readers, a book that became for many years prior to and after the Civil War, a best seller of its kind. The two men did not always see eye to eye, but they stimulated one another's thinking on a wide range of subjects, Emerson remaining always optimistic, romantic in contrast to Carlyle's wry skepticism.

Emerson returned to America a more cosmopolitan man than when he had left and with increased confidence in his own genius and in that of his country.

> Glad I bid adieu to England, the old, the rich, the strong nation, full of arts & men and memories; nor can I feel any regret in the presence of the best of its sons that I was not born here. I am thankful that I am an American as I am thankful that I am a man.

No longer did he feel need to lean on European thinkers; no longer would he ever be patient with himself or any other American who bowed to the taste of the Old World to the exclusion of native ability. Self-Reliance! What energy lay behind that simple phrase. It signified the Original Man, the Non-Conformist Man, the man leaning on his own ideas in religion as well as in politics and the arts. At every possible opportunity, Emerson decided, he'd bid American scholars, poets, architects, indeed all his countrymen to be done with copying, to build always on the premise: have I not my own experience—my own native genius?

The first few months after his return home Emerson spent in Newton with his mother, and there, in the peace and quiet of the Massachusetts countryside feasted on the works of oriental poets and philosophers, on the works of Goethe and Kant. Feasted, too, on the beauty of the surrounding landscape. In the opinion of John Jay Chapman, one of Emerson's earliest biographers, Emerson's worship of the New England landscape "amounts to a religion." In all that Emerson wrote, sermons, essays, poetry, he evoked the quality of that landscape as man's connection with the infinite. "We tend to see the world piece by piece," he wrote, "sun, moon, animal, tree, but the whole of which these are the shining parts is the soul." In the woods, in the fields, in the uplands of Newton, with all his faculties open to receive, Emerson was inspired to sum up the essence of his religious faith:

A man contains all that is needful to his government within himself
. . . All real good or evil that can befall him must be from himself.
He only can do himself any good or any harm. Nothing can be given
to him or taken from him, but always there's a compensation. There
is a correspondence between the human soul and everything that
exists in the world; more properly everything that is known to man
. . . The purpose of life seems to be to acquaint man with himself.
He is not to live to the future as described to him, but to live to the
future by living to the real present. The highest revelation is that God
is in every man . . . it is the "open secret" of the universe . . . I
believe in *this* life.

Moving out from Newton, traveling from village to village to spread
this liberating gospel, Ralph Waldo Emerson, in the role of itinerant
philosopher-poet, felt as strong a sense of mission as any of the revival-
meeting evangelists of the 1830s then barnstorming through the country
whipping up religious frenzy. But he was a soul saver of a new breed,
preaching possibility and hope. "I plainly read my duties as writ with
pencil of fire," he said, "they speak not of death; they are woven of
immortal thread."

His lectures became increasingly popular, especially with students.
The long, thin man with the dark hair, blue eyes, and eagle nose, became
revered by some as a prophet, by others as a saint. But Emerson was
under no illusion that all who came out to hear his "Emersonese" (as
the critics liked to refer to his highly intellectual, poetic discourses) were
making the connection he intended between poetry and religion. "In
all my lectures," he said, "I have taught one doctrine, namely the infinitude of the private man. This the people accept readily enough, &
even with loud commendation as long as I call the lecture Art; or Politics; or Literature; or the Household; but the moment I call it Religion,—
they are shocked."

One who was not shocked was Miss Lydia Jackson of Plymouth,
Massachusetts. Mutual friends confided to Emerson that this young lady
was sympathetic to his "new light" enthusiasms, and he soon became
aware of some sly maneuvering to bring them romantically together.
Riding forth one day to meet Miss Jackson, he prayed she would also
be sympathetic to his intense dislike of "fancy dinners, tailors, gigs, and
balls," and be unspoiled enough—should he find her to his taste for
marriage—to leave her comfortable Plymouth home for his more isolated
bucolic life in Concord where he now intended permanently to settle.

Lydia (or Lydian as he soon preferred to call her), gave a madonna-like impression with her mass of dark hair pulled up to expose a high forehead and features of quiet, classic beauty. Long a hero worshiper of Waldo Emerson, she offered no resistance to his proposal except for a stubbornly expressed desire not to leave Plymouth. "But Plymouth is streets," Emerson argued, "I live in the wide champaign . . . I am born a poet, of a low class without doubt, yet a poet. That is my nature and vocation. A sunset, a forest, a snowstorm, a certain river-view are more to me than many friends & do ordinarily divide my day with my books."

Lydian melted, promising by letter to come at once to marry and "live in Concord with Mr. Emerson." Emerson then felt free to tell her what he had not yet dared allow himself to feel: "I expect to love you & that you will love me better and better every hour whilst the world stands," ending by way of signature: "Waldo Emerson, for whom I hope you will be *able* to find a more affectionate name than 'Mr. E.'"

In September 1835 the two were married, going to live in The Old Manse, still occupied by Emerson's step-grandfather, Ezra Ripley. While Emerson occupied himself in the upstairs north study writing the first draft of an extended essay to be called *Nature*, "The Good old Pastor," as his neighbors called Ezra Ripley, helped acquaint Lydian with Concord and Emerson history. There had been an Emerson in Concord village since the first of them, fleeing England in the seventeenth century, had made his way to Musketaquid country and helped found Concord along the shore of the river. From the windows of the Old Manse in April 1775 Emerson's paternal grandmother had been eyewitness to the battle of Concord. Her husband, the Reverend William Emerson, had been among the first to recruit minutemen, joined the Army at Ticonderoga and died there of camp fever at age thirty-three. He was but one among many in the family touted as a hero. According to legend one of Waldo Emerson's clergyman-ancestors had saved Concord from the Indians. Listening to these and other tales, Lydian knew that her husband must have been reared on them which no doubt explained why, in his youth, he had etched and initialed onto a wooden panel beside the fireplace of one of the upper rooms in this homestead: "Peace to the soul of the blessed dead, honor to the ambition of the living."

The newlyweds did not long remain in The Old Manse. With a sizable inheritance which had been left to him by his deceased wife, Emerson bought a house of his own lying not quite a half mile from the center of Concord village. Here, for the first time, Lydian seriously took over hostessing for her husband's family and friends. "Promised Mr. E.

that I will be contented to give our many visitors only things comfortable dispensing wholly with luxury and show," she wrote to her mother. "Sometimes it comes over me as *so* strange that I should be housed with these two wonderful beings [Emerson's brother, Charles was now living with them] turning out coffee for them and helping them to pie! Consulting also about the keeping of pigs and hens and telling Waldo to be sure to stop at the grocers in his morning expedition . . . to inquire about the price of molasses & rinsing tubs." Lovingly dubbing her "Lydian Queen" of their new mansion, Emerson let her send him on any missions she pleased. "A man's wife," he observed in his journal, "has more power over him than the state."

He, meanwhile, was readying his manuscript of *Nature* for the printer. When it at last appeared in 1836 his reputation soared, both as philosopher and author. The first edition of the little book, a modest five hundred copies, quickly sold out as word spread of its poetic power and revolutionary theme—the same theme Emerson had been preaching from the outset: "Who can set bounds to the possibilities of man. Man has access to the entire mind of the Creator, is himself the creator in the finite." One among many students at Harvard College enthusiastically responding to the book and hailing its author as a prophet, was a young man by the name of Henry David Thoreau who thrilled to the knowledge that Ralph Waldo Emerson was his own townsman. Upon reading such a passage as—

> In the woods we return to reason and faith . . . Standing on the bare ground, my head bathed by the blithe air and uplifted into infinite space, all mean egotism vanishes. I become a transparent eyeball; I am nothing; I see all; the currents of the Universal being circulate me; I am part or parcel of God.

Thoreau knew he had come across a kindred spirit. At the first opportunity he hastened home to make Emerson's acquaintance, and when the older man wholeheartedly welcomed him, there began a relationship destined to be lifelong, to have profound influence upon Thoreau's life— indeed upon the times, and beyond the times in which both men lived. At the moment, in the upsurge for freedom just beginning to tear away at the old structures of nineteenth-century society in which more and more young men and women were daring to challenge the values of the past and insist on change, the philosophy of Emerson became the support on which they leaned, his word their word, his book their new bible.

As a result of *Nature*, so many liberal-minded clergymen, scholars, writers, scientists, students, farmers, housewives found their way to Emerson's door that Concord became the Mecca of New England, the press dubbing the man attracting so many disciples the "Concord Sage." The Phi Beta Kappa Society of Harvard, despite, or perhaps because of Emerson's controversial philosophy, invited him in 1837 to give its major address. Young James Russell Lowell, then a student at Harvard, described the occasion as "an event without former parallel . . . a scene to be always treasured in the memory for its picturesqueness and its inspiration. What crowded and breathless aisles, what windows clustering with eager heads, what enthusiasm of approval, what foregone dissent."

No one expected Emerson to follow traditional formula in his address and he did not disappoint his listeners. Titling his remarks "The American Scholar," he took full advantage of this opportunity (as on similar occasion before the graduates of Harvard Divinity School the following year) to call for the new man, the new American who once and for all would stop groping "in the dry bones of the past" and, with true sense of the dignity of his labors, begin to exercise the whole of his creative faculties for original thought and work. What is needed, he told his young audience, is Man Thinking, not men who believe that all thinking has already been done for him.

> The planter who is Man sent out into the field to gather food is seldom cheered by any idea of the true dignity of his ministry. He sees his bushel and his cart and nothing beyond, and sinks into the farmer, instead of Man on the Farm. The tradesman scarcely ever gives an ideal worth to his work, but is ridden by the routine of his craft, and the soul is subject to dollars. The priest becomes a form; the attorney, a statute book; the mechanic, a machine; the sailor, a rope of a ship.

Deploring the number of disconsolate students who, under the pressure of their frightening and restrictive world committed suicide, Emerson bid young and old alike to awaken to new hope, new dreams in a time ripe for change. He hit hard at scholars, accusing most of doing little more than parrot other men's thinking. Come out of the library into the fresh air, be modern men learning from *life*, he counseled his colleagues. "Free should the scholar be—free and brave." To aspiring poets and novelists in the room, as well as those unseen, he threw out similar challenge, asking why, in a country so filled with materials for imagination there was yet no voice singing America. "Our day of dependence, our long apprenticeship to the learning of other lands draws to a close," he said, "events, actions arise, that must be sung, that will sing themselves."

In his own recent traveling to give lectures, Emerson had begun

to realize not only the energy and adventurousness that took whole popu-
lations to break new territory westward, but the people themselves, a
conglomeration of cultures which he thought the greatest source of strength
the nation—and its creative artists if they would but take advantage of it—
possessed:

> This continent, asylum of all nations, the energy of Irish, Germans,
> Swedes, Poles, & Cossacks, & all the European tribes—of the Africans
> & of the Polynesians will construct a new race, a new religion, a new
> state, a new literature which will be as vigorous as the new Europe
> which came out of the melting pot of the Dark Ages.

His enthusiasm for America grew as he continued his travels in the bustling 1840s and 1850s; he became king of all Yankee boosters. Speaking
one day in a small church in Illinois (where a then unknown Abe Lincoln
came to listen), the next in a mining camp of Nevada or California,
Emerson was overjoyed to discover with what eagerness people of all
degrees of learning turned out to hear him. Commenting on this phenomenon, James Russell Lowell, the poet-critic who had had his earliest inspiration from Emerson, remarked that though practical folk would much
rather hear about a new air-tight stove than Plato they wouldn't miss a
chance to hear Mr. Emerson even if it did cost 27½ cents, would sit for
hours in whatever discomfort not only for the now famous oratory,
but for the practical good sense this tall Yankee philosopher brought
along whenever he came to town. "Is it not that he out-Yankees us all?"
Lowell asked, "that his range includes us all? that he is equally at home
with the potato-disease and original sin; with pegging shoes and the Over
Soul? that as we try all trades, so has he tried all cultures?"

And that indeed was what made Ralph Waldo Emerson more influential than his learned colleages—his willingness to leave his study and be
—to the degree he could—both a man of action (the rigors of his mule-
back journeys through western hills did sometimes give him that illusion)
and a mingler among all kinds of people. He not only gave inspiration,
he was receiving it; he not only shared his learning, but was himself
learning from his countrymen. His ideal American, he said, was "a stal-
wart Yankee man with a coat on his back" for whom he wanted a
rugged and uninhibited poet to sing the democracy of an adventurous,
earthy people. "We want a genius," he cried. "When I see how much
work is to be done, what room for a poet, for any spiritualist in this
great, intelligent, sensual, and avaricious America, I lament my fumbling
fingers and stammering tongue."

Already he had reluctantly faced the fact that his poems, exercises in experimental form and thought, were not measuring up to his own idea of what the new poetry had to be. "We have yet had no genius in America with tyrannous eye which knew the value of our incomparable materials," he wrote to his friend Carlyle, "our fisheries, our Negroes and Indians, the northern trade, the southern planting, the western clearing. Oregon and Texas are yet unsung. Yet America is a poem in our eyes."

Little wonder that Emerson was the first to welcome Walt Whitman's *Leaves of Grass* when it was published in 1855, for this was just such a poet and poem as he had anticipated. "I give you joy of your free and brave thought," he wrote to Whitman. "I have great joy in it. . . . I greet you at the beginning of a great career, which yet must have had a long foreground somewhere for such a start." In that "foreground" was Emerson himself. "I was simmering, simmering, simmering," Whitman later admitted, "Emerson brought me to a boil."

He brought others to a boil too, most notably, Henry David Thoreau, but also one unknown in her day, young Emily Dickinson who, like so many others of her generation in the 1850s, was as one observer put it "turning to Mr. Emerson as to the rising sun." The spreading of Emersonian philosophy helped break the Calvinist yoke of fear that for so long had damaged the spirit of the young in New England, opened a floodgate of long repressed emotions in the Puritan stronghold. Some converts to Emersonianism were striking out on new paths in literature, others finding new life styles, still others entering the arena of political and social struggle, all intent upon breaking free of ignorance, prejudice, and hypocrisy; all espousing the *new* morality based on individual conscience, all elevating soul and renouncing "things" which Emerson said were "in the saddle and riding mankind."

The author of *Nature; Essays* First & Second Series, 1841, 1844; *Poems*, 1846, *Representative Men*, 1850, was pleased by the impact he was having on the young as long as they were not simply following him blindly without original thought of their own. But it always alarmed him to hear of anyone making a cult of his teachings, or living to the letter all that he spoke. Emerson wanted liberated men and women, originators not apostles. "I am only an experimenter," he warned. "Do not, I pray you, set the least value on what I do, or the least discredit on what I do not, as if I had settled anything as true or false. I unsettle all things. No facts are to me sacred, none are profane; I simply experiment, an endless seeker, with no Past at my back."

Idealistic New Englanders who broke with Calvinism to become Emerson's followers came to be known as *transcendentalists*, epousers of a philosophy commonly associated with the German philosopher, Kant, which held that man has faculties transcending the senses through which, intuitively, he comprehends the universe. Actually Emerson's brand of transcendentalism was derived not alone from the German idealists, but from many different sources including his reading in Coleridge and oriental philosophers and poets. It had in it traces of the mystical, the romantic, the ideal, but always highlighting his central thought: "Man is all. In yourself is the law of all nature. It is for you to know all—to dare all." It was no ivory tower philosophy, but a highly practical one, meaning nothing if it did not teach people how to live—that is, entirely self-reliant, requiring no church, preacher, Bible, no intermediary whatsoever, to intervene between the individual soul and the center of all things of which man is part—call it Nature, call it God, call it Oversoul.

When not traveling, Emerson opened his house on Monday nights to all who wished to come discuss ideas with him. One small group that visited regularly came to be known as The Transcendental Club though it was never an official organization. The most important result of its free-flowing discussions was the birth of the magazine *Dial* to which Thoreau, Bronson Alcott (philosopher-teacher who was Louisa May's father), and others prominent in the transcendental circle contributed poems and articles. The *Dial* was coedited by Emerson and the brilliant Bostonian, Margaret Fuller (1810–50). Herself a controversial figure, Miss Fuller had been conducting for five winters what she called "Conversations" with a devoted following of young men and women who came to learn and share in her knowledge of philosophy and the arts. "She not only did not speak lies after our foolish social customs," said one of her pupils, "but she met you fairly. . . . Encountering her glance, something like an electric shock was felt. Her eye pierced through your disguises . . . you were at her mercy . . . she spoke rudely searching words, and told you startling truths . . . to be with her was the most powerful stimulus, intellectual and moral." Until her tragic death by drowning off the coast of Fire Island in 1850, Margaret Fuller was one of the most stimulating of Emerson's friends, a woman who dared challenge conventions and break with traditions, whose name was often slandered in her native Boston.

For almost two decades before the Civil War that city and its environs was center for most of the revolutionary activities of the times in which enlightened men and women were holding up the banner word Freedom —freedom for the slaves, freedom for women, freedom in religion. It was also center for all varieties of cults taking advantage of the new times to espouse peculiar callings. Indeed so many were the organizations springing up and meeting in convention from one week to the next in Boston that Emerson quipped once in amusement that his native city was entertaining "madmen, madwomen, men with beards, Dunkers, Muggletonians, Come-Outers, Groaners, Agrarians, Seventh-Day Baptists, Quakers, Abolitionists, Calvinists, Unitarians, and Philosophers." But he was glad to be alive in such dynamic times.

> If there is any period one would desire to be born in, is it not the age of Revolution; when the old and the new stand side by side and admit of being compared . . . when the historic glories of the old can be compensated by the rich possibilities of the new era. This time like all times is a very good one if we but know what to do with it.

One small group of his transcendentalist friends, thinking *they* knew what to do with it, had left their individual homes in 1841 to participate in a utopian commune known as Brook Farm, property bought, shared, and worked in common. Emerson refused to join the Brook Farmers in their "heaven on earth," though he went often to visit and lecture. While expressing great admiration for the high ideals of his friends, he was critical of their communal style of living. In his opinion "their solitary and fastidious manners not only withdraw them from the conversation, but from the labors of the world: they are not good citizens, not good members of society." Besides not participating in the abolition of the slave trade, "they do not even like to vote," he said.

Though many conservative Americans tended to pin on Emerson and his newfangled philosophy responsibility for everything from communistic communities springing up to "free love," alleged to be one of the goals of the women's rights movement, the truth was that Emerson renounced "extremes" in any direction, and of all his friends, was probably the most conventional in daily life style. He was an owner of property, a taxpayer, a member of the school board, above all a devoted family man. At the birth of his first child, a son, Waldo, his joy had been so great that Lydian wrote to her family, "I feel as if a volume might be filled before one could duly set forth all this child is to him, both as possession & hope."

As a father, Emerson had Pygmalian fantasies of molding his son into a truly ideal human being, and could not contain his excitement as, day by day, the boy developed under his careful guidance. All in the Emerson circle saw, through the father's eyes, the highest ideals of beauty, spirit, and intellect in young Waldo, and were aware that he had become center to Emerson's heart and dreams. Thoreau, especially, loved the boy whose care often fell to him when Emerson was off on a lecture-tour. This child, it was thought, would grow up to have that perfection called for in all the language of the transcendentalists. But young Waldo—quite unaware of what he was a symbol, or of whose great dream was perishing along with him—took sick and died of scarlatina when he was six years old. The tragedy had stunning repercussion on Emerson.

For weeks he walked in a daze about the grounds of his estate touching the swing upon which his son had so recently played, eyeing a small toy left in the grass, trying to understand what had befallen him. He could comprehend nothing of the fact of his loss but the bitterness. Not the comfort of his friends or of his wife, who for his sake tried to subdue her own mourning, seemed able to win him back to himself. At last, with further passage of time, Emerson returned to normal occupations—writing, lecturing, meetings with colleagues and friends, but he never fully recovered from this shattering experience. Two daughters— Ellen, born in 1839; Edith in 1841; and a son, Edward, born in 1844— each of whose thoughts and ambitions he also carefully nurtured—were dearly loved and vital to his daily existence; yet, for the forty years that Emerson lived past the terrible January day when young Waldo died, the loss of his first born remained a haunting grief. Five years after the event he wrote "Threnody" a long poem in memory of the child, many of its lines as freshly poignant as if spoken in those early weeks of mourning—

> *The South-wind brings*
> *Life, sunshine, and desire*
> *And on every mount and meadow*
> *Breathes aromatic fire;*
> *But over the dead he has no power,*
> *The lost, the lost, he cannot restore;*
> *And looking over the hills, I mourn*
> *The darling who shall not return.*
>
> *I see my empty house,*
> *I see my trees repair their bough;*
> *And he, the wondrous child*
> *. . . . .*
> *The hyacinthine boy, for whom*
> *Morn well might break and April bloom*
> *. . . . .*

> *Has disappeared from the Day's eye;*
> *Far and wide she cannot find him;*
> *My hopes pursue, they cannot bind him.*
> *O child of paradise,*
> *Boy who made dear his father's home,*
> *In whose deep eyes*
> *Men read the welfare of the times to come,*
> *I am too much bereft.*
>
> . . . .
>
> *O trusted broken prophecy!*
> *O richest fortune sourly crossed!*
> *Born for the future, to the future lost!*

The last words Emerson was to speak to Lydian when he himself lay dying in 1882 were, "Oh, that beautiful boy!" Yet the world at large had long since forgotten that he had ever known tragedy in his life. Throughout the years it had been his visions and inspiration that had helped keep the hope of a disintegrating nation alive. Tirelessly he chipped away at the influence of narrow-minded bigots whether that influence was in the Congress, in the pulpit, or in the neighborhood. He deplored false patriotism, false piety, and false morality. "I think that only is real which men love and rejoice in—not the things which starve and freeze & terrify them." Enthusiastically he welcomed every scientific advance, every new invention in a fast-industrializing America. Unlike many of his idealistic friends, he refused to indulge in nostalgic dreams of a more simple, graceful past which the coming of the railroad had interrupted. Thoreau would point to the evil of the iron horse—the sacrifice of precious timber and woodland, the lives of immigrant workmen sacrificed in its building, the speeding up of modern life; Emerson would see both the evil and the good. No longer would affluent Americans be going abroad at every opportunity, "the nervous rocky West is intruding a new & continental element into our national mind, & we shall have an American genius."

At the passage of the infamous Fugitive Slave Law in 1850 commanding "all good citizens to aid and assist" federal marshals and their deputies in the speedy return of escaped slaves, and imposing heavy penalties upon those who assisted in their escape, Emerson turned his attention to active participation in the anti-slavery struggle. Speaking in meetings throughout the East, he directed his sharpest attack against his once revered hero, Daniel Webster, Senator of Massachusetts, whose political compromise had permitted the passage of the law. "Under the shadow of his great name," cried Emerson, "inferior men sheltered themselves, threw their ballots for it, and made the law . . . Nobody doubts that Daniel Webster could make a good speech . . . but the question which history will ask is broader. In the final hour when he was forced by the peremptory necessity of the closing armies to take a side—did he take the part of great principles, the side of humanity and justice, or the side of abuse, and the oppression and chaos?"

As he had at the outbreak of the Mexican War, which he considered an immoral adventure on the part of his country, Emerson continued throughout the 1850s to denounce whoever or whatever in his view was hastening the corruption or disintegration of the nation he so loved. "One thing appears certain to me, that the Union is at an end as soon as an immoral law is enacted. He who writes a crime into the statute books digs under the foundations of the Capitol."

"It is rather painful to see Emerson in the arena of politics hissed and hooted at by young law students," wrote Henry Wadsworth Longfellow in his diary May 14, 1857. Painful for Emerson, too, but having entered the arena, he took all the consequences, and at that they were not half so dangerous for him as for men like William Lloyd Garrison, Wendell Phillips, Thomas Wentworth Higginson, Theodore Parker, all of whom had suffered either physical abuse in the streets or imprisonment. "The mob roared whenever I attempted to speak," he said of one rally in Boston, "and after several beginnings I withdrew." But at least the world knew that he was taking a side—the part of great principles, the side of humanity and justice.

As a philosopher Emerson deplored the waste and brutality of war, but he never considered himself a pacifist. "There never was a nation great except through trial," he said when it became clear that war was the tragic inevitability for his country. "A Civil War sweeps away all false issues on which it began, and arrives presently at real and lasting questions." He was critical of Lincoln for delaying the Emancipation Proclamation, but became among the first to announce Lincoln's greatness when the document was at last published in January 1863. A year earlier he had gone to Washington to confer with the President, and Lincoln had invited his Cabinet in to hear what America's great philosopher had to say. It is possible that in his excruciating dilemma as President of a divided nation, Lincoln may have gained confidence from this brief contact with Emerson to exercise individual conscience in a matter in which millions of human beings were the victims not only of southern slaveholders but corrupt northern politicians as well.

Throughout the war years Emerson continued to write, cherishing his country house in Concord for the solitude it gave him especially during the long New England winters. "The northwest wind, with all his snows, took me in charge," he said, "and defended me from company." One of the finest of his poems was written in the solitude of a snowbound evening.

THE SNOW-STORM

Announced by all the trumpets of the sky,
Arrives the snow, and, driving o'er the fields,
Seems nowhere to alight: the whited air
Hides hills and woods, the river, and the heaven,
And veils the farm-house at the garden's end.
The sled and traveller stopped, the courier's feet
Delayed, all friends shut out, the housemates sit
Around the radiant fireplace, enclosed
In a tumultuous privacy of storm.

Come see the north wind's masonry.
Out of an unseen quarry evermore
Furnished with tile, the fierce artificer
Curves his white bastions with projected roof
Round every windward stake, or tree, or door.
Speeding, the myriad-handed, his wild work
So fanciful, so savage, nought cares he
For number or proportion. Mockingly,
On coop or kennel he hangs Parian wreaths;
A swan-like form invests the hidden thorn;
Fills up the farmer's lane from wall to wall,

Maugre the farmer's sighs; and at the gate
A tapering turret overtops the work.
And when his hours are numbered, and the world
Is all his own, retiring, as he were not,
Leaves, when the sun appears, astonished Art
To mimic in slow structures, stone by stone,
Built in an age, the mad wind's night-work,
The frolic architecture of the snow.

In the summer Emerson liked to think that the hills and sandbanks that intervened between him and the city kept guard over his privacy, but as fame has its price, there was always some visitor at his door. Like all artists and scholars he would sometimes grow impatient when too many such interruptions interfered with his work. "A self-denial no less austere than the saint's is demanded of the scholar," he wrote. "He must embrace solitude as a bride." But when asked the secret of his energy it was not removal from his fellows of which Emerson spoke, but contact: "My only secret was that all men were my masters," he said. "The one event which never loses its romance is the alighting of superior persons at my gate."

In 1867 *May Day and Other Pieces* (poems) was published. Two years later came *Society and Solitude*. *Letters and Social Aims* was published in 1875, and the following year *Selected Poems*. Emerson was now seventy-three, age creeping upon him almost unnoticed. His life was full with family, friends, and travel. One of the most exciting adventures during this period was a railroad trip to the far west where he lectured in San Francisco, visited Salt Lake City and Yosemite. He also traveled to England, France, Italy, and Egypt, but for him America was still the nation of nations. While admitting reluctantly that the outcome of the Civil War had not brought the greater freedom in politics, religion, social science, education he had hoped, he retained his customary optimism, saying that there had been at least a general "opening up in the seams of tradition." "The very constitution is amended & is construed in a new spirit. Things once not possible are probable now. Women dispose of their own property. Women will vote. Women lecture, preach, are physicians, artists . . . I not only see a career at home for more genius than we have, but for more than there is now in the world." Having, in his own way, helped bring on such change, it was his life's reward.

"We Americans have lived fast in ten years," he wrote. "We have seen our rocks covered with gold, our states floored with coal, the rifts are now gushing oil. We have seen railroad & telegraph subdue our enormous geography. We have seen the snowy deserts on the northwest, the seals & Esquimaux become lands of promise: we have seen slavery disappear like a painted scene in the theatre. We have seen the old oligarchs tumbled out of their powerful chairs . . . those who were their victims occupy their places and dictate their fate. . . . We have seen

China opened to European & American ministers & commerce. Japan likewise. Our arts & our productions begin to penetrate both. Negroes, too, are a new nation of customers. Now we are working the new Siberian Telegraph & mean to perforate & deal with the old ball of the Earth as a carpenter does with wood." With his unabated interest in science, he recorded how the "tough old planet" was yielding to "man's power and convenience."

> The splendors of this age outshine all other recorded ages. In my lifetime have been wrought five miracles . . . steam boat, railroad, the electric telegraph, the application of the spectroscope to astronomy; the photograph . . . and what of cheap postage, the sewing machine, the mowing machine & the horse rake; the power loom, power press for printers, machines for pegging shoes, anaesthesia, the identity of electricity & magnetism; in geology the discovery of correspondence of the age of stratified remains to the ascending scale of structure in animal life; predictions of the weather for the next twenty-four hours for North America can be forecast by the Observatory at Washington.

In his last years Emerson's memory began to fail, a fact especially poignant as those who loved him watched him struggle for a lost thought or word while delivering a lecture titled "Memory." On attending Longfellow's funeral in March 1882, he could not remember the name of the man he had come to mourn. His own death seemed not far behind; indeed one month later, April 27, 1882, Ralph Waldo Emerson died, the churchbells of Concord tolling as if he had been king—but, sadly, with no king to replace him.

Emerson's influence upon his times had been more profound than even he was aware. In announcing his death, British critics called him and his friend Carlyle the "two fathers of the century," saying of Emerson that he was "the wiseman whose voice is heard round the world." His thought, interpreted so originally by Henry Thoreau, influenced men as diverse as Nietzsche and Gandhi, and continues to be an influence as the twentieth century draws to a close. Hardly a day passes that he is not quoted somewhere in the world either by a statesman, a commentator, a writer, or the humblest of men seeking what he sought—freedom to live to the highest of man's potential unobstructed by false values or false gods. Though never counting himself a great poet, all of the New England poets who followed Emerson, whether greater or lesser than he, took cue from him as to the goal to be reached:

> *Great is the art,*
> *Great be the manners of the bard.*
> *He shall not his brain encumber*
> *With the coil of rhythm and number;*
> *But leaving rule and pale forethought*
> *He shall aye climb high*
> *For his rhyme.*
> *"Pass in, pass in" the angels say,*
> *"In to the upper doors,*
> *Nor count compartments of the floors,*
> *But mount to paradise*
> *By the stairway of surprise."*

It would not be amiss to say that with the publishing of "Merlin" came the on-rolling tide of modern poetry.

No better epitaph for Emerson can be given than the lines he wrote in his diary the month his son Waldo was born: "The love that is in me, the justice, the truth can never die & that is all of me that will not die."

Henry David Thoreau
(1817–1862)

"Rather than love, than money, than fame, give
me truth."

Henry David Thoreau, native son of Concord, Massachusetts, was a
curiosity to his neighbors and sometimes a curiosity to himself. He came
home from college in 1837 moody, restless, impatient, showing no inclination to enter any of the professions or trades expected of a Harvard graduate like himself, nor any interest in achieving what his family or neighbors
called success. "The fear of displeasing the world ought not in the least
to influence my actions," he wrote in his journal. And in a bold, still
boyish hand put down his optimistic estimate for an exciting future:
"The world is a fit theatre today in which any part may be acted. There
is this moment proposed to me every kind of life that men lead anywhere,
or that imagination can paint."

It was his own mind, of course, doing the proposing, his own imagination doing the painting. At age twenty—and, indeed all the days of his
life—Henry had a romantic concept of himself as a poet, not one who
merely wrote, but who *lived* hour by hour a poetic existence. He had a
singular sense of adventure, too, which called him not to any faraway
place but deep into the heart of his own beloved New England. Asked
once by an acquaintance to join him in a trip abroad, Henry replied:
"Why go to the Indies in search of riches when riches are to be found
by other routes and other methods of travel?" In Concord alone was
there not poetry to be found in the meadow, drama in the woods,
silence in the river, and mystery and beauty and knowledge in all three?

The only part he yearned to play in the world's great theater was
that of a free-roaming naturalist-poet. And having learned from his distinguished Concord neighbor, Ralph Waldo Emerson, that "the reason

the world lacks unity and lies broken and in heaps is because man is
disunited with himself. He cannot be a naturalist until he satisfies all
the demands of the spirit," Henry decided that not until he had
achieved a style of life which answered all the demands of his spirit,
making him a man united with himself, would he consider himself a
success.

> As to conforming outwardly and living your own life inwardly, I have
> not a very high opinion of that course. If I were confined to a corner
> in a garret all my days, like a spider, the world would be just as large
> to me while I had my thoughts. . . . Perhaps I am more than usually
> jealous of my freedom . . . If I should sell both my forenoons and
> afternoons to society, neglecting my own peculiar calling, there would
> be nothing left worth living for.

Going one's own way in the neighborhood of a small New England
village was not easy. The young graduate did not, as is commonly believed,
fly at once in the face of all opinion and live exactly as he pleased.
There was the practical problem of finances to be solved, and a great
deal of soul-searching to do to find the inner resources necessary to face
up to all the obstacles against a man committed to living totally independent of institutions. Indeed, it took Thoreau almost eight years before
he fully came to terms with himself; it was not until 1845 that he went
to live alone in the woods at Walden determined "to meet myself face
to face at last."

> I went to the woods to front only the essential facts of life, and see if
> I could not learn what it had to teach, and not, when I came to die,
> discover that I had not lived. I did not wish to live what was not life,
> living is so dear; nor did I wish to practice resignation . . . I wanted
> to live deep and suck the marrow of life . . . to drive life into a
> corner and reduce it to its lowest terms, and if it proved to be mean,
> why then to get the whole and genuine meanness of it and publish its
> meanness to the world; or if it were sublime, to know it by experience
> and be able to give a true account of it.

Giving a true account of what he learned in the woods was the sum and
substance of the life Henry David Thoreau lived thereafter. A quiet man,
he made an unquiet sound in his village; a small man, he loomed large
over the landscape; a solitary man, he was a vivid presence everywhere
among his neighbors. Throughout two dramatic decades preceding the
Civil War, it was his "free and erect mind," as Emerson termed it, that

acted as the conscience of Concord society, fearlessly speaking hard truths and passionately ringing bells for justice.

"On the 1st of August 1844, when I read my Discourse on Emancipation in the Town Hall in Concord, and the selectmen would not direct the sexton to ring the meeting-house bell, Henry went himself and rung the bell at the appointed hour," said Emerson.

"This man," said Bronson Alcott, who sent his young daughter, Louisa May, and her sisters to be educated by Thoreau, "is a Revolution in himself." So compelling a revolution, apparently, that once when Henry was jailed for refusing to pay a tax levied to support the Mexican War which he vehemently opposed, even the local constable, Sam Staples, commented on his unique prisoner. Said Sam: "I never heerd a man talk honester."

Like all dissenters and non-conformists Thoreau was often singled out for abuse by frightened and narrow-minded people. Even those not so narrow-minded—James Russell Lowell and Nathaniel Hawthorne, for example—carped at him because of his purist habits. (Thoreau would not smoke, drink coffee, tea, alcohol; would not own more than one decent suit, would not ride if he could walk; and, when in the woods, disregarded modern implements in favor of surviving Indian style.) "Mr. Thoreau seems to me to insist in public on going back to flint and steel when there is a matchbox in his pocket which he knows very well how to use at a pinch," snapped Lowell.

Emerson, though he became Thoreau's staunchest defender, also had differences with his independent-minded, inflexible young friend, criticized him for refusing to vote, for not using his talents in a way that would have benefitted the entire country. He regretted that "it was not the Ship of State Henry was aching to captain, but only a huckleberry party or a search for chestnuts or grapes." When Thoreau died prematurely at age forty-five, having seldom ventured outside New England, and, aside from his townspeople, known but to a few devoted disciples, Emerson expressed great sadness that this undeniable genius should have been so content to let his superiority shine only "in his simple and hidden life. The country," he said, "knows not yet, or in the least part, how great a son it has lost."

A century later it is clear that the nation does know. That which Thoreau said of John Brown stands peculiarly true of him: "He is the only one who *has not* died. I meet him at every turn. He is more alive than he ever was . . . no longer working in secret only . . . he has earned immortality."

John Thoreau, father of two young children—Helen and John, Jr., —must have looked with concern upon the arrival of his third child, christened David Henry at birth in Concord, July 12, 1817. The little boy had come at a particularly bad time, for creditors were about to take over the family's general store. Bankruptcies were not uncommon in New England during this period, a sharp economic slump having set in after the War of 1812. But the cause of John Thoreau's failure seemed due less to external factors than to his gentle, studious nature, ill-suited to the business world. If, in his youth, Henry's father had dreamed of becoming something more romantic than a village merchant, the realities of a growing family and a demanding society had long since crushed the dream. He had had other business failures before this one; now with five in the family he knew he could afford no more. Once again he would try to borrow money, once again try to prove to himself and to his critical Boston relatives that he did not lack what they called true Yankee drive.

Almost all accounts that have come down about John Thoreau, Sr., picture him as a silent, plodding man, hovering always in the shadow of his more able, garrulous wife, Cynthia. Legend even puts him in the shadow of his children, for it is Henry who, in the end, gets the credit for making a success of his father's last business venture by introducing a process by which the Thoreau Pencil Factory turned out one of the most sought-after pencils in the country. But in recounting the history of the son, the father cannot be brushed aside so lightly. First and foremost in Henry Thoreau's observation of the world around him as he was growing up was the figure of his father—factory-enclosed, debt-burdened, anxiety-ridden—a man of whom Thoreau could easily have said, like Emily Dickinson of her father, "Father never played." That sad fact alone was enough to stimulate in Henry a desire to plot for himself a different kind of life, freer and happier in every respect.

Being third in a brood of four children (his sister Sophia having been born in 1819) never for a moment threatened to put Henry in the shadows. From the beginning this sharp-eyed, sensitive, bright little boy, who showed more than a trace of his father's owlish solemnity, struck the Thoreau clan, particularly the women of the family, as being something special. He was "Our Henry" to them, favored somewhat to

John, Jr., whom they expected would probably make a higher mark in the world. The brothers themselves made no such distinction, early became inseparable friends, and determined to make together whatever mark was to be made in the world.

Shortly after the failure of her husband's general store, Cynthia Thoreau moved the family out of the home of her in-laws and took a house close to the center of Concord village, which in due time she turned into one of the most popular boarding establishments in town. Itinerant preachers, politicians, lecturers, summer visitors, came to stay for varying lengths of time, as did, now and then, a student entrusted to Mrs. Thoreau's care. "Mrs. Thoreau *is a woman*," wrote one of the latter home to his mother. "She told me how she used to sit up nights and wait until a young man whom she had to board with her came home, a stranger to her, still she insists that she must treat all the same as her own. . . . If you were to see her, mother, you would be perfectly satisfied that I have fallen into good hands & have met with a second mother."

Into Mrs. Thoreau's good hands there fell also, on occasion, an escaped slave in need of temporary shelter, hurriedly ushered inside the boarding house under cover of dark by Henry's two aunts, Maria and Louisa, who had helped found Concord's Anti-Slavery Society. Early in childhood, then, Henry was aware not only of abolitionist sentiment in his home (his father refused to go to First Parish Church because it endorsed slavery) but heard that kind of conversation which exposed his young mind to the clashing views of varying personalities momentarily meeting in a boarding house environment. It was by no means an arid intellectual climate in which to grow up. Cynthia Thoreau, whose favorite pastime was escorting her family out on sunset strolls to woods and river to awaken in them an appreciation for Concord's natural beauties, encouraged her young children to see, listen, think high thoughts, and speak out their individual ideas.

Henry and John liked the bustling atmosphere of the boarding house and its interesting visitors, but for the most part they preferred their own company. Early in the morning with fowling pieces slung over their shoulders, the two boys would set out for escapades of animal tracking and hunting, never staying for anything so tame as playing on the village common. In those days, according to Henry's memory in later years, hunting and fishing grounds in Concord "were not limited like the preserves of an English nobleman, but were more boundless even than those of a savage." Within a matter of minutes Walden Woods could

enclose them in a private and ecstatic world of their own where, ruled
only by their own laws, they became masters of the chase, exulting in
their skill at bringing down game.

Or, should they prefer, they could escape to that other paradise
for boys—the river—ribboning the landscape as an enticement whatever
the season. Concord it was called, but the boys liked better the ancient
name given to it by the Indians before the English arrived to settle
by its banks in 1635—Musketaquid, or Grass-ground River. Most villagers shrugged the river off as being little more than a sluggish stream;
to the Thoreau brothers, it abounded with mysterious life below, and
had currents suggestive of the most romantic adventures. Here, where
no boat bigger than a canoe was to be seen, and no whistle other than
the cry of meadow or river birds, imagination contrived for John and
Henry an exciting port of entry and departure. Longing to be part of
the river's history, the brothers dreamed of a time when they could build
their own boat, sail through the thick, entangling lilypads to other woods
and meadows of New England like a pair of Columbuses on a voyage
of discovery.

What Henry David Thoreau was to be for the whole of his adult
life took root by this river and in these woods of Concord. The transition
of a hunter into a preserver and cherisher of life had had to begin with
his first conscious recognition as a boy that "a hare in its extremity cries
like a child." "No humane being past the thoughtless age of boyhood
will wantonly murder any creature which holds its life by the same
tenure that he does," Thoreau was to say in *Walden*, expressing no guilt
for the hunter role he had once played in the woods. "Such is oftenest
the young man's introduction to the forest and the most original part of
himself. He goes thither at first as a hunter and fisher, until, at last,
if he has the seeds of a better life in him, he distinguishes the proper
objects as a poet or naturalist and leaves the gun and fishpole behind."

What he would not leave behind was the truthfulness and spontaneous quality of childhood which he so idealized as to let it color
his strongest opinions of what adult life could and ought to be. Forever
close to the surface of Thoreau's memory was the vision of the bony-
cheeked boy he had been, healthfully, joyously alive, taking full advantage
of all his faculties to make the most of his days, of the natural world
he was heir to. To him one of the saddest facts of life was that the
majority of people lost not only their childhood too soon, but lost use

of its greatest gift—the ability to rise fresh to the day with all the senses alert and ready for new experiences.

His own childhood came to an end when he was barely into his teens. Bookish, idealistic, with a taste for poetry as strong as his taste for nature, he—and though with less intensity, John too—had dreamed of combining poetry and adventure, extending boyhood pleasures into a man's world. But he quickly learned that the structured society in which he lived had well-laid plans for its young men, in no way resembling boyhood dreams. His mother, with dreams of her own, was struggling to find the money to finance her two bright sons through Harvard College so that they might enter one of the customary professions such as law, medicine, or theology. Thinking in practical terms only, she had already sent Helen, the oldest of her two daughters, out to work as a tutor. The younger, Sophia, was being trained on the piano with the idea that she would later on earn her living as a music teacher. Far more was expected of Henry and John; in them lay Cynthia Thoreau's hope of solving once and for all the borderline poverty hounding the family. Well aware of this, however much the brothers dreaded preparing for one of the professions, neither wished to be the one to disappoint their resourceful mother.

Cynthia Thoreau's upbringing had been Tory-rebel, her mother the daughter of a British colonel, her father a hard-working, impoverished New England minister proud of having, in his youth, led a rebellion at Harvard College protesting the bad food. In her character Cynthia reflected both sides of this heritage. She had a flair for elegance put to good use in running a boardinghouse; and a highly practical mind which knew how to make-do when funds were low. Not by accident would her son Henry also know how to make-do when he finally came to the decision to be rich by owning little. Scottish practicality and French romanticism intertwined curiously in all the Thoreaus. Henry's paternal grandfather, the son of a French wine merchant, had sailed from the Channel Islands to New England in his youth and, before settling down to what he termed "a good marriage and a good fortune" in Boston, had deliberately allowed himself a few exciting years as a privateer.

Very little of his good fortune had been handed down to John and Cynthia Thoreau, but Cynthia determined that whatever other families could afford for their children, she would have for hers. All four young Thoreaus had music and dancing lessons, for which one son, at least, was always to be grateful. Outdoorsman Henry Thoreau, moving with

the grace of an Indian through narrow mountain passes would never
have a disparaging word to say for the dancing lessons given to him
as a boy though he disdained ever to put such skill to use in a social
parlor. As for music, his flute would accompany him wherever and whenever he went, whether for a night, a fortnight, or a year or more.

> In warm evenings I frequently sat in the boat playing the flute, and
> saw the perch which I seemed to have charmed, hovering around me
> and the moon traveling over the ribbed bottom which was strewed
> with the wrecks of the forest.

The music of Henry's flute floating across Walden Pond on an icy
winter evening into the vicinity of his native village would serve as a
testimonial to his mother who, to inquisitive neighbors wondering if she
were not anxious about Henry alone in his home by the shore, could
smile and say, "but he's not alone—he has his flute."

An easygoing woman in many ways, Mrs. Thoreau had been fiercely
tyrannical when it came to her children's formal education. Through her
planning and stinting, John and Henry had had the finest of private
school training at Concord Academy. Legend says that the moment the
academy closed its doors for the quarterly vacation, she would ship the
boys off to the girls' school in order that they waste no time which might
be spent at learning. When the Concord Lyceum first opened its doors
in 1829, she was among the first to take her brood to hear lectures on
geology, botany, ornithology. Cynthia had a zest for life, people said,
making her an excellent partner for the quieter kind of man she had
married. There is no doubt that she was just the antidote her unusually
sensitive sons required to shield them from excessive morbidity.

A story is told of Mrs. Thoreau going one day to call on Emerson's
somewhat formidable Aunt Mary who, shocked at the gay appearance of
her guest, told her that the yellow-ribboned bonnet she was wearing
suited neither her age nor her presence in the sight of God. Cynthia
Thoreau's response was to go happily on wearing whatever bright color
suited her fancy in the certainty that yellow was as proper an adornment
for man as for nature. It is hardly to be wondered at, then, that Henry
David Thoreau's *Walden* would also renounce those melancholy customs
of dress and thought inspired by New England Calvinism. In one of the
most passionate affirmations of life ever recorded, *Walden*, with its repeated word symbols—*morning, awakening, rebirth, renewal, yellow, green*
—would invite New Englanders into the life-that-is rather than the

heaven-to-come; bid them welcome each new day as if they were first
born again and seeing the universe with fresh vision—.

> Little is to be expected of that day if it can be called a day, to which
> we are not awakened by our Genius . . . are not awakened by our
> own newly-acquired force and aspirations from within. . . . That
> man who does not believe that each day contains an earlier, more
> sacred, and auroral hour than he has yet profaned, has despaired of
> life, and is pursuing a descending and darkening way . . . To him
> whose elastic and vigorous thought keeps pace with the sun, the day
> is a perpetual morning. It matters not what the clocks say or the
> attitudes and labors of men. Morning is when I am awake and there
> is a dawn in me . . . To be awake is to be alive.

The deeper Henry believed that to be awake is to be alive, the
more unhappy he was to see his dream of living a free life as poet-
adventurer shattered by the confinement of a work-a-day commercial
world. While his family was meeting in council trying to resolve the
financial difficulties that threatened to deprive him and John from having
a college education, he and his brother were meanwhile put to work
in their father's pencil factory. The long hours and atmosphere heavy
with dust had a deleterious effect upon his spirits, more so upon
John's health, for the older brother developed symptoms of tuberculosis.
This settled the fate of both boys. John was not to be put under
the strain of four years of higher education, but would go out to work
as a tutor alongside Helen. The combined earnings of all in the
family would see Henry through Harvard.

Thus it was that in 1833, at age sixteen, Henry went off to college
with a sense of awesome responsibility; he who least desired it was to
become the professional upon whom all the dreams of his family depended. Whether due to this pressure, or to the not uncommon adolescent
restlessness, he did not fare well on campus. A most untypical freshman,
he seemed out of place with his country-style clothing and his lack of
enthusiasm for any of the extra-curricular activities. He spent whatever
free time he had either burrowing among the fifty thousand volumes
of the college library, or going for long, solitary walks.

"An odd stick" was the way one professor characterized him.
Those few of his classmates who had consciously observed him said
the same. One, who many years later sought out the author of *Walden*
and became his friend, said that while at Harvard Thoreau never
signaled a desire for friendship, that his sober, gray-blue eyes were

almost always down, either on a book, or on the ground "as if he
had dropped or expected to find something."

Despite a modest showing in grades putting him only in the middle
of his class, Thoreau benefitted greatly from the broad education he
received at Harvard. He became adept in languages—Latin, Greek,
French, and German—preferring to read philosophy and poetry in the
original then write his own translations. Under Edward Channing,
professor of rhetoric and oratory, he learned how to express his ideas
with some degree of order and literary style. Especially important to
his development as writer and thinker was his introduction to German
transcendentalism through reading the works of poet-critic Samuel Coleridge. But for all the hard facts he acquired, Thoreau, like Emerson
before him felt much too harnessed away from "real life" during these
student years and was chafing at the bit to be free. As with all other
institutions of society, he now put college under his critical microscope,
deciding that much taught in its classrooms was no longer relevant to
his modern world, or if relevant, could quicker be learned from direct
experience. Whenever opportunity arose he argued the point, as later
he was to argue it in *Walden*:

> "But," says one, "you do not mean that the students should go to
> work with their hands instead of their heads?" I do not mean that,
> exactly, but I mean something which he might think a good deal like
> that; I mean that they should not *play* life, or *study* it, merely, . . .
> but earnestly *live* it from beginning to end.
>
> • • •
>
> If I wished a boy to know something about the arts and sciences, I
> would not pursue the common course which is merely to send him
> into the neighborhood of some professor where anything is professed
> and practiced but the art of life; to survey the world through a tele-
> scope or a microscope and never, with his natural eye; to study chem-
> istry, and not learn how his bread is made, and mechanics, and not
> learn how it is earned. . . . Which would have advanced the most at
> the end of a month, the boy who had made his own jackknife . . .
> or the boy who had attended lectures on metallurgy at the Institute
> in the meanwhile and had received a Rodgers penknife from his
> father? . . . To my astonishment I was informed on leaving college
> that I had studied navigation! Why, if I had taken one turn down
> the harbor I should have known more about it.

Still not reconciled to any of the customary professions, Thoreau
came into the last year of his studies wanting more than ever to go

back to the river and woods he had known as a boy and bring
to them a naturalist's talent, a poet's quest for beauty and truth. But,
understandably, he was deeply troubled by the thought that the cost
of not betraying himself in this aspiration was to betray the hopes
of his family. Neither by character nor intent could he live dependent
upon others, yet this life he wished to lead required that he have
boundless freedom.

The more closely Thoreau looked into the world he was expected
to enter after graduation, the less he wanted to compete in it. Values
in the middle-class world to which he belonged seemed to him topsy-
turvy. The standard by which even a man's morality was judged was
monetary success. The poor were "shiftless," the debtor a "criminal."
Originality was suspect; conformity sane and safe. Yet the very system
which taught these values was now itself caught in a tailspin. After
years of heady prosperity, when President Andrew Jackson set out to
put an end to reckless land speculation and spiraling inflation the result
was the worst economic depression the nation had yet known. A run
on the banks in May 1837 having brought suspended payments, creditors
could no longer collect, debtor's prisons were filling, the farmer groaning
under the weight of his mortgage, the bankrupt merchant in panic.
Three of the largest cotton firms in the East failed. And while hungry
farm laborers were drifting from rural communities to the larger towns
in search of employment, unemployed, hungry city laborers were gathering in mobs on the streets rioting. Grim statistics were predicted of the
number likely to die during the coming winter from starvation or
exposure, so many were the families already evicted from their homes.
Yet this was a time of ostentatious spending by the wealthy, a con-
tradiction easily detected not only by the workers but by idealistic
students about to pocket their diplomas. Many among the latter were
dismayed by the fact that the government had no ready solution to
meet the crisis. Congress was beset with mounting conflict over the not
unrelated issue of slavery. Southern and northern politicians, each rep-
resenting economic interests of their region, were leaving the moral
question of buying and selling human beings to a few isolated men and
women in New England who were only just beginning to gather force
for what William Lloyd Garrison of the *Liberator* promised would be
a war to the death against the slaveowners.

Thus, what lay ahead for the class of 1837 of which twenty-year-
old Henry David Thoreau was a member, was a disorderly society with

problems further complicated by the repressive measures relied upon by civil authorities who thought only in terms of maintaining law and order. Dangling somewhere in the middle of things, being neither workers nor owners of property, students of the upper and middle class, especially in the New England states, argued the need for reform on all levels of American life. A glance at a few of the titles of debates and themes put forward at Harvard in the 1830s indicates the degree of concern:

The Commercial Spirit of Modern Times.

*Ought there to be any restrictions on
publication of opinions?*

Ought Capital Punishment to be abolished.

Conformity in things Unessential

At commencement exercises August 1837, Thoreau argued the negative side in a debate on the Commercial Spirit. If there was a difference between him and his classmates it was not that he was the originator of radical ideas, but that he was imbued with a stern set of principles that would not allow him to think one way and act another. Everyone who knew him in the Harvard years testified to his fierce and unshakable integrity.

More valuable to Thoreau than his diploma when he returned to Concord after graduation was a little book he had in his possession— Ralph Waldo Emerson's *Nature* that had been published in 1836. This brief philosophical essay, which had excited so many students at Harvard, gave order to Thoreau's hitherto disjointed ideas about religion and society, bolstered his bravest thoughts as to how men ought to live. "The foregoing generations beheld God and nature face to face; we through their eyes. Why should not we also enjoy an original relation to the universe?" asked Emerson. "Why should not we have a poetry and philosophy of insight and not of traditions?" Which was precisely the argument Thoreau had been putting forward in a kind of internal dialogue he had been carrying on trying to anticipate family discussion about his future. And, as if linked in spiritual kinship, Emerson expressed precisely his own yet unstated argument for keeping alive the child inside the man, for keeping fresh the visions and sensory experiences that unite the man with his wondrous universe.

To speak truly few adult persons can see nature. Most persons do not see the sun. At least they have a very superficial seeing. The sun illuminates only the eye of the man, but shines into the eye and the heart of the child. The lover of nature is he whose inward and outward senses are still truly adjusted to each other; who has retained the spirit of infancy even into the era of manhood. . . . In the woods a man casts off his years as the snake his slough, and at what period soever of life is always a child. In the woods is perpetual youth.

Thoreau's wish to meet the man who wrote those words was almost immediately fulfilled. Emerson's sister-in-law, Mrs. Lucy Jackson Brown, who was at the moment living at the Thoreau boardinghouse, took the young graduate under her wing, escorted him, along with some of his writings, to the home of the Concord Sage. Emerson was then thirty-four and, at the start of a brilliant career, but he struck up a friendship with the younger man as if they two were equals. "I delight much in my young friend, who seems to have as free and erect a mind as any I have ever seen," he wrote in his journal.

Basking in the affectionate warmth of the Emerson household, highly stimulated by the intellectual talk of which he nightly partook there, Thoreau soon lost some of his cold reserve. At home, and sometimes over back yard fences to neighbors as he passed their houses on his walks, he would expound with boyish enthusiasm his opinions on a wide range of subjects including religion, often startling his maiden aunts who thought their favorite nephew was taking his youthful independence too far. His mother, on being told by one or another of her acquaintances that Mr. Emerson in a lecture had said such and such would interrupt to say, "Why, he talks just like our Henry." If this brought smiles to her listeners it was because it seemed to most Concordians that young Henry Thoreau was spouting word for word Mr. Emerson's ideas. Emerson himself wrote of his young protégé, "I am familiar with all his thoughts. They are my own quite originally drest." But in reality it was a case of master and student blending well. Thoreau was Emerson's ideal American, a man ready to practice the philosophy they both were preaching.

In the beginning things did not exactly go Henry's way, however. Though he made clear to his family all his reasons for not wishing to enter the professional world, why he preferred, if necessary, even to work as a day laborer to earn his keep, his aunts, being somewhat less sparing of his sensibilities than his mother, insisted that he at least try his hand at a respectable job like schoolteaching. They apparently pressured Emerson into counseling him in that same direction, for it was Emerson who got him a position in the Concord public school. As he did not wish to be ungrateful, Thoreau accepted, but he began his teaching with strong misgivings. And with good reason, for he had unorthodox ideas about education that he had no intention of yielding up for the sake of a salary. Needless to say, the job did not last very long. According to one version handed down by legend, on being instructed by his superior to flog an unruly student, Thoreau refused and in this insubordinate posture simply walked out of the schoolyard never to return. Another version states that after arguing against the wisdom of flogging, and having his argument soundly rejected, he chose six students at random, flogged all, the innocent along with the guilty, to show his disdain for this disciplinary method. Perhaps neither version is true (the latter hardly seems consistent with Thoreau's character), but he did instruct his class at first meeting that he "should not flog, but would talk morals as a punishment instead," and this attitude brought about dismissal finally by the Concord school board.

Emerson next tried to get his young friend employment in schools elsewhere in New England, saying in the letter of recommendation which Thoreau obligingly carried with him as far as Maine, "I shall esteem the town fortunate that secures his services." But apparently no town to which Thoreau wandered agreed with that sentiment, so he returned to the only place on earth he was ever to feel native to. "Am I not made of Concord dust? I carry Concord ground in my boots and in my hat," he wrote.

Still one more scheme to get him settled was plotted, this one turning out more to Henry's liking for it united him once again with his brother John. The two brothers were to take over the now abandoned Concord Academy and set up a school of their own, John acting as business manager, Henry as headmaster-instructor. A prospectus was sent out and the academy soon began to draw students from many liberal-minded families of New England. In this school there would be no flogging, no endless hours over desks, but as many outdoor sessions as weather permitted. Perhaps to the surprise of many, Thoreau turned out to be no overindulgent master. He believed that while children should be free to think, explore, and speak, they must not be allowed to forget who was teacher and who pupil. Stern authority was seldom necessary, however, for Headmaster Thoreau kept the interest of his students at high

Nathaniel Hawthorne. Portrait by Charles Osgood.

"Old Manse" where Hawthorne wrote Mosses from an Old Manse. It was built by Emerson's grandfather just before the Revolutionary War.

Ralph Waldo Emerson, 1844.

Concord, Massachusetts, as it was in Emerson's boyhood.

Concord Bridge.

Henry David Thoreau.
CONCORD ANTIQUARIAN MUSEUM

Thoreau's home, Concord, Massachusetts.

Concord River. Thoreau called it by its Indian name, the "Musketaquid, or Grass-ground River."
"It will be Grass-ground River as long as grass grows and water runs here; it will be Concord River only while men lead peaceable lives on its banks."

Harriet Beecher Stowe, 1853
Portrait by Alanson Fisher.
STOWE-DAY FOUNDATION

Violence in the 1840s. William Lloyd Garrison, editor of the Liberator, being dragged through a Boston street.

Civil Disobedience in 1851. This sign and others like it inspired abolitionists to defy the Fugitive Slave Law. A group led by Thomas Wentworth Higginson and Theodore Parker stormed the city jail to free Thomas Sims.

CAUTION!!

COLORED PEOPLE

OF BOSTON, ONE & ALL,

You are hereby respectfully CAUTIONED and advised, to avoid conversing with the

Watchmen and Police Officers of Boston,

For since the recent ORDER OF THE MAYOR & ALDERMEN, they are empowered to act as

KIDNAPPERS

AND

Slave Catchers,

And they have already been actually employed in KIDNAPPING, CATCHING, AND KEEPING SLAVES. Therefore, if you value your LIBERTY, and the *Welfare of the Fugitives* among you, *Shun* them in every possible manner, as so many *HOUNDS* on the track of the most unfortunate of your race.

Keep a Sharp Look Out for KIDNAPPERS, and have TOP EYE open.

APRIL 24, 1851.

THEODORE PARKER'S PLACARD

Placard written by Theodore Parker and printed and posted by the Vigilance Committee of Boston after the rendition of Thomas Sims to slavery in April, 1851.

peak by the surprise and flexibility of curriculum. Field trips provided lessons in botany and philosophy. An afternoon of boatbuilding, log floating, tree measuring turned into lessons in mathematics. Thoreau impressed upon the flock of children walking at his heels on these out-door excursions that "What everybody echoes as true today may turn out falsehood tomorrow," thus they had best keep open minds, see and think out problems for themselves. "There are as many ways as there can be drawn radii from one center. All change is a miracle to contemplate; but it is a miracle which is taking place every instant."

"Mr. Thoreau," said one of his pupils who must have had cause to remember, "was a person you would never feel inclined to fool with." Another—young Edmund Sewall—fared so well on the other hand, he did not like to part company from the headmaster at term's end. Indeed he found Mr. Thoreau so warm a friend that he was anxious to have his sister Ellen come from their home in Connecticut to meet him. In the spring Ellen Sewall did come to Concord, bringing feminine beauty and romance into Henry's life. Pain, too, unfortunately, for as might have been expected with two brothers of one mind, John also fell in love with Ellen. The older brother escorted the pretty girl to country dances, the younger took her for canoe rides on the Concord River. What was said between the parties of this little drama, the world may never know. In Henry's first book, *A Week on the Concord and Merrimack Rivers*, he gives a swift, but poetic view of a moonlight riverboat ride with an unnamed companion—". . . . as she sat in the prow there was nothing but herself between the steersman and the sky. I could then say with the poet,

> Sweet falls the summer air
> Over her frame who sails with me
> Her way like that is beautifully free,
> Her nature far more rare,
> And is her constant heart of virgin purity."

This passage, with the long poem that follows it, written so many years after the event, indicates the impact Ellen Sewall had made on Thoreau's heart. Legend says that when Ellen returned to Connecticut, John followed her there, asked for her hand in marriage and was gently turned down. Legend also claims that had Henry come, she would have said yes to him. At John's return to Concord an unhappy silence fell for the first time between the two brothers.

"In human intercourse the tragedy begins, not when there is mis-understanding about words, but when silence is not understood," Henry was later to write in his essay on friendship. What seems clear is that John never confided to Henry what had happened in Connecticut; and Henry never confided to John his own mixed feelings about how to resolve this problem of two brothers and a girl. When at last Henry thought the way clear for himself, and proposed to Ellen by letter rather than in person, apparently it was too late. Ellen's parents thought neither of the Thoreau brothers a good risk for their daughter. In the end Ellen Sewall married a New England minister, but she, and her husband as well, remained Thoreau's friend for life.

No doubt, this all worked out for the best. Henry could hardly have made a suitable husband feeling as he did: "My love must be as free as is the eagle's wing"—that it would be an interruption "to spend my time in earning rich carpets or other fine furniture or delicate cookery or a house in the Grecian or the Gothic style." In his view "a taste for the beautiful is most cultivated out of doors where there is no house and no housekeeper." Wisely, he was to remain a bachelor.

Whether due to John's rapidly declining health, or Henry's dislike of staying too long in any one occupation, the brothers closed down their school before its second year was out. Henry later offered as explanation in *Walden* that as he "did not teach for the good of my fellow men, but simply for a livelihood" he had considered the venture a failure. Thus ended his attempts at "respectable" professions to appease his elders. He began instead to design his own days and nights, comfortably pocketing money for necessities by trimming hedges, painting fences, or whatever he could do with his hands, working one day a week only so as not to interrupt what he called "true living" the balance of the week. Later on when the Harvard Alumni Association sent its customary request asking its members for the history of their careers since leaving school, Henry wryly replied with an accounting of the number of fences mended, roofs repaired, but generously offered to instruct any of his former classmates, who might wish to improve their lot, in the art of joyful living. Not until *Walden*, did he explain in detail why, by ordinary standards, he was so "unsuccessful."

> I tried trade: (the pencil factory) but I found that it would take ten years to get underway in that, and that then I should probably be on my way to the devil. I was actually afraid that I might by that time be doing what is called a good business. I thought often and seriously of picking huckleberries; *that* surely I could do, and its

small profits might suffice—for my greatest skill has been to want
but little . . . While my acquaintances went unhesitatingly into
trade or the professions, I contemplated this occupation as most like
theirs; ranging the hills all summer to pick the berries which came
in my way, and thereafter carelessly to dispose of them. I also
dreamed that I might gather the wild herbs, or carry evergreens to
such villagers as love to be reminded of the woods, even to the city
by haycart loads. But I have since learned that trade curses everything
it handles; and though you trade in messages from heaven, the whole
curse of trade attaches to the business.

Starting out, then, in his twenty-second year to practice his own
profession of naturalist-poet, Thoreau began a series of remarkable adventures in living, growing, in the course of each, more mature as man
and artist. His first adventure realized the dream he and John had had in
their youth—a trip on the Concord River to other New England shores.
For their journey the brothers spent a week building their boat, and when
it was done christened it *Musketaquid*. As designed by Henry she was
fifteen feet long by three and a half in breadth at the widest part, and
shaped like a fisherman's dory, rigged with two small masts and a sail,
and furnished with wheels for going over falls, poles for the shallow
places. To prove that she was seaworthy Henry allowed his sisters, and
then, one by one all in Emerson's "Transcendental Club," the informal
philosophical discussion group of which he, too, was a member, to take a
ride in her. Emerson thought it highly romantic to be pushed out into
the "delicate realm of sunset and moonlight" where, as he wrote in his
diary, he could "leave the world of villages and personalities behind."
The little boat symbolized to Henry precisely the same combination of
freedom, romance, and philosophical detachment—"the land seemed to
grow fairer as we withdrew from it." He looked forward to the coming
expedition—a week forward, a week to home again—as two weeks in the
study of rivers, fishes, men, and stars. He and John made ready a store of
supplies, each considering his diary as important to the project as the
potatoes and melons they loaded aboard.

At length on Saturday, the last day of August 1839 we two brothers,
and natives of Concord, weighed anchor in this river port. . . . A
warm, drizzling rain had obscured the morning and threatened to
delay our voyage, but at length the leaves and grass were dried and
it came out a mild afternoon, as serene and fresh as if nature were
maturing some vigorous scheme of her own. . . . So, with a vigorous
shove we launched our boat from the bank . . . and dropped silently
down the stream.

From different points along the shore his friends and family came to wave farewell. Envious, admiring, Emerson that night wrote in his journal:

> We are shut up in schools and college recitation rooms for ten or fifteen years and come out at last with a bellyfull of words and do not know anything. We cannot use our hands or our legs or our eyes or our arms. We do not know an edible root in the woods. We cannot tell our course by the stars, nor the hour of the day by the sun . . . Now here are my wise young neighbors who instead of getting like wordsmen into a railroad car where they have not even the activity of holding the reins, have got into a boat which they have built with their own hands with sails which they have contrived to serve as a tent by night and gone up the river Merrimack to live by their wits on the fish of the stream & the berries of the wood.

Their plan was to keep with the Concord as she gathered in the Assabet, mile upon mile, brushing past New England towns, Bedford, Carlisle, Bilerica; be with her still as she broadened to "deep, dark, and dead stream" just before narrowing to channel at Middlesex where she brushed gently in to feed the Merrimack. Then, charging over rapids, past falls, through shoals, in view of all the isles that kept the Merrimack's course, have the joy of knowing they had gone as far as the river would take them.

With barely a mishap, and yet enough excitement to meet their highest expectations, Henry and John followed "nature's nearest pathway" to New Hampshire and back, sometimes racing scows along the way, sometimes visiting with shorefolk who hailed their boat; stopping off at islands to pick berries, to sleep under the stars.

> Whenever we awoke in the night, still eking out our dreams with half-awakened thoughts, it was not till after an interval, when the wind breathed harder than usual, flapping the curtains of the tent, and causing its cords to vibrate, that we remembered that we lay on the bank of the Merrimack, and not in our chamber at home. With our heads so low in the grass, we heard the river whirling and sucking, and lasping downward, kissing the shore as it went, sometimes rippling louder than usual, and again its mighty current making only a slight limpid, trickling sound, as if our water-pail had sprung a leak, and the water were flowing into the grass by our side. The wind, rustling the oaks and hazels, impressed us like a wakeful and inconsiderate person up at midnight, moving about, and putting things to rights, occasionally stirring up whole drawers full of leaves at a puff. There seemed to be a great haste and preparation throughout Nature, as for a distinguished visitor; all her aisles had to be swept in the night by a thousand handmaidens, and a thousand pots to be boiled

for the next day's feasting,—such a whispering bustle, as if ten thousand fairies made their fingers fly, silently sewing at the new carpet with which the earth was to be clothed, and the new drapery which was to adorn the trees. And then the wind would lull and die away, and we like it fell asleep again.

Emerson's comment about Thoreau that "He liked to throw every thought into symbol. For this reason his presence was poetic—he knew well how to throw a poetic veil over his experience," is nowhere better illustrated than in A Week on the Concord and Merrimack Rivers, the book finally to grow out of this river journey. As carefully as he had designed his boat, so did Thoreau carefully design each on-flowing chapter, making it both a prose-hymn to the memory of John (who three years after the journey died of lockjaw), and a religious (transcendentalist) exercise in which he propagandizes for heaven on earth, challenging man to reassess his relationship to nature, to reawaken to the possibilities of his own innate genius. In the book Thoreau reopens the gates of Eden, demonstrates how, by taking fate in his own hands, modern man can make the hours of the day, the days of the week, the highest tribute to whatever God he believes in. One of its most brilliant passages draws a parallel between sounds in the world of nature and in the world of man. As the life-death force beats steadily on, the young philosopher who is listening cannot be put off his optimistic course because, in the case of man, the music musters to war.

> Then when supper was done and we had written our journal of our voyage, we wrapped our buffaloes about us and lay down with our heads pillowed on our arms, listening awhile to the distant baying of a dog, or the murmurs of the river, or to the wind, which had not gone to rest. . . . It was pleasant to lie with our heads so low in the grass, and hear what a tinkling, ever-busy laboratory it was. A thousand little artisans beat on their anvils all night long.
> Far in the night, as we were falling asleep on the bank of the Merrimack, we heard some tyro beating a drum incessantly, in preparation for a country muster, as we learned, and we thought of the line,—
> "When the drum beat at dead of night."

We could have assured him that his beat would be answered, and the forces be mustered. Fear not, thou drummer of the night, we too will be there. And still he drummed on in the silence and the dark. This stray sound from a far-off sphere came to our ears from time to time, far, sweet, and significant, and we listened with such an unprejudiced sense as if for the first time we heard at all. No doubt he was an insignificant drummer enough, but his music afforded us a prime and leisure hour, and we felt that we were in season wholly. These simple sounds related us to the stars. Ay, there was a logic in them so convincing that the combined sense of mankind could never make me doubt their conclusions. I stop my habitual thinking, as if the plow has suddenly run deeper in its furrow through the crust of the world. How can I go on, who have just stepped over such a bottomless skylight in the bog of my life? Suddenly old Time winked at me,—Ah, you know me, you rogue,—and news had come that IT was well. That ancient universe is in such capital health, I think undoubtedly it will never die. Heal yourselves, doctors; by God I live.

And live he did. Home again from the river journey, his notebooks filled with data on nature, and early New England history, Thoreau became ever more clearly defined to his neighbors as a village character, one to be contended with as he continued to defy all established custom. Public officials trembled lest his example lead other youth astray, for not only was he content to work erratically, loafing (in their view) the rest of the time; he also would not vote, pay taxes, or even go to church. His mother defended whatever her son did or did not do, as did his two adoring sisters; what his father thought no one knew, but Aunt Maria went about Concord saying she *wished* her nephew "could find something better to do than always walking off somewhere," and that *she*, for one, could not understand why he would willingly spend a whole day knee-deep in water listening to a bullfrog when he would not give one minute of his time on Sunday to hear what the preacher had to say. In due time she, and the preacher, too, was to have Henry's answer in the chapter titled "Sunday" in *A Week on the Concord and Merrimack Rivers*.

> In dark places and dungeons the preacher's words might perhaps strike root and grow but not in broad daylight in any part of the world that I know. The sound of the Sabbath bell far away, now breaking on these shores, does not awaken pleasing associations, but melancholy and sombre ones rather . . . It is as the sound of many catechisms and religious books twanging a canting peal around the earth, seeming to issue from some Egyptian temple and echo along the shore of the Nile . . . startling a multitude of storks and alligators basking in the sun.
>
> Everywhere "good men" sound a retreat, and the word has gone forth to fall back on innocence . . .

Like young Emily Dickinson, who, in her turn, also was to fall back on innocence rather than attend Calvinist services, Thoreau stubbornly insisted that he least profaned when he made mountains, woods, or fields his temple, not on Sabbath only, for all the days of the week were holy.

> To anticipate not the sunrise and the dawn merely but if possible, Nature herself! How many mornings, summer and winter, before yet any neighbor was stirring about his business, have I been about mine!

This business which he took so seriously—recording the arrival of birds, detecting the change of weather and reading it for his farmer neighbors, standing at attention for sunrise or moonrise, studying ferns, moss, bass trees, spotted toads, the water lily, the beaver—most oldtimers among the farmers of Concord took for "tomfoolery" and said so. As Thoreau had earlier predicted more than one called him "loafer" behind his back. But he looked first to his own opinion of himself and stuck to his course as if his life depended on it. As he was to write in *Walden:* "The mass of men lead lives of quiet desperation. . . . A stereotyped but unconscious despair is concealed even under what are called the games and amusements of mankind. There is no play in them, for this comes after work." But as his avocation and vocation were one—

> I had this advantage, at least, in my mode of life over those who were obliged to look abroad for amusement, to society, and the theater, that my life itself was become my amusement and never ceased to be novel. It was a drama of many scenes and without an end.

The man for whose opinion Thoreau cared most after his own—Ralph Waldo Emerson—fully comprehending what Henry David Thoreau was all about, called him *"the* man of Concord," described his way of life as "holy living." Perhaps Thoreau would have had a harder time of it in Concord had he not had for friend this highly respected citizen who did vote, who did pay taxes, who did own property.

In 1841, hoping to further assist his young friend, Emerson invited Thoreau to live with him saying he could earn his keep by acting both as caretaker of his estate and of his family while he was away on lecture-tours. The plan appealed to Thoreau for it made him for the first time independent of the life at the boardinghouse. Also he had meanwhile come to love like a sister Emerson's beautiful wife, Lydian, and like a father, young Waldo Emerson, then age five. Thus, for a year, Thoreau lived in the protective shelter of his host-employer, upon whose insistence he put before all chores his nature walks and his writing. The result was beneficial both on an emotional and professional level; on the one hand Thoreau (especially in Emerson's absence) had an adopted family on which to expend manly protection and tenderness, and on the other, his sense of total well-being resulting from his relationship inspired an increasing output of creative writing.

During the course of the year he saw his poem "Sympathy" and an essay on the Roman poet, Flaccus, published in the *Dial*, the Transcendentalist magazine of which Emerson and Margaret Fuller were co-editors. When other poems and essays submitted came back to him from Miss Fuller with suggestions for changes, Thoreau characteristically balked. As his life style was original, so did he have his own original style of writing and did not like to conform to anyone else's idea of form. The dispute between Thoreau and Margaret Fuller put Emerson in a peculiar position for he, too, saw mannerisms in Thoreau's writing that he thought obscured the meaning. Nevertheless, as always, he came to his young friend's rescue, telling his coeditor, "Our tough Yankee must have his tough verse." One of Thoreau's great ambitions, expressed as early as his Harvard days, was to write a poem to be called "Concord." "For argument," he wrote in his journal, "I should have the River, the Woods, the Ponds, the Hills, the Fields, the Swamps and Meadows, the Streets and Buildings, and the Villagers. Then Morning, Noon, and Evening, Spring, Summer, Autumn, and Winter, Night, Indian Summer, and the Mountains in the Horizon." He would indeed write such a poem, but not in the form he originally intended. It was to take shape in the great prose poem *Walden*, the book destined to grow out of his second great adventure.

One night in 1841 he wrote in his journal: "I want to go soon and live away by the pond where I shall hear only the wind whispering among the reeds. It shall be a success if I shall have left myself behind. But, my friends ask, What will I do when I get there? Will it not be employment enough to watch the progress of the seasons?" Two momentous events occurred to stay this plan—the sudden death in January 1842 of young Waldo Emerson from scarlatina, followed shortly thereafter by the loss of John Thoreau who, in the midst of the most excruciating suffering, died in Henry's arms. The double tragedy brought on a depression deep enough in Thoreau to warrant his seeking a change of scene. Hardly prepared now for such solitude as he would have had to endure had he chosen to go live by the pond, he took Emerson's advice and went to live for a time in Staten Island, New York, working there as companion-tutor for the children of Emerson's brother, William. But away from New England and from the comfort of his family and Lydian Emerson, Thoreau grew even more dispirited. Homesickness soon brought him to Concord again.

The depth of friendship existing between Thoreau and Lydian Emerson has led some biographers to speculate that for the second time in his life Thoreau had fallen in love—such speculation based on letters Thoreau wrote to her from Staten Island. However, it was not uncommon during this period of the nineteenth century (often referred to as the Romantic Age) for idealistic men and women to engage in platonic friendships, using all the language of love to express their feelings. It was a time when the word "sister," for example, took on a connotation implying (as Thoreau used it to Lydian, as Emily Dickinson used it to her friends) "one in whom you have unbounded faith . . . a gentle spirit, a wise spirit, a loving spirit." When from New York, lonely, hungering for consolation, Thoreau writes to Mrs. Emerson, "you are of me and I of you. I cannot tell when I leave off and you begin," his sincerity is not to be doubted; but the phrase itself was one widely used at the time on both sides of the Atlantic, and particularly in Germany, the source from which New Englanders derived the language of romanticism. Emerson's essay "Friendship" exemplifies one aspect of the romantic movement. Thoreau wrote poems and incorporated into his books essays describing the ideal friendship. "A true Friendship is as wise as it is tender," he said, conceding that it was "more rare between the sexes than between two of the same sex." In his lifetime he was to know few who so nearly fulfilled his ideal as did Lydian Emerson.

After returning to Concord, Thoreau once again took up residence in his mother's boardinghouse, but the bustling atmosphere interfered too much with his privacy and his writing, causing him to revive his plan of living alone by the pond. When Emerson generously offered him a piece of land on which to build a hut in the woods, he veritably leaped at the offer, and thus began his second great adventure.

> Near the end of March, 1845, I borrowed an ax and went down to the woods by Walden Pond, nearest to where I intended to build my house, and began to cut down some tall arrowy white pines, still in their youth, for timber. It is difficult to begin without borrowing, but perhaps it is the most generous course thus to permit your fellow men to have an interest in your enterprise.

By May with the generous help of two poets and two philosophers,* who came to do some lifting and hammering, the frame of the little hut was set up. ("No man was ever more honored in the character of his raisers than I.") By July, though the chimney was still unfinished and not to be completed until it grew cold enough to necessitate a fire, all was ready for the moving in. Most of the furniture Thoreau had made himself; as for the rest, he took only what was absolutely essential. "Thank God," he said, "I can sit and I can stand without the aid of a furniture warehouse." A bed, table, desk, three chairs, a looking glass, a pair of tongs and andirons, a kettle, a skillet and a frying pan, a dipper, a washbowl, two knives and forks, three plates, one cup, one spoon, a jug for oil, a jug for molasses, and a japanned lamp—these, besides his books were all his worldly possessions. "A lady . . . offered me a mat, but as I had no room to spare within the house, nor time to spare within or without to shake it, I declined it, preferring to wipe my feet on the sod before my door. It is best to avoid the beginnings of evil."

Thoreau's actual residency in the hut began, significantly enough, on Independence Day, July 4, 1845, while the celebration drums were sounding loudly in the village behind him.

For the first two months, because of the unfinished chimney, he did all his cooking out of doors, blissful whatever the weather, for if "it stormed before my bread was baked, I fixed a few boards over the fire and sat under them to watch my loaf, and passed some pleasant hours in that way." As usual he cast a poetic veil over every experience, even the hoeing of an adjoining field to plant a crop of beans.

> When my hoe tinkled against the stones, that music echoed to the woods and the sky, and was an accompaniment to my labor which yielded an instant and immeasurable crop. It was no longer beans that I hoed, nor I that hoed beans. . . . The nighthawk circled overhead in the sunny afternoons . . . like a mote in the eye, or in heaven's eye, falling from time to time with a swoop and a sound as if the heavens were rent, torn at last to very rags and tatters. . . . Sometimes I watched a pair of hen-hawks circling high in the sky, alternately soaring and descending, approaching, leaving one another, as if they were the embodiment of my own thoughts. Or I was attracted by the passage of wild pigeons from this wood to that, with a slight quivering winnowing sound . . . When I paused to lean on my hoe, these sounds and sights I heard and saw . . . part of the inexhaustible entertainment which the country offers.

* Ellery Channing, William Curtis, Waldo Emerson, Bronson Alcott.

In no way did he feel or intend to be different or eccentric by retiring to a woodland hut. He had, as he said, a piece of business to do there (writing a book), and the setting provided necessary solitude and more. Like any other writer he ordered his day to suit his needs, no greater proof of the fact that he was not, by any definition, a loafer being the three great documents—A Week on the Concord and Merrimack Rivers, Walden, "Civil Disobedience"—all for the most part written or conceived during the two years he lived in the woods. Of his flexible, but disciplined daily schedule which usually began at dawn with a swim in the pond (until the pond was well iced-over) Thoreau wrote in Walden:

> After hoeing, or perhaps reading and writing, in the forenoon, I usually bathed again in the pond, swimming across one of its coves for a stint, and washed the dust of labor from my person, or smoothed out the last wrinkle which study had made, and for the afternoon was absolutely free. Every day or two I strolled to the village to hear some of the gossip which is incessantly going on there, circulating either from mouth to mouth, or from newspaper to newspaper, and which, taken in homeopathic doses, was really as refreshing in its way as the rustle of leaves and the peeping of frogs. As I walked in the woods to see the birds and squirrels, so I walked in the village to see the men and boys; instead of the wind among the pines I heard the carts rattle. . . . It was very pleasant when I stayed late in town to launch myself into the night, especially if it was dark and tempestuous, and set sail from some bright village parlor or lecture room, with a bag of rye or Indian meal upon my shoulder, for my snug harbor in the woods . . .

When he could not, or did not wish to leave his snug harbor, he was not so far away that the sounds of the village did not remind him of civilization, some being pleasant, others less so. "When there were several bands of musicians, it sounded as if all the village was a ,vast bellows, and all the buildings expanded and collapsed alternately with a din." Once the town fired its great guns which echoed "like popguns to these woods," and Thoreau, with his usual rejection of any noise signifying man's taste for war, burrowed deeper into his hideaway pursuing his own war against weeds or invaders into his cellar where dry food was stored. "The moles nested in my cellar, nibbling every 3rd potato."

Often the sound of a train would shatter the quiet and rouse up thoughts concerning the speed of the modern world, of how much, with this new invention, man would be missing by cutting himself off more and more from his natural environment. Unlike Emerson, Thoreau had

almost nothing good to say for the train. "So is your pastoral life whirled
past and away. But the bell rings, and I must get off the track and let
the cars go by. . . . I will not have my eyes put out and my ears spoiled
by its smoke and steam and hissing." And yet, like Emily Dickinson
after him, there was a kind of fascination which made him evoke images
of the iron horse into his art. One passage in *Walden* almost matches
the famous train poem of Emily Dickinson's beginning "I like to see it
lap the miles/and lick the valleys up." It is as though each poet in their
separate worlds had bridged a distance to read the thought of the other.

> All day the fire-steed flies over the country stopping only that his
> master may rest, and I am awakened by his tramp and defiant snort
> at midnight, when in some remote glen in the woods he fronts the
> elements incased in ice and snow; and he will reach his stall only with
> the morning star, to start once more on his travels without rest or
> slumber.

By contrast, and because he was far removed from the formality
of the churches from which they came, Thoreau liked, on Sundays to
hear the bells, "the Lincoln, Acton, Bedford, or Concord bell, when the
wind was favorable, a faint, sweet, and, as it were, natural melody, worth
importing into the wilderness. At a sufficient distance over the woods
this sound acquires a certain vibratory hum, as if the pine needles in the
horizon were the strings of a harp which it swept." In this passage from
Walden, as in all others, Thoreau invites his fellow men away from the
formal into the free atmosphere of the natural. His most seemingly casual
utterances are proselytizing for casting off dogma and tuning in on in-
stinctual responses to the beauty and wonder of the universe.

Only for one hour, a few weeks after he had first come to live in
Walden, did Thoreau have a bad time because of solitude, "thinking it
unpleasant to be alone and shut off from the near neighborhood of man."
But he quickly recovered, and afterward drew even sharper pleasure from
the company he did have, seen or unseen. "I found myself suddenly
neighbor to the birds; not by having imprisoned one, but having caged
myself near them." At night the sound of owls accompanied the sound
of his pen as he wrote his day's experience into his journal, or he would
draw comfort from hearing the scratching of small animals outside his
door. On many a winter evening he thrilled to the cry of the fox, identifying with it, feeling that *he*, Henry David Thoreau, was the wild neighbor to the rightful resident of these woods. His hut stood on the side of
a hill in the midst of a young forest of pitch pines and hickories, and

these trees, too, were companions. "Every little pine needle expanded
and swelled with sympathy and befriended me. I was so distinctly made
aware of the presence of something kindred to me, even in scenes which
we are accustomed to call wild and dreary, and also that the nearest of
blood to me and humanest was not a person nor a villager, that I thought
no place could ever be strange to me again."

> Men frequently say to me, "I should think you would feel lonesome
> down there, and want to be nearer to folks, rainy and snowy days and
> nights especially." I am tempted to reply to such: This whole earth
> which we inhabit is but a point in space. How far apart, think you,
> dwell the most distant inhabitants of yonder star, the breadth of
> whose disk cannot be appreciated by our instruments? Why should I
> feel lonely? Is not our planet in the Milky Way? . . . What sort of
> space is that which separates a man from his fellows and makes him
> solitary?

In a sense Walden Woods was like the boat *Musketaquid*, a corner
of the universe cut off from the laws of civilization from which Thoreau
could see in better perspective how men lived, what false gods they
worshiped, what better ways there were to make the most of time and
energy. He hoped that the knowledge he gained in his search for reality
he could impart to others in such a way as to help affect a change in
society. "Authors more than kings or emperors exert an influence on
mankind," he believed.

But Thoreau was realistic enough to know that his ideals and utopian
dreams, like those of prophets and philosophers before him, would probably go unheeded in his own day and fall on more fertile ground some
ages hence. "The poet or the artist never yet had so fair and noble a
design but some of his posterity at least could accomplish it." With that
optimism, he proceeded to say his piece to his contemporaries whether
or not it alarmed authority or marked him for a dangerous man. His
advice to the young people of the day was nothing more, nothing less
than what he himself was at that moment practicing.

> If the engine whistles, let it whistle till it is hoarse for its pains. If
> the bell rings why should we run? We will consider what kind of
> music they are like. Let us settle ourselves, and work and wedge
> our feet downward through the mud and slush of opinion, and preju-
> dice, and tradition, and delusion, and appearance, that allusion which
> covers the globe, through Paris and London, through New York and
> Boston and Concord, through church and state, through poetry and

philosophy and religion, till we come to a hard bottom and rocks in place which we can call *reality* and say, This is, and no mistake; and then begin . . .

While living in the woods Thoreau spent many hours reading the works of India's philosophers and poets. In the Hindu poem, *Bhagavad Gita*, a special favorite, he found lines which well might stand for the central text of his life—

> *If you do not fight this just battle*
> *You will fail in your own law*
> *And in your honor*
> *And you will incur sin.*

Such sentiment reinforced his resoluteness each time he confronted difficulties resulting from his principled stand on current issues. One such difficulty occurred not too long after he had begun his experimental living at Walden.

> One afternoon, near the end of the first summer, when I went to the village to get a shoe from the cobbler's I was seized and put into jail because . . . I did not pay a tax to or recognize the authority of the state which buys and sells men, women, and children like cattle, at the door of the senate house. . . . It is true I might have resisted forcibly with more or less effect, might have run "amok" against society; but I preferred that society should run "amok" against me, it being the desperate party.

The incident formed the basis for Thoreau's revolutionary essay, "Civil Disobedience." First published without much fanfare in 1849, the work has survived to be one of the most influential documents of the twentieth century, known in all parts of the modern world. Its text, an example of Thoreau's unflinching integrity, was a hard-hitting attack against the country's domestic and foreign policy, pointing up not only the immorality of slavery but the unpopular Mexican War as well. It spoke for Thoreau alone as one man's way of dissuading the government from its wrong policies; but, in this essay, as in all his writing, Thoreau was proselytizing, holding up *his* revolutionary method before the citizenry as the better way to end violence on all sides.

> The majority is not ruling because it is in the right but because it is the strongest. Conscience should decide—not majorities. Must the citizen ever for a moment, or in the least degree resign his conscience to the legislator? Why has every man a conscience then? I think we

should be men first, and subjects afterward. It is not desirable to cultivate a respect for the law so much as for the right.

• • •

When a whole country is unjustly overrun and conquered by a foreign army, and subjected to military law, I think that it is not too soon for honest men to rebel and revolutionize. . . . What makes this duty the more urgent is the fact that the country so overrun is not our own, but ours is the invading army.

• • •

If I have unjustly wrested a plank from a drowning man, I must restore it to him though I drown myself. . . . He that would save his life, in such a case, shall lose it. This people must cease to hold slaves, and to make war on Mexico though it cost them their existence as a people.

• • •

Under a government which imprisons any unjustly, the true place for a just man is also a prison. . . . the only house in a slave state in which a free man can abide with honor. . . . If the alternative is to keep all just men in prison, or give up war and slavery, the State will not hesitate which to choose.

• • •

A very few—as heroes, patriots, martyrs, reformers in the great sense, and *men* serve the state with their consciences and so necessarily resist it for the most part; and they are commonly treated as enemies by it.

As one of those "enemies," Thoreau said of his experience in jail:

I did not for a moment feel confined, and the walls seemed a great waste of stone and mortar. I felt as if I alone of all my townsmen had paid my tax. . . . They plainly did not know how to treat me but behaved like persons who are underbred . . . I could not but smile to see how industriously they locked the door on my meditations, which followed them out again without let or hindrance, and *they* were really all that was dangerous. . . . I saw that the State did not know its friends from its foes, and I lost all my remaining respect for it, and pitied it.

When he was released from jail the next morning (a friend, without his knowledge or consent having paid his tax), Thoreau proceeded on to the cobblers, "and having put on my mended shoe, joined a huckleberry party who were impatient to put themselves under my conduct, and in half an hour in the midst of a huckleberry field on one of our highest mountains two miles off, and then the State was nowhere to be seen."

By nature an intensely private man, Thoreau nevertheless drew at-

tention to himself by the very fact of his nonconformity. To his dismay
he and the hut he had built at a cost of $28.12½ became victims of
sightseers. If he was not at home his uninvited guests took advantage of
his unlocked door, and, like Goldilocks in the forest, tried out his home-
made furniture, his eating utensils, even poked into his closets to see if
he kept clean linen. A pair of pretty young girls who thought it great fun
to run off with his dipper later on found themselves publicly scolded in
Walden as "a disgrace to their sex and to humanity. They will never
know peace 'til they have returned the dipper. In all worlds this is
decreed." But other than the dipper nothing else of his property was ever
stolen. "I had no lock nor bolt but for the desk which held my papers, not
even a nail to put over my latch or windows. I never fastened my door
night or day, though I was to be absent several days; not even when the
next fall I spent a fortnight in the woods of Maine. And yet my house
was more respected than if it had been surrounded by a file of soldiers."
"I am convinced," he went on, "that if all men were to live as simply as
I then did, thieving and robbery would be unknown. These take place
only in communities where some have got more than is sufficient while
others have not enough."

On September 6, 1847, Thoreau closed the door of his hut in
Walden for the last time and returned to live in Concord. "I left the
woods for as good a reason as I went there," he wrote. "Perhaps it seemed
to me that I had several more lives to live, and could not spare any
more time for that one." After his sister Helen's death in 1849, he became a professional surveyor in order to make up for her earnings otherwise lost to his family, but his daily activities did not greatly alter from
what they had been before. He camped, sometimes alone, sometimes
with friends; led expeditions into the mountains, to Cape Cod, to the
Maine woods; led escaped slaves safely to the underground railway heading north to Canada; and he continued to write. In 1849 he saw through
the press the book he had finished in the woods, *A Week on the Concord
and Merrimack Rivers*. Reviewing it in the Massachusetts *Quarterly Review*, James Russell Lowell called Thoreau "the Boswell of Musketaquid and Merrimack, but criticized the many philosophical digressions
in his book, saying, "We were bid to a river-party,—not to be preached
at." The public ignored the book altogether. In 1853 Thoreau's discouraged publisher, needing the space being taken up by the unsold copies,
wrote asking the author what disposition he wanted made of them.
Thoreau bought up the 706 copies, writing with acid humor in his diary,

"They are something more substantial than fame, as my back knows, which has borne them up two flights of stairs. . . . Of the remaining two hundred and ninety and odd, seventy-five were given away, the rest sold. I have now a library of nearly nine hundred volumes, over seven hundred of which I wrote myself. Is it not well that the author should behold the fruits of his labor?"

Meanwhile Thoreau, as a result of traveling to New York to see to the business end of his writing, had come to know some of the leading personalities in the literary and publishing world. One of these, Horace Greeley of the New York *Tribune*, who was so taken with Thoreau's knowledge of nature that he invited him to stay in his home at Chappaqua, wrote an editorial in his widely read newspaper saying that if more young men in America would go to hear what Henry David Thoreau had to say in his lectures, they'd be less inclined to pick up stakes and leave home in hopes of finding gold in California or fame in New York. But Thoreau's lectures continued to draw only small audiences, and understandably enough, for his subjects, as he himself described them, were "not scientific but rather transcendental and aesthetic." Unlike Emerson, he had not a reputation for oratorical delivery and it was rumored that people fell asleep while he was talking. Not until *Walden* was published in 1854, on terms that for the first time made Thoreau—in his own words—"a first class author," did a wider audience sit at attention for his transcendental views.

With its long poetic passages contrasting sound and silence, civilization and wilderness; detailing habits of birds, animals, insects; describing the seasons, the skies, the pond—*Walden* is more than a nature book; it is, above all, a book about man. Man coming to grips with aloneness, with darkness, with melancholy, with weather, with limited resources and tools for survival—coming to grips, conquering, surviving. We witness all that simultaneously attracts and repels man in civilization, all in the wilderness that he finds true to his native instincts. A philosophical book, a religious book, a romantic book, *Walden* is also, as Thoreau intended it to be, a practical book of the "how-to" variety, explaining the ways— not necessarily, in the woods, but wherever one may live or in whatever circumstances—the individual, through *total* self-reliance can live freely, creatively, and in spiritual peace. It is Thoreau's document of faith, his undaunted "yes" to life. The things he says "no" to are only those things which crush the spirits of men, stifle their freedom, love, honesty, and joy. It is a happy book.

A reviewer for the *Unitarian Christian Register* said of *Walden,*
"We suppose its author does not reverence many things which we reverence; but the fact has not prevented our seeing that he has a reverential,
tender, and devoted spirit at bottom. Rarely have we enjoyed a book
more." The *Boston Atlas* found it without "one spark of genial warmth,"
called Thoreau "a would-be savage." *Graham's Magazine* at least paid
tribute to Henry David Thoreau's "powerful and accomplished mind."
On the whole the critical reception was mild for so revolutionary a piece
of work. Emerson said that Thoreau in his excitement at seeing his book
in print looked like "the undoubted king of all American lions."

After reading some of the passages in *Walden,* there must have been
many a Concordian who wished the lion would go away and roar somewhere else for from top to bottom, class society in the village (a microcosm
of society everywhere in America) fell victim to Thoreau's biting wit or
blunt exposure. In his depiction of hypocrisy, false values, and self-decep-
tions, even his "do-gooder" liberal friends came in for a share of censure.
It no doubt shocked the local philanthrophist to read: "There are a
thousand hacking at the branches of evil to one who is striking at the
root, and it may be that he who bestows the largest amount of time and
money on the needy is doing the most by his mode of life to produce
that misery which he strives in vain to relieve." Self-satisfied public officials
of Concord doubtless, bristled to be told: "This town is said to have the
largest houses for oxen, cows, and horses hereabouts, and it is not behind-
hand in its public buildings; but there are very few halls for free worship
or free speech in this country."

To merchant, farmer, professional man—to the entire middle class
of which he was a part—Thoreau said: "Our life is frittered away by
detail. An honest man has hardly need to count more than his ten fingers,
or, in extreme cases he may add his ten toes and lump the rest. Simplicity, simplicity, simplicity! I say, let your affairs be as two or three,
and not a hundred or a thousand; instead of a million count half a
dozen, and keep your accounts on your thumb nail . . . Simplify,
simplify."

He scolded housewives, too, for their insatiable hunger for "things,"
for their fancy furniture, for the baubles and gewgaws collected on the
mantelpiece. "At present our houses are cluttered and defiled with it,
and a good housewife would sweep out the greater part into the dust
hole and not leave her morning's work undone. Morning work! . . .
what should be man's *morning* work in this world? . . . I would rather

sit in the open air, for no dust gathers on the grass unless where man has broken ground." And he had a word to say of his tailoress, too, who, when he had asked her for a garment of a particular style had replied: "They do not make them so now." "Of what use this measuring of me," he asked sternly, "if she does not measure my character, but only the breadth of my shoulders, as it were a peg to hang the coat on." *Fashion* was anathema to Thoreau. "The head monkey at Paris puts on a traveler's cap," he said, "and all the monkeys in America do the same."

A sincere belief that overindulgence by America's middle class in luxuries, in intoxicants and drugs as well, was ruinous to the country, prompted Thoreau to his brash criticism. "Such apparent slight causes destroyed Greece and Rome, and will destroy England and America," he warned. "For my part, I prefer the natural sky to an opium-eater's heaven. . . . who does not prefer to be intoxicated by the air he breathes?" As a social critic, he kept an anxious eye on all the changes in his fast-industrializing country, took note that factories, such as the textile mill at Lowell, Massachusetts, were emptying waste products into New England waters resulting in pollution; that building expansion was encroaching more and more upon the wilderness. All this he thought a danger not only to the natural resources, but to the spirit of man.

> Our village life would stagnate if it were not for the unexplored forests and meadows which surround it. We need the tonic of wildness—to wade sometimes in marshes where the bittern and the meadow hen lurk, and hear the booming of the snipe; to smell the whispering sedge where only some wilder and more solitary fowl builds her nest, and the mink crawls with its belly close to the ground. At the same time that we are earnest to explore and learn all things, we require that all things be mysterious and unexplorable, that land and sea be infinitely wild, unsurveyed and unfathomed by us because unfathomable. We can never have enough of nature.

His best hope lay in the young. For them, because it was also for himself, his advice was urgent, sharp to the point.

However mean your life is, meet it and live it.

Let not to get a living be thy trade, but thy sport.

Say what you have to say, and not what you ought. Any truth is better than make believe.

It is never too late to give up our prejudices. No way of thinking or doing, however ancient, can be trusted without proof. . . . What old

people say you cannot do you try and find that you can do. Old
deeds for old people, and new deeds for new.

Every path but your own is the path of fate. Keep on your own
track then.

Rise free from care before the dawn, and seek adventures. . . . Enjoy
the land but own it not.

We must learn to reawaken and keep ourself awake, not by mechanical aids, but by an infinite expectation of the dawn which does not
forsake us in our soundest sleep. I know of no more encouraging fact
than the unquestionable ability of man to elevate his life by a conscious endeavor.

Explore your higher latitude, nay be a Columbus to whole new
continents and worlds within you, opening new channels, not of trade,
but of thought.

Though with *Walden* he had become the author of two books,
and had, besides, poems and essays published in various magazines,
Thoreau's reputation as an author was not widespread. In the environs
of Concord his fame was still more for what people thought of as his
eccentricity than for his writing. Many stories circulated about him, some
true, others apocryphal, but all catching the spirit of the man. The one
most often told recounts that when he went to jail for not paying his
taxes, Emerson (it probably was not Emerson) came to see him, asking
from between the bars, "What are you doing in there, Henry?" "What
are *you* doing out there?" came the cryptic reply. Another anecdote
says that Thoreau went one day to a shop in his village asking to buy
a bolt for his front door. The shopkeeper thinking such a purchase
most unusual in his case, asked "why?" "The Governor is coming,"
Thoreau said soberly. At this the shrewd merchant decided to play
Henry's game. "But the legislature is coming, too," he said. "True,"
replied his unique customer, who at once bought a second bolt for his
back door.

In 1857 John Brown, the fervent abolitionist, came to Concord to
raise money for his cause. Thoreau, who was meeting him for the first
time, was so impressed with his sincerity and courage he did what he
could to help him. Others came forward, too, as Brown asked to meet with
all the leading thinkers and liberals of this and other New England
communities. Two years later, when news came of Brown's raid on
Harpers Ferry, many of these supporters, frightened lest they be connected somehow with the incident, turned their back on him. Thoreau

was one of the very few who did not. Ill at the time, he rose from his sick bed to organize a public meeting to plead for Brown's life. Despite frantic advice sent to him from friends and from leaders of the abolitionist organization that to openly identify with Brown was dangerous, Thoreau, on the appointed day, delivered his speech. It would have been even more dangerous, he said, to let the moral and physical courage of a man like John Brown go unsung.

The illness which had befallen Thoreau had meanwhile been diagnosed as tuberculosis. By the time the Civil War began, it had progressed to a critical stage. A trip to Minnesota in the hope of restoring his health having proved futile, he returned home resigned to his coming death. Confined to his room, no longer able to go even for a short walk, he lay brooding less over his health than the bloodshed of the war. His friends, who came daily to see him, thought it impossible for him to get well while the war lasted. To distract his thoughts, they would lightheartedly recount all their daily activities. One day Thoreau said to one of these visitors: "You have been skating on this river, perhaps I am going to skate on some other—perhaps I am going up country."

As the months went by, though he grew ever weaker physically, Thoreau's spirits revived enough so that he was able, once again, to work at his writing. For the *Atlantic Monthly* he wrote "Walking," knowing he probably would never see the essay in print. To a correspondent writing at this time to ask after his health, he replied that he supposed he had not many months to live, but added: "I am enjoying existence as much as ever and regret nothing." It was spring. His bed was drawn close to the open window. New life was flooding the world and the vision filled him with joy. His sister Sophia, in constant attendance at his bedside, told a friend grieving over his condition, "He is so happy, I feel as if he were being translated rather than dying in the ordinary way of most mortals." To the end Thoreau remained alert, maintained his humor. As he lay dying his Aunt Maria approached his bed saying, "Henry, have you made peace with God?" "Why, Aunt," he replied, "I didn't know we had ever quarreled."

On May 6, 1862, Henry David Thoreau went "up country," and on that day all the children of Concord, whose friend he had ever been, were let out of school to say a last farewell. "No truer American existed than Thoreau," they heard Emerson say in the funeral oration.

It was a pleasure and a privilege to walk with him. He knew the country like a fox or a bird, and passed through it as freely by paths of his own. He knew every track in the snow or on the ground and what creatures had taken this path before him. . . . Snakes coiled round his leg, the fishes swam into his hand, and he took them out of the water; he pulled the woodchuck out of its hole by the tail, and took the foxes under his protection from the hunters. . . .

No college ever offered him a diploma, or a professor's chair; no academy made him its corresponding secretary, its discoverer, or even its member. Perhaps these learned bodies feared the satire of his presence. Yet so much knowledge of Nature's secret and genius few others possessed. . . .

It seems an injury that he should leave in the midst his broken task, which none else can finish—a kind of indignity to so noble a soul that he should depart out of Nature before yet he has been really shown to his peers for what he is. But he, at least, is content. His soul was made for the noblest society; he had in a short life exhausted the capabilities of this world; wherever there is knowledge, wherever there is virtue, wherever there is beauty, he will find a home.

And then came the ringing of the bells of Concord—forty-five tolls to signify the number of years Henry David Thoreau had lived his life of "singular purity and kindness." Whenever friends had spoken to him of immortality, he had replied, "one world at a time," assuring them that he dreamed of "no heaven but that which lies about me." In that heaven he was buried, in the good earth of New England at Sleepy Hollow near friends and neighbors and the flora and fauna of his most familiar world.

Harriet Beecher Stowe

(1811–1896)

"The time is come when a woman or a child who can speak a word for freedom and humanity is bound to speak."

Harriet Surprised would be an apt title for the story of "the little woman who made this big war"—as Lincoln said of Harriet Beecher Stowe—for little conscious planning went into the author's life experiences. Circumstance lifted her out of the innocence of a sheltered New England girlhood in Litchfield, Connecticut, to the realities of life in an Ohio rivertown; from a world of splintering religious sects into a world of splintering political sects; from a resigned spinsterhood into a loveless marriage; from obscurity and backbreaking domesticity into sudden world-wide fame, wealth, and notoriety. Harriet's dream since childhood had been to be an author in the classical tradition, not a crusader like her minister father and brothers. But caught up by the threads of heritage and the circumstances of history, she was surprised to find herself one day using her pen with all the fervor of an evangelist and—as she was so often to claim—directed by an unseen force more eloquent than herself: in her view God and not she was the true author of *Uncle Tom's Cabin*.

However that might be, it was Harriet Beecher Stowe the public acclaimed. From 1852, the year *Uncle Tom's Cabin* was published, until shortly before her death forty years later, she was the most sought after, most highly paid author in America. It was said of her with justification that with a stroke of her pen she had moved the world's heart the way Emerson had moved its mind. But, ironically, the very fact that she was living in a moment of history when the ability to move hearts became a potent weapon for rooting out an evil in American society—when, as she said, any woman or child who can speak a word for freedom and humanity is bound to speak—served in the end to undermine her reputation in the world of letters.

Once read by millions of people, the story of *Uncle Tom's Cabin* (subtitled *Life Among the Lowly*) has, since the Civil War, become familiar to succeeding generations through its telling in many forms including ballet, but the actual text of the book is seldom, if ever, read. This has worked to the disadvantage of the author, for these dramatic presentations have often exaggerated out of all proportion the events and characters in her book, left an impression undermining the value of *Uncle Tom's Cabin* even as a historical document. Further complicating objective assessment of Harriet Beecher Stowe as an artist is the fact that in the continuing struggle for Negro rights, the character, Uncle Tom, whom within the religious framework of her appeal the author conceived as a Christ figure, has evolved over the years to represent something quite different—a negative symbol in the minds of millions of oppressed people who, in rejecting Uncle Tom, question the basic premise of Mrs. Stowe's anti-slavery novel. Did she in fact present the true face of slavery, or misrepresent even the will of the oppressed to shake off master and shackle? In her own century, surprised that *anyone* North or South should question her facts or her understanding of the issues involved, Harriet fearlessly defended herself. Could she but know that most of the issues raised in her book are still alive, are still being hotly debated a century past the day *Uncle Tom's Cabin* first blazed its way across the world, this, for Harriet, would surely be the sharpest surprise of all.

Whatever the sociopolitical assessment of *Uncle Tom's Cabin* either in her own day or by posterity, Harriet Beecher Stowe never dreamed that her literary reputation would rest solely on that controversial novel. Because she had written it more for the urgency of its message than for display of her artistic ability, she thought it had served its purpose once it had succeeded in arousing the conscience of her contemporaries—especially in the North—to the immorality and the danger of remaining silent about slavery. It was the books Harriet wrote after the war that she hoped would live and give her status in the ranks of American authors. The sad fact is that these books are no longer read, indeed, few except scholars know that they even exist.

"Posterity neglects her to its peril," warns Professor Edward Wagenknecht, Mrs. Stowe's twentieth-century biographer. Most other literary historians and critics dismiss Harriet Beecher Stowe as a sentimental propagandist unworthy of serious discussion. Yet passage after passage even in *Uncle Tom's Cabin* reveal a mastery of dialogue, plot development, characterization, and psychological insight indicating a talent far superior to that of a mere sentimentalist or propagandist. *Old Town Folks* (1869), *Poganuc People* (1878), even the more pietistic *Minister's Wooing* (1859), and *The Pearl of Orr's Island* (1862), lie quietly waiting to be rediscovered not alone for quality of writing but for the deeper understanding they give of New England life, especially of the impact Calvinist doctrine had upon people and events in the nineteenth century. When that day of discovery comes Harriet Beecher Stowe may yet be restored to her rightful place among the significant New England authors.

From the beginning Harriet had to be a fighter in order to be recognized. Legend says that on the day of her birth June 14, 1811, her father, looking for the first time at his newest child, threw up his hands and said, "I wish't been a boy." His reason would have been well understood by his contemporaries. Since women were barred from the professions and seldom trained for any kind of employment outside of the home, daughters—and in the Beecher family Harriet was now the third—were considered a financial liability, a lifelong burden to their fathers should they by some unhappy chance never marry. The Reverend Lyman Beecher undoubtedly would have spent the day rejoicing if he could have announced to his parish that he now had another son to add to the three boys already in the family. It was the ambition of this nationally known Calvinist minister to build himself an army of home-grown young evangelists who under his leadership would go barnstorming through the country keeping alive the old-time religion.

As Harriet in due time discovered, growing up under Papa Beecher was an exciting experience even for a girl. He was a lively man, a curious combination of earthly and spiritual passions. Possessed of keen intellect and a high sense of drama, he had a leapfrog way of thinking that led him to take first one side and then the other during the course of debate or public controversy, a habit most unsteadying to his opponents. Whether this vacillating was a deliberate theatrical device to keep him always center stage before the public (as many of his critics believed), or merely his peculiar way of arriving at truth, the net effect was to bring down upon the minister a host of enemies in and out of his field accusing him of being either too liberal or too conservative as the case might be. More than once he had charges of heresy brought against him. The air of surprise and innocence he wore while defending himself in these widely publicized disputes only added to the drama surrounding this amazing man. Always eager to plunge into life and grapple with every problem even at the risk of error, Papa Beecher throughout his career was the butt of many a newspaper or magazine cartoon picturing him a bungling buffoon one day, a saint with one of his wings slightly off balance the next. In their turn more than one of his children, including Harriet, would be held up before the public in exactly the same way.

At home Papa Beecher could do no wrong. He adored and was adored in return by his children and by his young wife, Roxanna—"Angel" as he called her—who put matters to rights for him after the disappointment of Harriet by adding to his flock Henry Ward in 1813, Charles in 1815. She would have done more for the cause but, worn out by domesticity and childbearing as well as the tuberculosis from which she was suffering, she died in 1816. Roxanne Stowe's one consolation on her deathbed was that of her eight children five were boys destined for a life of glory; as for the three girls, what had been true in the past would probably be true for all time—they'd dedicate themselves to servicing father, brothers, husbands, be angels on earth as well as in heaven.

Harriet, who was six when her mother died, had started out early a rebellious angel. As if sensing what was required to win her father's attention, even as a toddler she ignored sisters Catherine and Mary in favor of older brothers William, Edward, and George. She imitated the boys at their games, hung around them while they did their farm chores, pestered them at their studies asking as many questions—usually of a religious nature—as her little head could conjure up. Legend says that her grasp of words and ideas was phenomenal and that when Papa was home she would show off what she had learned. But she was such a curious, comical minx of a child with her full, pouting mouth, passionately sincere brown eyes, and tomboyish habits that instead of winning his praise as she expected, he would rock with laughter as did all the other men in the family, wounding her babyish dignity. A temper tantrum expressing her outrage only made Papa laugh the more. But one day, not long after her mother's death she put such a penetrating question to him on the subject of "election"—the method by which some souls were selected for paradise and others were not—that on the spot Lyman Beecher became convinced that he had struck gold in this child. "Harriet is a genius!" he proclaimed before the entire family, after which all her idiosyncrasies, her unpredictable, shifting moods, startling statements, visions of demons and angels, her "shakes" at night, her funny, boyish escapades and histrionic posture in the parlor were covered by the definition. In the Reverend Lyman Beecher's sprawling Litchfield household one could do almost anything and get away with it as long as it was inspired by what inspired Papa himself—genius.

In her childhood Harriet thought her father the most fascinating man in the world, loved nothing better than to listen at table while he engaged his sons in theological debate. Often too excited to eat what was on the plate before her, she had a veritable feast of language rich in biblical rhythm, the allegory and poetry intermixed with generous flavorings of dry humor and spicy denunciations of Unitarians, "tolerationists," and other New England-style heathens. A famous latter-day heathen, Robert Ingersoll, was to call the Reverend Dr. Beecher "one of the wardens of the Puritan penitentiary," colorfully denouncing him for his inflexible position on infant damnation, "election," and other Calvinist precepts. Despite the fact that her girlhood was beset with problems growing out of her Calvinist upbringing, Harriet would have been the first to deny that her father ever imprisoned her mind or her spirit. However terrifying to sinners elsewhere in the world with his famed sermons on the tortures of hell, at home the minister was peculiarly lenient and gentle. He encouraged argument among his children, heard with patience their questions, delighted in sharpening their intellects through debate. If on occasion he was firm in upholding a precept that frightened or puzzled them, it did not dim his light in their eyes. He did not forbid Harriet in her childhood to read the poetry of Lord Byron (next to Papa Harriet thought Lord Byron the most fascinating man in the world) even though the poet's private life was said to be scandalous. If anyone was "warden" in the Beecher household, as far as Harriet was concerned it was her sister Catherine who took over the role of mother immediately after Roxanna's death. Thinking that Harriet needed a stern hand, Catherine dominated this young sister of hers even after their father brought home a strapping young woman by the name of Harriet Porter to be their new mother.

With the advent of Harriet Porter into the family, young Harriet Beecher's life became a complex of problems. She resented her stepmother the more because now there were two to tell her that she should be doing samplers instead of reading poetry (Catherine thought Lord Byron disgraceful); that daydreaming was idleness and idleness devil's work; that arguing was unladylike, that to want praise because she was gifted at writing showed "sin of pride." Clinging always to the memory of her dead mother, Harriet, sinning again, resisted all efforts of the new one to turn her into a lady. However, as the stepmother soon had children of her own to care for—Isabella, born in 1822, Thomas in 1824; and James in 1828, she left it up to Miss Pierce's Academy on North Street to make a lady of Harriet.

The school fared better. Harriet had lessons in history, rhetoric, and religion, with main emphasis on the latter and "winsome womanhood." A woman's highest duty was to God not self, she was taught. All personal ambition and vanity must be put aside in favor of service to home and society. For the first time Harriet admitted to herself that she did most wickedly love praise, and yearn to use her intelligence freely and boldly like a man. It was sinful to want to write poetry like Lord Byron, drama like Shakespeare, novels like Sir Walter Scott. As a minister's daughter she had example to set. By trying hard to curb her desires and to overcome her weaknesses, romantic Harriet managed to get through Miss Pierce's Academy with few bad marks against her name. But she was far from cured. At closing exercises in her graduation year, one of her teachers rose in the assembly hall to read aloud a composition chosen for its excellence of construction written by a student whose name—according to custom—was withheld. The title of the composition was "Can the Immortality of the Soul be Proved by the Light of Nature." At the conclusion of the reading one of the dignitaries seated on the platform leaned over to ask Miss Pierce which among her girls had written so excellent a piece of work. Miss Pierce nodded in Harriet's direction, and the dignitary, none other than the Reverend Lyman Beecher himself, beamed with pride as he met his daughter's equally proud and smiling eyes. In that blissful moment father and daughter revealed themselves to one another. They were Beechers. They were exceptional. The Lord had blessed them with talent which it was their duty to use. They could not help that it also gave them joy to be recognized for their worth. To be anonymous was not their style.

The subject of immortality had been a burdensome one to Harriet ever since in early childhood she had been taught that every individual (in Jonathan Edward's words) "had to descend agonizingly to a full acceptance of God's foreordained plan for themselves, eternal life for some, eternal damnation for others, and only then, if he truly was one of

God's elect would Divine Grace come to his assistance and inform him of his salvation." Her shakes at night had come from fear lest she die before morning without having had word direct from Deity of her salvation. Now fear and trembling were at an end for she had convinced her father (who challenged her word at the first telling) that she had arrived at a perfect understanding with God who had made known to her "in a flash" her election for heaven.

But no sooner did she come to a state of peace concerning her fate in the afterlife than her earthly fate as a woman began to haunt and terrify her. In adolescence this emotional, passionate-natured girl, who thought herself different from her sisters, began to live out fantasies in which she alternately played swooning heroine to a brilliant Lord Byron, or was herself the brilliant writer so dazzling society by the art she practiced that it forgot what she owed it in the way of "good works." Coming out of that world of fantasy to perform the dull arts of house-keeping under the critical eyes of Catherine or her stepmother grew daily more difficult. Those three cardinal rules of winsome womanhood— obedience, piety, and submission became the tormenting devils of Harriet's life. Unable to confide her troubles to anyone, she sank into a state of morbidity which no amount of prayer seemed able to overcome. Working out the salvation of her soul, she thought, had been far easier than working out her salvation on earth where clearly eternal suffering was to be her fate. "I do nothing right! I yield to temptation!" she cried out one day to a puzzled Catherine.

Sister Katy, as the family called Catherine, was going through a crisis of her own. A tragedy at sea had claimed the life of her fiancé, Alexander Fisher, newly appointed professor of mathematics at Yale University who had set off for Europe in 1822 on the packet ship *Albion* and gone down with it in a storm off the Irish coast. With the news that Alexander Fisher would never return to claim his bride, a deep gloom settled over the Beecher household. Twenty-two-year-old Catherine begged her father for some reassurance that though Professor Fisher had not yet to anyone's knowledge come to his "perfect understanding with God," it did not necessarily follow that she would not be reunited with her one and only love in heaven. The Reverend Lyman Beecher refused to give his daughter such reassurance and her lamentations filled the house.

The aftermath of the conflict between daughter and father was that Catherine Beecher renounced those aspects of Calvinism which she thought unreasonable and cruel. Harriet, a witness to it all, would have cause to remember many years later when a loss of her own, under similar circumstances, put her through the same suffering and the same bitter renunciation. Even at the moment her compassion for her sister had her secretly vacillating between the more lenient Episcopalian Deity worshiped by her mother's relatives in Nutplains and the sterner God to whom by upbringing she owed allegiance.

The tragedy brought about another change in sister Katy's life. Professor Fisher had left to her, along with his library, a sizable sum of money. The unhappy girl decided now to use this as a means of escape from home. She made up her mind to go to Hartford, Connecticut, and open up a school for girls the purpose of which would be to "enhance the sphere of usefulness open to women." Typically Lyman Beecher did not hold back his daughter, nor balk even when she took fifteen-year-old Mary along with her to work as an assistant teacher. For Harriet the loss of her sisters piled trouble upon trouble, for she now was the lone girl at home with all the household chores to do, without the aid even of her stepmother who had just given birth to baby Isabella. On top of this came her father's decision to move to Boston where in taking over the pulpit in the Hanover Street Church he would have a higher salary and a livelier fight against Unitarianism.

Harriet had completely taken for granted her life in rural Litchfield. In the company of Mary and schoolfriends she had on occasion enjoyed the simple pleasures of family living in the village—hayrides, church suppers, boatrides, now and then a lecture—the only forms of entertainment there were. In the more sophisticated Boston environment, without sisters or friends, she felt an outsider, desolate, abandoned. Catherine wrote promising to bring her to Hartford if the school there prospered, but to Harriet that time seemed a long way off. By now, writing had become the driving passion of her life, but domestic duties made it almost impossible to spend the time necessary for creative work. The result was a short-tempered young girl in trouble with her stepmother, and—in trouble with herself. "I wish I could die young and let the remembrance of me and my faults perish in the grave," she wrote to Catherine.

In 1823 a religious upheaval in Boston allowed the Reverend Lyman Beecher little time for his introspective young daughter; or for a troublesome young man by the name of William Lloyd Garrison, a church member who kept urging him to take a public stand calling for instant abolition of slavery. Having enough to do trying to bring instant abolition of Unitarians, the harrassed minister told young Garrison that he was not out of sympathy with the slaves but that he had "other irons in the fire" —a phrase destined to come home to haunt him. There had been slaves in New Haven where Lyman Beecher was born, slaves in Litchfield when he arrived there in manhood to take over as minister of the Congregational Meetinghouse. He had taken this state of affairs more for granted than he did dueling, against which he had become an ardent crusader while a student at Yale. He was equally eloquent on the subject of alcoholic beverages, writing six sermons against their use which by popular demand had been brought out in many American and English editions. But in these strange times so many young men, including his own son Edward, wanted him to put all causes aside except slavery, and were continually trying to convince him that it was the business of the church to play a leadership role in abolition. Not until many years later when in *Uncle Tom's Cabin* he came across this passage—

> Oh, Church of Christ, read the signs of the times . . . This is an age of the world when nations are trembling and convulsed. A mighty influence is abroad, surging and heaving the world as with an earthquake. And is America safe? Every nation that carries in its bosom great and unredressed injustice has in it the elements of this last convulsion . . . Both north and south have been guilty before God; and the Christian church has a heavy account to answer . . .

did the Reverend Lyman Beecher get the message. By then every other member of his family was supporting the activities of William Lloyd Garrison whose cry "no union with slaveholders" was putting terror into slavery's defenders on both sides of the Mason-Dixon line.

At age sixteen Harriet was not yet thinking about slavery, not yet inclined to defend anyone's rights except her own. She had, after a long struggle with herself, come to the conclusion that if as a woman she must meet the world's standards as a domestic creature, then so be it, but as she was God's servant as well she would not abandon her true, creative self. Someday, somehow, she'd be an author. "I do not mean to live in vain," she argued defensively to her brother Edward. "God has given me talents which I must use. I will lay them at His feet, well satisfied if He will accept them."

Catherine, who had written poetry before "real-life," as she said, put an end to such nonsense, thought Harriet's talents could be put to better use as a teacher of religion. In part to lift her younger sister out of dejection, she brought her to Hartford even before the Beecher school reached a peak of success. Delighted to be free of the Boston life, Harriet blossomed in Hartford, liking particularly the room she had all to herself in Mrs. Bull's boardinghouse. There for the first time she read to her heart's content, and began to fill notebooks with ideas for stories, in due time copying them out, allowing sheaf after sheaf to pile up on her little desk. But on discovering what she was up to, Catherine took away the precious sheafs, exchanged the Scott novels which she had been reading for inspiration, for Cotton Mather's *Magnalia* and Butler's *Analogy of Religion*. Sulking, Harriet buried her nose in these dry texts as she needed them to prepare her for her teaching, but she by no means had abandoned her determination to become an author. On Sundays, in company with a newfound friend, fellow teacher, Miss Georgiana May, she would go strolling along the river, her thoughts as always on her future as a writer. "There will come a time when I will be both rich and famous through the novels I write, and then I'll come back to Hartford and build a mansion here near the river," she told Georgiana.

Even as the two girls walked arm in arm in the Connecticut sunlight confiding their dreams, forces of history were gathering that were to determine the fate of one of them. "The Peculiar Institution," as New Englanders fastidiously referred to slavery, was more and more becoming the issue around which the politics of America were shaping. With the appetite of the entire nation whetted for economic growth since the War of 1812, in human terms this meant an influx of immigrants into the North for paid labor in mills and factories; a deepening of the exploitation of slaves in the South, and a drive on the part of the agrarian economy to widen the boundaries of their holdings in which to increase their "stock of manpower."

Self-interest became the dominating motive of most lawmakers in Congress who rose to champion or put down any bill that threatened to cut into the profits of the section they represented. In the 1820s the dispute over slavery was a battle of words fought in legislative chambers, village lyceums, schools, inns, and parlors. By the 1830s tensions mounted and the battle began to spill over into the streets—especially in New England —with fists, stones, and sometimes swords accompanying the words. Public disorder gave rise to the ominous phrase "a gathering storm."

For the most part educated young New Englanders sided with the "instant" abolitionists, angrily challenging the gradualist approach of state and national leaders including teachers and churchmen. In Hartford the Beecher sisters could not help being aware of the anti-slavery movement, for its propaganda throughout the region was deliberately designed to be loud, aggressively sharp "stinging as with salt to make the guilty wince." But while on Christian principles they sympathized with the slaves, the girls followed their training at Miss Pierce's Academy, which said that respectable young women kept out of controversy. Out of loyalty to their father they were, however, quite vocal in his behalf whenever he or the Congregationalist Church of New England came under attack. As a result of its refusal to intervene on the slavery question, the Church was beginning to lose ground in New England, many of its members breaking away either to give up religion altogether or to join more liberal sects. While to the government these abolitionists were saying: "We do not *play* politics. Anti-slavery is not half-jest with us; it is a terrible, earnest-with-life-or-death, worse than life or death issue," to the church hierarchy they were saying: "We do not *play* religion." To every leader upon whom they were putting pressure, they issued a warning: join us in our struggle for freedom or—

> We will write out judgment with the iron pen of a century to come and it shall never be forgotten, if we can help it that you were false in your generation to the claims of the slave.

In the course of time, names of the "false" began to be put down— Henry Clay, Daniel Webster, the Reverend Lyman Beecher. . . .

One New England churchman on returning to Boston from a trip to Europe reported that all he was asked as an American traveling abroad was his opinion of immediate emancipation. "Is an American," he asked, "never to travel anywhere in the world but men will throw this troublesome question in his face?" Leaving his stormy pulpit in Boston for a new assignment in Ohio in 1832, the Reverend Lyman Beecher was soon uttering that same cry. He hadn't imagined that even in the West theological students would be hounding him, telling him that when it came to taking a stand on slavery he had no right to vacillate, "moderate, or beg delay." Everywhere he turned someone was thrusting a pamphlet under his nose, or spouting verbatim from Wendell Phillips or that fellow Garrison—

> Our clients are three millions of Christian slaves. They have no voice but ours to utter their complaints, or to demand justice. The press, the pulpit, the wealth, the literature, the prejudices, the political arrangements, the present self-interest of the country are all against us. God has given us no weapon but the truth . . . there are sluggards to be awakened . . . doubters to be convinced.

Twenty-one-year-old Harriet had also thought that when she left New England she would be leaving the slave controversy behind. Indeed, despite misgivings about the quality of life one might find in Ohio (to her as to most New Englanders the very word *West* suggested heathenism, loose women, gambling, and imbibing), she had welcomed the relief of getting away from the quarreling factions that kept her region in a constant state of turmoil. Catherine, who had gone ahead to survey the environs of Cincinnati had reported back to the family that she had never seen "a place so capable of being rendered a paradise." The city itself was built on cliffs overlooking the Ohio River. Its roads were muddy, rutted, and pigs ran wild along them. But two miles distant from the center of the city was a place called Walnut Hills, a truly peaceful spot in which, at Lane Seminary, Papa could train and inspire his soldiers of God, while Catherine, Mary, and Harriet could establish nearby a religiously oriented school to uplift and educate the neglected children of frontier Ohio.

A small girl, dark complexioned, with languorous, dreamy eyes, and quite pretty now, Harriet entered this new life with excitement and curiosity. The years in Hartford had turned her from child to woman, developed her teaching skill, but there had been no romance for her, no adventures. From the moment her skirts swept into the Ohio mud, and her eyes surveyed the wild hills and river, she sensed that life would be different in this less genteel milieu. She made up her mind to quit for a while her "internal world of emotions," as she wrote to Georgiana, and face head-on the external world; pioneers had little time for dreaming, and besides, it would be good to fill up with some new experiences. In her next report to Georgiana she describes herself as "scarcely alive" due to exhaustion from her duties: the school had already been set up; Catherine, a strict headmistress, had her working long hours at teaching by day, and by night writing a geography book to be used by her pupils. Both Catherine and Papa had a sense of mission in Ohio: "What will become of the West if her prosperity rushes up to such a majesty of power, while those great institutions linger which are necessary to inform the mind, and the conscience, and the heart of that vast world?" Papa wrote. To guarantee that institutions did not linger, all in the family worked hard and long. It was up to the Beechers to bring the "moral culture" that would save the soul of the West.

While Harriet worked away at the geography, Catherine, along with her teaching and running of the school, became a mainstay writer for the *McGuffey Eclectic Readers*, the first of which was published in Ohio in 1836. Papa, too, did his share of writing for the series. These books soon became a "must" for nineteenth-century children, educating them not only in history, language, and literature, but also indoctrinating them in the Puritan ethics and conservative philosophy which governed the lives of those editing the *Readers*. In the fourth *McGuffey Reader* Catherine chose Harriet's beloved Lord Byron to use as an example of one who had spent his days in search of selfish enjoyment, who, though gifted, did not understand that happiness was only to be attained by self-denial. "Lord Byron," wrote Catherine, "had every source of earthly bliss laid open, and drank to the very dregs." Meanwhile Catherine was keeping strict watch over the emotions of romantic Harriet, testing Harriet's self-denial by giving her tasks that kept her "scarcely alive." Only "in the law of God is the true path of happiness," said sister Katy.

When *Geography for Children* was completed, it was published under Catherine's name, but it earned its true author her first money as a professional writer, the grand sum of $187. All the old vanity and pride of accomplishment came soaring up in Harriet when she saw her work in print. She decided it was high time she slipped from under the iron thumb of her elder sister and did the kind of writing Catherine called selfish enjoyment. Luckily Harriet had on her side a friend of her father's, Judge James Hall who informed her that there was an organization in Cincinnati called the Semi Colon Club which met every Monday evening to hear poetry, stories, and plays written by its members. Himself a charter member, he would, he said, gladly sponsor her if she would like to join. What Sister Katy and Papa Beecher had to say about this new development in Harriet's life is nowhere recorded, but it is in their favor that she was allowed to burn the midnight candle now, not for a second textbook, but for a short story to read at her literary debut.

In selecting a subject for the story, Harriet for the first time rejected the temptation to write pure romance. As foreign as the West had been to her before coming to Ohio, so, she realized, was New England to most Westerners. With all the artistry at her command, she wanted now to write a story that would bring to life the flavor and color of the New England she recalled so nostalgically, especially when thinking about her mother's people in Nutplains. Further incentive was the realization that New England folklore had hardly been tapped for literature though it was American to the core, and colorful and entertaining besides. When, finally, the story was completed and read before the members of the

Semi Colon Club, it so entranced her listeners that Judge Hall begged her to write more such sketches and enter one of them into a contest he was sponsoring in the *Western Monthly*. This kind of encouragement was all she needed. When "A New England Tale" by Harriet Beecher took first prize, the young author in a state of almost delirious excitement ran home to put another fifty dollars in the family pot. The moment was of profound significance to Harriet for it offered proof that she was capable of writing professionally not only for the "trade," which Catherine considered acceptable, but for the literary market as well. Two works in print had her smiling now into the eyes of the world as once, when her essay had been read at the academy, she had smiled into the eyes of her father. To her joy this new self-esteem helped give her a bit more respect at home. Away from home she was now much in demand by her new western friends who considered it prestigious to have so highly gifted a writer at their social affairs. The result was as good for Harriet's art as it was for her growth as a woman. With her keen feeling for language, her insight into character, and excellent eye for detail she was studying now these Ohio people, listening to their tales, learning something about their politics and mores—herself entering into the spirit of frontier culture. She was not conscious of the refreshing effect this western experience was having on her New England sensibilities, that it had taken the edge off of romantic fantasy, added the toughness of realism to her style. She was a New Englander whose genius was flourishing far from the scenes of home.

Quite the opposite was true of her father. As president of Lane Seminary the Reverend Lyman Beecher was getting into ever deeper trouble, hounded by financial problems in the running of his school, hounded by local ministers who did not see eye to eye with him on religious matters, hounded by students who wanted him to join in their radical activities in the anti-slavery movement. In campus rallies he was accused of hypocrisy, bigotry, and excoriated for declaring himself in favor of colonization as a solution to the disposal of the slaves. Put on the defensive in what soon became an issue involving the community surrounding the campus, Dr. Beecher pointed out to his young critics that under his administration at Lane Seminary he had admitted a "free" Negro as a student and was this not proof that he was no bigot? He admitted the inhumanity of slavery—said he was opposed only to the methods of the abolitionists and the solutions put forward by them. But his arguments did not satisfy Theodore Weld, militant leader of the student dissenters. Speaking in the name of his followers, young Weld demanded that Dr. Beecher use his nationwide reputation as leader of the Congregationalist Church and announce at once for instant abolition. The minister told Weld what he had told William Lloyd Garrison when once, in Boston, Garrison had come to him asking for use of the church for an anti-slavery meeting: "Your zeal is commendable, but you are misguided." Garrison had left the church and gone over to The First Society of Free Enquirers who had not denied him their meetinghall. Now Weld seemed ready, in the spirit of Garrison's notorious anti-slavery newspaper, the *Liberator*—"I will be as harsh as truth, and as uncompromising as justice"—to lead a breakaway from Lane Seminary if his demands were not met, including that of admitting more Negroes and establishing equality on a social as well as educational basis for all students on campus. When Dr. Beecher hedged, the student leader sent a letter to a group of philanthropists in the East whose money had made possible the establishment of the school, accusing him of prohibiting free speech and of having left out of a reception given in his honor the one Negro student on campus. This letter resulted in the withdrawing of funds by one of the leading philanthropists of Boston whose sympathies were strongly abolitionist. It seemed the beginning of the end for Lane, and for Beecher influence both in the East and the West.

Harriet, Catherine, and their brothers, the eldest of whom were now churchmen themselves and ardent Garrison followers, stood loyally by their harrassed parent in his difficulties. He was in a particularly trying position, they thought, since in Ohio the pro-slavery forces were in violent opposition to him, accusing him of being too liberal, while his students, erstwhile financial backers, former churchmembers, and even many among his close friends (Judge Hall among them), had turned on him for not being liberal enough. The whole issue of slavery had now become one of keen interest to Harriet as she followed the arguments of Judge Hall and others and was forced to sort out her own thinking in the course of defending the role of the church and her father. She decided to take an opportunity offered to her by an Ohio friend who had relatives living across the river in Kentucky to see for herself the conditions under which the slaves lived on a southern plantation.

One of the first things Harriet observed as the somewhat uncomfortable recipient of the hospitality of the plantation, was the attitude of her charming hostess (who later was to show up as Mrs. Shelby in the opening chapters of *Uncle Tom's Cabin*). "Mrs. Shelby" was gentle, "a woman of a high class, both intellectually and morally," a woman of "religious sensibility" yet gave not a second thought that her life of ease and splendor was had at the expense of other human beings who could be bought and sold like cattle. The observation was an education for Harriet—far more so than all the rhetoric she had been hearing from the abolitionists. Returning to the Ohio side of the river, she allowed herself to be taken again and again to hear the tales of runaway slaves being sheltered by friends in the Cincinnati "underground." Curiously, she seems not, at this time, to have recorded her impressions nor thought to use them as the basis for stories. She was still preoccupied with her New England tales, indeed was readying her first collection for publication— *The Mayflower: or sketches of Scenes and Characters among the Descendants of the Pilgrims.*

As an indignant spectator, she was also spending a great deal of time at the trial of her father who, among all his other problems, had awakened one morning to find himself accused of heresy by a fellow theologian. It was an experience to watch Papa take on his opponent. Taken aback and confused at first, he quickly recovered and began to employ every oratorical trick of the trade to defend himself. He was so passionately earnest and sincere in the manner in which he gave evidence that somewhat to everyone's amazement he managed not only to come through the trial triumphant, but even to get a sizable donation for Lane Seminary from Arthur Tappan, the very man who at the instigation of young Weld, had recently cut off his funds. This sudden acquisition of money saved the school—for the moment, at least—and had significance for Harriet of which she was not aware at the time.

With the additional money at his disposal, Lyman Beecher decided to increase his staff at Lane and hire a professor of biblical literature. His choice for the position fell to Calvin Stowe, an ardently religious and learned little man who had been one of his assistants in Boston. Professor Stowe arrived in due time, but not alone as expected. He brought along his new bride, Eliza, the hazel-eyed daughter of the president of Dartmouth College. According to Harriet's description of her, Eliza was a "delicate, pretty little woman" who instantly won her sympathy. The friendship between the two women deepened as the months went by, Eliza more than replacing Georgiana May in Harriet's affection. Having not yet met a man who lived up to her romantic conception of Lord Byron, or one who equalled in intellectual force her dynamic father, Harriet seemed resigned to spinsterhood, tended to drift into strong, sentimental relationships with women. All of her friends, including Eliza, were in a constant conspiracy to find a husband for her, but when she learned of this Harriet quite firmly told them to leave such matters to God. Some of those concerned were soon to have cause to remember her words.

In June—the year was 1834—an impulse seized Harriet to attend the graduation exercises at Amherst College where her dazzling young brother, Henry Ward, was going to take his degree. Emboldened by her Kentucky-Ohio experiences she made the journey alone, going by stage-coach to Toledo, then steamship across Lake Erie to Buffalo, and stagecoach again to Albany and Massachusetts. Her motive was really a double one—sisterly affection and a writer's instinct to return to the place of her roots for renewal. After the graduation exercises were over, she planned to go to Nutplains in search of still more family lore for a second volume of New England tales.

With Henry Ward who, like his brothers, was slated to be a church-man, Harriet traveled to Connecticut, brother and sister finding much in common as they recounted to one another their experiences of the past few years. Henry Ward had a flair for poetic prose, and in tempera-ment was as romantic and impressionable as Harriet. His strong anti-slavery sentiment was later on to lead to his participation in underground activities in which boxes mailed to Kansas supposedly containing Bibles in reality contained weapons for those abolitionists defending Kansas as a free state ("Beecher Bibles"—these boxes would be called in the under-ground). At the moment Henry Ward was twenty-one, entirely unaware that he was destined within a few years to become one of the great religious leaders of the day, and, for his ideas and activities, be almost as controversial as the favorite sister now at his side. When Harriet arrived with him in Connecticut they were greeted with unexpected news. Their father and Catherine were on their way to join them—the former coming East to raise still more money for Lane Seminary, Catherine to recruit teachers, and talk over with the family her desire to give up her own teaching in order to crusade throughout the West for "higher edu-cation for females."

Thus it was that the entire Beecher clan was out of Cincinnati that fateful summer when a cholera epidemic hit the city taking a heavy toll of lives, among them Harriet's beloved friend, Eliza Stowe. Almost un-consolable at her loss, Harriet wept also out of sympathy for Calvin Stowe, the brilliant, childlike man Eliza had left behind. On her return to Ohio she tried to ease her grief by comforting the bereaved husband, and together, gradually, they both emerged out of mourning. Harriet persuaded Professor Stowe to join her in attending Monday evening meetings of the Semi Colon Club where, on occasion, he read to the group a scholarly paper. Much to her distress, members of the club began to whisper among themselves that a marriage between her and the widower seemed an ideal solution for both of them. Professor Stowe, emboldened by the whispers, began to look upon her more romantically. As she could not reciprocate his feeling, Harriet braced herself to refuse his proposal. Yet, when it came, she surprised herself by how quickly she accepted, hardly knowing whether her yes was out of duty to the dead Eliza, or for the opening it gave her to set up her own home away from the dominating Catherine. Like so many other young women of her day, Harriet Beecher loved romance but secretly dreaded marriage considering it to be "a sacrifice." Under the law women had no rights but were completely subservient to their husbands. Their lives were shortened if not by diseases stemming from childbirth, then by exhaustion from what usually amounted to a good sixteen hours a day at cooking, sewing, laundering, house cleaning. For a woman of Harriet's creative temperament to whom time was essential if she was to be a writer, marriage seemed a double threat. Thus it is not surprising that on the morning she was to be married to Calvin Stowe—January 6, 1836—her mood as she dashed off a letter to her Hartford friend, Georgiana May, was far from ecstatic.

> Well, my dear Geo., about half an hour more and your old friend, companion, schoolmate, sister, etc., will cease to be Hattie Beecher and change to nobody knows who. My dear, you are engaged and pledged in a year or two to encounter a similar fate . . . I have been dreading and dreading the time, and lying awake all last week wondering how I should live through this overwhelming crisis, and lo! it has come, and I feel nothing at all. . . . Sister Katy's not here, so she will not witness my departure from her care and guidance to that of another. None of my numerous friends and acquaintances who have taken such a deep interest in making the connection for me even know the day, and it will be all done and over before they know anything about it . . . Well, here comes Mr. S., so farewell, and for the last time I subscribe Your own Harriet E. Beecher.

As Mrs. Stowe she was surprised a few months later to find herself "tranquil, quiet, and happy." Her husband, who was nine years her elder, idolized her for her superior talent, her skill at managing so well his house and her writing; when her little tales published in the *Western Monthly* brought in extra money to supplement his scant salary, not only he, but she too, thought it the best of all possible worlds. They decided, however, that as soon as his contract at Lane terminated, he would take up an offer to teach at his alma mater in Maine—Bowdoin College. (As a graduate of the class of 1824 Calvin Stowe had known both Hawthorne and Longfellow.) Harriet was longing to get back to New England.

Late in 1836 she became the mother of twins, naming them, appropriately enough, Eliza and Harriet. These two were followed by Henry Ellis born in 1838; Frederic William (named after a German monarch) born in 1840; Georgiana May born in 1843; and Samuel Charles born in 1848—bringing to their often frantic mother all the domestic duties she had so feared in the sleepless weeks before her marriage. Though physically strong, Harriet indulged in numerous "nervous collapses" complaining endlessly of them to friends, giving as cause "writer's block" though she did manage between feedings, moppings, sewing, and nursing to get in a few hours of writing each day. Once, when Calvin was away on church business, leaving her altogether without help, the distressed mother of six, still living in Cincinnati, poured out her heart to her usual confidante in Hartford—Georgiana May:

> I have been working hard (for me) all day in the kitchen, washing dishes, looking into closets, and seeing a great deal of that dark side of domestic life. . . . I am sick of the smell of sour milk, and sour meat, and sour everything, and then the clothes will not dry . . . and everything smells mouldy. I feel no life, no energy, no appetite.

Thus, sour tempered, she waited impatiently for Mr. S. to return. With gratitude she called him "housefather" for he never minded lending a hand at domestic chores. It must be admitted, however, that she sometimes took advantage of his good nature, and could not help laughing at her gentle scholar, considering him a comical figure "in his spectacles, gravely marching the little troop in their nightgowns up to bed, tagging after them . . . like an old hen after a flock of ducks." Dragging herself up to bed hours later when her pen was put aside, she would lie awake disgruntled by the thought that she was getting along in years, and, though a working writer, still had no fame, no wealth, no mansion on the Connecticut River. Meanwhile her husband and her father were still struggling to make a go of Lane Seminary, on the decline since the radical young Weld had bolted the school taking along with him a great many of the students to set up a college of their own in Oberlin,

Ohio. Oberlin was already underway and being run on a basis of "freedom
and self-help." Despite the loss this had meant to Lane, and consequently
to her own fortune, Harriet could not help admiring Weld's courage. In
her own state of slough, action of any kind seemed glorious. She fairly
hero-worshiped her brothers Edward and Henry Ward because they were
doing something about slavery.

Looking in the mirror one night in 1849 Harriet Beecher Stowe
performed for the hundredth or more time the ritual of resignation to
womanhood, etc., etc., then wrote to Georgiana: "I am thirty-seven years
old. I am glad of it. I like to grow old and have six children and cares
endless. I wish you could see me with my flock all around me. They sum
up my cares, and were they gone I should ask myself, what now remains
to be done? They are my work over which I fear and tremble." But that
they were not her *true* work she well knew, and no amount of shouting
or confessing could still her fear and trembling that life and glory were
passing her by.

A few weeks later the youngest of Harriet's children, Samuel Charles,
died in the "fresh harvest of death" reaped by Asiatic cholera in
Cincinnati. The epidemic was severe enough to prompt President Zachary Taylor to proclaim a "Day of National Fasting, Humiliation, and
Prayer." Unable to comprehend her personal disaster, Harriet could do
nothing but sit and moan "My Charley—my beautiful, loving gladsome
baby, so loving, so sweet, so full of life and hope and strength." For a
time it looked as if she would not recover her spirits, this nervous breakdown making all past ones seem frauds. But she did come through with
that toughness of spirit so characteristic of all the Beechers. "I write as
though there were no sorrow like my sorrow, yet there has been in this
city, as in the land of Egypt, scarce a house without its dead," she told
Georgiana.

Fortunately her husband's contract with the seminary terminated at
this time enabling her to leave the city which held so many memories of
her lost child.

On touching New England soil again Harriet felt not only revived
in spirit but renewed in hope. Surely there was time yet for her dream of
fame to be realized. In the large house near Bowdoin College campus
where she waited out still another pregnancy, she announced to her husband and to Georgiana (and, this, too, for the hundredth or more time)
"I have determined not to be a mere domestic slave." This time, though,
things did seem to be looking up for her. Shortly after the birth of Charles

Edward in 1850, she received a letter from New York informing her that Harper and Brothers was interested in bringing out Harriet Beecher Stowe's collected New England stories. After reading aloud the letter, Calvin peered at his wife over his spectacles and said in sincere delight: "My dear, you must be a literary woman, it is so written in the book of fate." While Harriet sat smiling in triumph, he repeated the name "Harriet Beecher Stowe" again and again, saying it had a euphonious ring meant to be heard round the world. Then, in absolute awe of this woman he had married, the professor rose from his chair, stood with his hand lightly touching Harriet's head, and spoke a biblical passage. "Your husband," he said softly, "will lift up his head at the gate, and your children will rise up and call you blessed." The key had turned for Harriet. She was in time for history.

In March 1849 General Zachary Taylor had "assumed the presidency" (as the saying went) with no decision having been reached on the status of slavery in the Mexican cession lands. California and New Mexico territories were being administered by military officials. Had gold not been discovered just at this time, the subsequent "rush" booming the population of the territories to 100,000—well above the minimum for statehood —there would have been no immediate crisis further stirring up the dispute between North and South regarding the spread of slavery to the West.

Anxious to ease the tension the President encouraged both territories to apply immediately for statehood since as sovereign states they could do as they pleased about slavery. His private opinion was that they would choose to come in as free states. "Old Zach" as Horace Greeley called the general, was new at statesmanship and maneuvering in a far more complex business than his soldier mind could comprehend. He sent out two agents to prod the two territories to action; their report to Congress indicated that California's already prepared constitution prohibited slavery while New Mexico was well on the way to the same decision. The report put southern representatives in a fury. Two free states entering the union meant a drastic change in the sectional balance in Congress and an end to the power of slaveholders. In the view of Jefferson Davis, unless some compromise could be reached, the people of his state "would know how to meet an attack on their rights even by Civil War if that be provoked." The South charged President Taylor, himself a Louisiana slaveholder, with "gross injustice," "gross usurpation of powers."

Excitement mounted. An Ohio newspaper replied editorially to Davis, saying: "The north is determined that slavery shall not pollute the soil of lands now free even if it should come to a dissolution of the Union." The prospect of dissolution so terrified the moderates in Congress that, under the leadership of Daniel Webster of Massachusetts, they began to yield to southern pressure. Taking advantage of the weakening of their adversaries, South Carolina's John C. Calhoun, on coming back to Washington from a convention called in Nashville to plan resistance to "northern aggressions," rose to throw a final challenge at the mighty Webster. The price of peace, said Calhoun, was for the North to stop agitating against slavery, amend the Constitution to give the minority South a power of veto. "If you are unwilling we should part in peace, tell us so," he thundered, "and we shall know what to do when you reduce the question to submission or resistance."

Meanwhile, back in New England, Harriet with her flock of children was casually taking the air in Brunswick, trooping down the road from Bowdoin College to picnic on fine days in the woods, or, jostling along in the family carriage, to reach points of departure for nearby islands. Her big house, big family, and little New England tales were absorbing all her energies. The twins, Eliza and Harriet, now aged fourteen, helped with the younger children while their mother, happier than she had been in years, had time to sit perusing the last sentence jotted down in her notebook. Like everyone else Harriet was well aware of the crisis in Washington but confident that New England's Daniel Webster would not betray the cause of the slave. She little dreamed that it would be the great Daniel himself, who inadvertently would draw her stage center into the anti-slavery struggle.

Calhoun threw down his challenge to Congress for peace or war on March 4, 1850. Three days later, March 7, Daniel Webster rose to make reply, knowing the entire nation was at attention. Everyone knew that he was a "Liberty *and* Union" man. What they did not know was that he had now decided to forego liberty for sake of union in order to preserve the peace. Addressing himself not to the South but to his own friends in the North, Webster explained that no law was needed to exclude slavery from the territories since geography and economics would of themselves discourage its introduction. As for those places where slavery already existed, it was best to leave it untampered with. Furthermore, he went on, it was a wrong to the South when northern citizens harbored runaway slaves; he would back a law to put a stop to that practice. A shock wave went over New England. Overnight the star of Daniel Webster fell (two years later, just before his death, Webster was to admit that his March 7 speech was the greatest mistake he had made in his political career), and his once hero-worshiping constituency in New England tightened ranks to openly defy the infamous fugitive slave law he had proposed.

In the Beecher conclave it was, curiously enough, Sister Katy who egged Harriet on to action. "If I could use a pen as you can," she wrote, "I would write something that will make this whole nation feel what an accursed thing slavery is." The letter was followed up by Henry Ward coming in person from Brooklyn, New York, where he headed one of the largest churches in the area. "Do it, Hattie, do!" he said. "Write something about slavery." On the night of his visit Harriet went to sleep with his command in her ears. The following morning she awoke recalling in detail her visit to the Kentucky plantation, her talks with fugitive slaves in Ohio, and all the slogans and phrases of the anti-slavery movement which were burned into memory as deeply as the Bible itself. But was this enough, she asked her husband, to enable her to handle such a momentous subject? Professor Stowe had confidence that it was. To do his part, after hours of teaching he would come home to help with the household chores so that his "literary woman" could make the whole nation "feel what an accursed thing this slavery is."

Nightly, Harriet shut herself up in her room, writing a few lines, tearing them up, beginning again, coming out at last to say despairingly that it was of no use, she had tried but to no avail. Then one Sunday morning while at church she had a "vision"—an entire scene spreading out before her eyes as if "God Himself" were showing the way: A Negro slave, in the posture of the Christ figure, murmuring as he lay dying of whip wounds inflicted by an overseer, "Forgive them for they know not what they do." Rushing home to put down on paper what she had seen, the words poured out in a torrent seeming almost to write themselves. Thus began the first of a series of sketches which later were to make up the book titled *Uncle Tom's Cabin, or Life Among the Lowly.*

Harriet determined to keep religion, not politics, as the basis for argument against slavery. She would be strictly non-partisan, excusing neither North nor South from responsibility for the "peculiar institution" and, by demonstrating in human terms the degradation, cruelty, and injustice imposed upon the slaves, point up how such things turn back upon the inflicters. In this way she hoped to arouse all Americans to

the fact that it was in their own self-interest to work for slavery's repeal.
To be able to combine the fine art of storytelling with a message of such
import gave her great satisfaction. It was *her* holy mission.

None other than the solicitor-general of Alabama, himself a former
slaveholder, had called the nation's sleep on the subject of slavery so
deep that "nothing but a rude and almost ruffian-like shake could rouse
her to a contemplation of her danger." "If she is saved," he said, "it is
because she is so treated." In writing *Uncle Tom's Cabin* Harriet Beecher
Stowe meant to be neither rude nor ruffian-like but just loud enough
with her anti-slavery trumpet to reach into every home and end the deep
sleep. After the book was published, when southern critics branded her
"the vilest liar and exaggerator" she was genuinely shocked and hurt.
She thought she had been kinder in her presentation of Southerners
who, after all, were for the most part inheritors of the evil system, than
she had been of Northerners who in their insulated position disavowed
responsibility for slavery even while profiting from it. She had least
been sparing of people like herself—the do-gooder New Englanders, who
had fooled themselves into believing they were less guilty than others.
It amazed her how, from the moment her sketches began to appear in
the magazine *National Era*, followed in 1852 by wider circulation in book
form, people were given to ignoring all these subtleties, seeing only the
propaganda value of her dramatic exposé of slavery. Publisher and author
alike were flabbergasted by the sale of the book. Jewett and Company
of Boston had to keep its three power presses running twenty-four hours
a day, and still could not keep up with the demand for this runaway
best seller, destined to be the most controversial book in the nation's
history.

At age forty-one, out of total obscurity, Harriet Beecher Stowe
emerged as the most talked-about woman in America. Asked again and
again how it was possible that she, pious daughter and wife of religious
leaders, was able to so forcefully address the nation on a political question,
she asserted repeatedly that *Uncle Tom's Cabin* was not political, and
furthermore "It was not I, but God who wrote it." Actually her side line
position in which she could not be corrupted by sectional, economic,
or political ambition had made it possible for her to leap upon a pulpit,
deliver a stunning moral sermon, and inadvertently put her finger into
the political pie. So thoroughly did *Uncle Tom's Cabin* cover every phase
of racial prejudice, unveil every hypocrisy, expose every symptom and
wound of the "national disease" that it added fuel to the already explosive

situation dividing the nation. In the South *Uncle Tom's Cabin* was banned and booksellers prosecuted who were found smuggling it over the border. In the North the most dramatic passages were lifted from the book to be shown in theaters and lecture halls, often in the most crass, sentimental presentations. This was a time when passions of people on both sides were so aroused that an objective presentation of what Harriet Beecher Stowe had written to argue the case for freedom seemed impossible. Only the life and death realities were relevant. Harriet herself got swept along by this fact as she took to the lectern not only at home but in Europe. She was an activist now. She and her book were doing the job that men like Garrison, Phillips, Theodore Weld had been campaigning for—awakening the sluggards, convincing the doubters, gathering the army that would stand up to put an end to slavery.

Today a more dispassionate and critical reading of *Uncle Tom's Cabin* reveals both the literary skill and the depth of insight Harriet brought to her work. In the home of the disillusioned slaveholder, St. Clare, and his selfish, high-strung wife, Marie, self-indulgence, decadence, boredom of plantation life hover in the languorous atmosphere, making their own subtle argument for the dangers inherent in a complacent, slaveholding society. What was it in Harriet Beecher Stowe's limited experience that enabled her to understand so well the psychology of St. Clare, his self-hatred, the tortured self-awareness with which he describes to Marie his participation in tracking down the runaway slave Scipio:

> People, you know, can get up just as much enthusiasm in hunting a man as a deer if it is only customary; in fact, I got a little excited myself.

It was the hand of genius, surely, holding the pen, filling in the strokes of characterization that made of St. Clare more than a one-dimensional figure. In one of the book's most searing dialogues, this reluctant slaveowner reminds the pious Vermont-born Miss Ophelia—and through her the entire nation—"Owner and slave get brutalized together." He longs for punishment, a "sublime last judgment—a righting of all the wrongs of the ages; a solving of all moral problems by an unanswerable wisdom."

Moderates in the country did not think *Uncle Tom's Cabin* unanswerable wisdom. As far back as 1820 a member of Congress had sounded an "alarm bell" declaring that partisan passions on the subject of slavery could "shake the goodly fabric of the union to its foundations

. . . reduce it to a melancholy ruin." Those in 1852 who hated slavery but wanted to do everything possible to avoid a split in the Union and civil war (Abraham Lincoln among them) thought nothing more incendiary than this book likely at any moment, because of the passions it aroused, to reduce the nation to melancholy ruin. Harriet was as shocked by this charge as she was by the charge of "liar" thrown at her by Southerners. Accuse *her* of wanting to hasten war, stir up hatred! Quite the opposite. Concern for humanity, for the welfare of the country and lives of all of America's sons had been her motive for writing the book. It would take only a stroke of the President's pen to emancipate the slaves and avoid the melancholy ruin of a great nation. Failing in that, the deluge that would come must be credited to a higher authority than her own for, said she, "not surer is the eternal law by which the millstone sinks in the ocean, than that stronger law by which injustice and cruelty shall bring on nations the wrath of Almighty God!" As for exaggerations and lies, her book did not begin to tell in fiction what all Americans must know to be even more terrible in life:

> Nothing of tragedy can be written, can be spoken, can be conceived that equals the frightful reality of scenes daily and hourly acted on our shores beneath the shadow of the American law and the shadow of the Cross of Christ . . . Men and women of America, is this a thing to be trifled with, apologized for, and passed over in silence? Farmers of Massachusetts, of New Hampshire, of Vermont, of Connecticut who read this book by the blaze of your winter evening fire— strong hearted, generous sailors and ship owners of Maine—is this a thing for you to countenance and encourage? Brave and generous men of New York, farmers of rich and joyous Ohio, and yet of the wide prairie states—answer—Is this a thing for you to protect and countenance?

If Harriet thought the brickbats hurled at her from moderate and southern quarters were unfair, she was even more distressed that the slightest word of reproach should come from anti-slavery circles. Certain of its leaders seemed to resent that it was a Beecher now standing in the forefront of the battle against slavery as if from the beginning she had been part of that struggle. Wendell Phillips, friend and associate of William Lloyd Garrison, in speaking before the Massachusetts Anti-Slavery Society in 1853 reminded the audience that "if the old anti-slavery movement had not aroused the sympathies of Mrs. Stowe the book had never been written; if that movement had not raised up hundreds of thousands of hearts to sympathize with the slave, the book had never been read." He followed this up by what Harriet had least expected—an attack through her upon her father. Obviously it irked Garrison and his followers that anyone with any connection to the man whose influence twenty years earlier—an influence, said Phillips, that made that of Daniel Webster seem "as dust in the balance"—could have speeded up abolition, now because of a popular novel, wore a mantle of glory in the world.

Not that the genius of the author has not made the triumph all her own, not that the unrivaled felicity of its execution has not trebled, quadruped, increased tenfold, if you please the number of readers—

but, Phillips went on, let us not forget her father, the man who once

held the orthodoxy of Boston in his right hand and who has since taken up the West by its four corners and given it largely to Puritanism, I mean the Rev. Dr. Lyman Beecher. Mr. Garrison was one of those who bowed to the spell of that matchless eloquence when it flamed over Zion. He waited on his favorite divine and urged him to give to the new movement the incalculable aid of his name and countenance . . . The reply was: "Mr. Garrison, I have too many irons in the fire to put in another." My friend said, "Doctor, you had better take them all out and put this one in if you mean well either to the religion or to the civil liberty of our country." The great orthodox leader did not rest with merely refusing. . . . he attempted to limit the irons of other men. As President of Lane Theological Seminary he endeavored to prevent the students from investigating the subject of slavery. The result, we all remember, was a strenuous resistance on the part of a large number of the students led by that remarkable man, Theodore D. Weld. The right triumphed, and Lane Seminary lost her character and noblest pupils at the same time. She has languished ever since even with such a president.

And so the story had come full circle to take Harriet Beecher Stowe down a peg from her glory; for, said Phillips, directing his words directly to her, "There must be a spot even for Archimedes to rest his lever upon before he can move the world, and this effort of genius (*Uncle Tom's Cabin*), consecrated to the noblest purpose might have fallen dead and unnoticed in 1835. It is the anti-slavery movement which has changed 1835 to 1852."

Harriet owed to the abolitionist movement still another debt for her success. Leaders of that group had long been urging American writers to take up "this uniquely American theme" of slavery, assuring writers that from "this debatable land between freedom and slavery" the literature of America could "gather its freshest laurels." Now she was tasting the truth of that statement. Called to England she was tumultuously received, dining with Lords and Ladies, showered with money and gifts for her cause; and while not brought into the presence of royalty (who feared taking sides in the American quarrel over slavery), she at least had the honor of meeting personally other "greats"—Charles Dickens, Thackeray, the Brownings, Heinrich Heine, Turgenev, George Eliot, among others. She had come too late for Lord Byron, unfortunately already dead, but she did meet Lady Byron from whom she learned a few intimate details concerning the private life of the poet, which so shocked her Puritan sensibilities that she instantly discarded this idol of her youth from her list of romantic heroes. England was swept by "Tom-mania," as the *Spectator* called the rage for Harriet's book. It had a record sale in the country of a million and a half copies. Songs with lyrics about slavery, dolls and other trinkets based on the novel were flooding the market. Harriet had fame—Harriet was getting rich—but she hardly had time to think about that now.

On her return from England she found herself challenged by her enemies to produce facts substantiating the conditions under which she claimed the slaves lived. Though she had intended to get back to her New England tales, she found herself, instead, embroiled in a defensive sequel to *Uncle Tom*, preparing what she called a "Key" to prove her case. It was from this tireless research she took, finally, the material for *Dred: A Tale of the Great Dismal Swamp*, published in 1856. (This book sold a hundred thousand copies in four weeks.) In creating it the author sharply shifted her emphasis to focus on the difference between 1852 and 1856. Uncle Tom was dead; a new slave had risen to replace him, younger, more militant, less willing to turn the other cheek. In the story the hero escapes to the swamp to gather strength to strike back at his oppressors. The meaning was clear to the country. Time was running out.

The maturing pen of Harriet Beecher Stowe was demonstrating that she, too, had learned something of the nature of the struggle, and, regardless of consequences, would continue to fight on until the end. Structurally, *Dred* was not so effective as *Uncle Tom's Cabin*, but once again, Harriet's feeling for drama, for the language of the Bible, the power of the "Word," the rhetoric of anti-slavery had accumulated to make possible a novel thoroughly American. Her name was now a household word throughout the world.

By 1858 no one on either side of the slavery controversy thought war could be avoided. In an address at Rochester, New York, Henry Seward, senator from New York, and one of the leaders of the newly formed Republican party, warned that the mounting tension could not be laid at the feet of "fanatical agitators" (Harriet Beecher Stowe was so labeled), but was an "irrepressible conflict between opposing and enduring forces." "It means," he went on, "that the United States must and will, sooner or later, become either entirely a slaveholding nation or entirely a free labor nation." In that same year, June 17, 1858, Abraham Lincoln said it another way. "A House divided against itself cannot stand. I believe this government cannot endure permanently half slave and half free . . . It will become all one thing or all the other."

In personal terms war, when it came, meant for Harriet the enlistment of her son Fred who, though earmarked by her father for the pulpit, was one of the first marched off to battle with the Union army. As the bitter war years dragged on, the rank and file soldiers on both sides were said to have complained that it was "a rich man's war, a poor man's fight." But Harriet Beecher Stowe was among the rich, far richer than she had ever dreamed in the days of her Connecticut girlhood. She built her mansion on Hartford's river, as she had said she would, pouring into it as a testimony to the realization of a dream, the most lavish of furnishings as well as gifts which had come into her possession from all over the world. The highest paid of all women writers— indeed, perhaps, of all writers in her time except Bret Harte, it had been only on the promise of stories by Harriet Beecher Stowe to boost circulation that the *Atlantic Monthly* had begun to publish in 1857. But all this fame and wealth was not bringing happiness to Harriet. She lived in a constant state of surprise at how life turned back on her again and again to keep her either in agitation or in sorrow. Charles, her youngest son, drowned while a student at Dartmouth. Her soldier son, wounded at Gettysburg, returned home malcontent, addicted to alcohol. She, who at *Atlantic Monthly* dinners would have no wine set before her (but came wearing vine leaves in her hair) grieved over Fred's "downfall." Depressed by his mother's disappointment in him, young Fred Stowe wandered off to California, was reported to have been seen on the San Francisco waterfront after which he disappeared never to be heard from again. There were other tragedies: Isabella Stowe, Harriet's young half sister of whom she had grown particularly fond, went insane;

one of the half brothers died a suicide. And, coupled with all this sorrow in her personal life, there seemed no end of trouble in her professional life. As a result of her continued friendship with Lady Byron, she decided to expose the "true story" of Lord Byron's incestuous relationship with his half sister. She wrote an article on the subject which, when printed in 1869 in the *Atlantic Monthly* not only brought wrath down upon her head from devotees of the poet throughout the world, but almost resulted in the closing down of the magazine as readers rushed to withdraw their names from its subscription list. With her father's blood running in her veins, Harriet came back at her attackers in true Beecher style: she enlarged the article and brought it out in book form under the title *Lady Byron Vindicated.* The trouble was that publication of this book came at the very moment when a sensational scandal and court trial erupted involving her adored brother, the Reverend Henry Ward Beecher, whose name, linked with that of a woman not his wife, filled the gossip sheets of every paper in the country. Henry Ward, too, came through his troubles in exactly the same way Papa Beecher had stormed *his* way out of difficulties through the years—with words and more words, spellbinding his way to victory.

Wisely, Harriet had brought to fruition in the years just preceding and after the war her wealth of New England material: *The Minister's Wooing* (1859) an interesting study of the effect of Calvinist theology on the lives of New Englanders; *Pearl of Orr's Island* (1862) portraits of Maine characters drawn from observation in Brunswick; *Oldtown Folks* (1869) based on her husband's memories of his childhood in Natick, Massachusetts, written with sharp realism and humor; *Poganuc People* (1878) her own Litchfield memories. In *Agnes of Sorrento* (1862) pure romance set in Italy, Harriet was storytelling to her heart's content. Unwisely, for she had far less understanding of the postwar world, she attempted to write about the new times and, in particular, the "new woman." *My Wife and I; We and Our Neighbors; Pink and White Tyranny* did not make her popular with leaders of the feminist movement, some of whom saw themselves in her scathing portraits.

Harriet's friends, while listening to her personal and professional troubles, wondered what on earth drove her each day to her writing table when, already famous, rich, and loaded down with family responsibilities, she had the best of excuses for getting out from under. Harriet gave surface answers—the need for money (keeping up her Hartford and Florida estates was a continuing problem), the pressure of editors who hounded her for books, articles, even poetry, so rich a gold mine was her name. But deeper than all this was the brooding young girl of Litchfield still alive inside the successful woman, whose imagination would not rest even now, and whose secretive romantic world had to emerge somewhere—on paper, finally, since that was where she knew best how to bring it into the open. When her reputation among critics began to decline with her last books, Harriet clung to the knowledge of her popularity among the people. She had done what she could and no more. *"My dear, you must be a literary woman, it is so written in the book of fate. Your husband will lift up his head at the gate and your children will rise up and call you blessed."*

As if striving to get back to the romantic little girl she had once been, Harriet Beecher Stowe returned to infantilism in her old age, exhibiting all the fantasies and tantrums of the Harriet whose designation "genius" at age six had excused her the consequences of bizarre behavior. But now she was put under the care of a restraining nurse. From time to time her strong Beecher will asserted itself, however. She outwitted lock and key to run off into the neighborhood (one of the neighbors with whom she was well acquainted was Mark Twain) causing a good deal of consternation in Hartford by her strange antics. Until the last possible moment of breath she lived—sometimes, like Ophelia, flinging flowers and song; sometimes—like the biblical Rachel—lamenting her lost children. She died in her eighty-fifth year, an internationally known New England writer whose touch upon her own country was much too real to allow her, even in 1896, to be eulogized as an artist whose life had taken on an aura of romance or legend. She was still—according to which side one had been on—that "infamous" or "great" little lady who had "started this big war."

Emily Dickinson
(1830–1886)

"My Country is Truth."

"The worst fate that an artist can suffer is to be overwhelmed by her own legend, to have her work neglected for an interest in her personality." So Katherine Anne Porter wrote of the British author, Katherine Mansfield. It may well be said of Emily Dickinson too, for no American artist suffered that fate more than this great New England poet.

As late as 1926 Emily Dickinson was not thought of sufficient importance to be listed in the Encyclopaedia Britannica. For the better part of the next two decades she gained no recognition in scholarly works dedicated to the poets of her region and America. Yet, as heroine of what appeared to be one of the outstanding love stories of nineteenth-century New England, she had deeply stirred the imagination of scholars who, in succumbing to her legend along with the rest of the world, spoke of her as if she were some sainted nun gracing a mysterious ceremony of sacrifice, or some half mythical creature more fay than woman. For them her poems served merely as keys with which to try to unlock her secrets. What caused this talented, witty young girl, with every opportunity of shining in her father's court (Edward Dickinson was a distinguished Massachusetts legislator) to disappear inside the Dickinson mansion while she was still in her early twenties to be seen no more, to live out the rest of her life as an elusive spinster recluse? Why had she dressed only in white? What inspired those strange, cryptic poems found in her room after she died, poems whose themes heightened the sense of a tragedy having been enacted behind what the rector of one Boston church called "an innocent hedge?"

In her native Amherst, Emily Dickinson had been a legendary figure long before her poems were uncovered. Some of her neighbors believed that there had been a cousin she had loved and lost; others were certain that an elderly clergyman, already married, was the cause of her heartbreak and seclusion. And there were those who continued to spread rumors of physical disfigurement or incurable mental disease. The Dickinson family, tight-lipped, clannish, gave away no secrets, though Emily's younger sister, Vinnie, seemed to delight in dropping contradictory hints. Once to an inquisitive visitor she said simply: "Emily had to think. She was the only one of us with that to do."

Yet talk of an aborted romance could not be put down, especially after Emily's poems were published posthumously in 1890. While no one could say for certain these poems were autobiographical, no one wanted to doubt that they were. With feverish intensity countless literary detectives, making a cult of Emily Dickinson, set to work searching out every scrap of information written by or about her since the day of her death May 15, 1886—seeking not by what route she had become so remarkable a poet but the name of the beloved behind those provocative lines:

> *I live with him, I see his face,*
> *I go no more away*
> *For visitor or sundown.*
> *Death's single privacy*
> *The only one forestalling mine,*
> *And that by right that he*
> *Presents a claim invisible*
> *No wedlock granted me.*

Unfortunately—for it proved to the poet's disadvantage to have the search prolonged—answers to the identity of "him" were not easy to come by. The sly mistress of the poem, who cherished privacy, who had a genius for ambiguity even in her letters, used every clever trick of language at her command to tease and baffle the most expert of sleuths. Concerned with larger business—the quest for truth to unlock secrets of human nature and the universe, she had not dreamed that posterity, in reading her "letter to the world" (the poetry she left behind) would overlook the *thought* of Emily Dickinson for sake of prying into her personal life.

One who posterity hoped would know the intimate details of that life was Thomas Wentworth Higginson, the soldier-poet with whom she had corresponded for twenty years and to whom she had entrusted many of her poems for criticism. Colonel Higginson was willing to tell all he knew, but he had seen his little "scholar" (as Emily so often signed herself in her letters to him) face to face only twice, and just in brief interviews from which he had come away more confused than enlightened about his strange hostess. Of the first of these interviews, August 16, 1870, he wrote:

> It was at her father's house, one of those large square, brick mansions so familiar in our older New England towns, surrounded by trees and blossoming shrubs without, and within exquisitely neat, cool, spacious, and fragrant with flowers. After a little delay I heard an extremely faint and pattering footstep like that of a child in the hall, and in glided, almost noiselessly, a plain, shy little person, the face without a single good feature, but with eyes, as she herself said, "like the sherry the guest leaves in the glass," and with smooth bands of reddish chestnut hair. She had a quaint and nunlike look, as if she might be a German canoness of some religious order, whose prescribed garb was white pique, with blue net worsted shawl. She came toward me with two day lilies, which she put in a childlike way into my hand, saying, also under her breath in a childlike fashion, "forgive me if I am frightened; I never see strangers, and hardly know what I say."

Most that she did say quite took her visitor's breath away, "things quaint and aphoristic" such as: "Truth is such a rare thing, it is delightful to tell it," and "How do most people in the world—you must have noticed them in the street—how do they live? How do they get strength to put on their clothes in the morning?" To one question the colonel put to her, Emily replied: "If I read a book and it makes my whole body so cold no fire can ever warm me, I know that is poetry. If I feel physically as if the top of my head were taken off, I know that is poetry. These are the only ways I know it. Is there any other way?" Her words, her presence, made him feel as if the top of *his* head were taken off. "She was much too enigmatical a being for me to solve in an hour's interview," he confessed. "We met only once again, and I have no express record of the visit."

Actually the colonel had come to the conclusion that he was dealing with a "half-cracked poetess," but after publishing the poems Emily had not allowed him to put into print while she lived, he was amazed at the reception they received. "I feel," he wrote in 1891 to Mabel Loomis Todd, with whom he was preparing a second edition of *Poems*, "as if we had climbed a cloud, pulled it away and revealed a new star."

Mrs. Todd agreed. Her relationship with the Dickinson family had begun in 1881 when, as wife of a newly appointed professor to Amherst College, she had arrived in the village and been entertained by the college bursar, Austin Dickinson, Emily's brother. Almost at once she began to hear tales about him and his family, especially of the sister whom the local citizens referred to as "the myth." Mabel Todd could hardly wait to write home to her Washington family about Emily Dickinson:

> She is a sister of Mr. Dickinson & seems to be the climax of all the family oddity. She has not been outside of her own house in fifteen years except once to see a new church when she crept out at night & viewed it by moonlight. No one who calls upon her mother and sister ever see her, but she allows little children once in a great while and one at a time, to come in when she gives them cake or candy or some nicety, for she is very fond of little ones. But more often she lets down the sweetmeat by a string out of a window to them. She dresses wholly in white, and her mind is said to be perfectly wonderful! She writes finely, but no one *ever* sees her. Her sister . . . invited me to come & sing to her mother sometimes. . . . people tell me that *the myth* will hear every note—she will be near, but unseen. Isn't that like a book? So interesting. No one knows the cause of her isolation, but of course there are dozens of reasons assigned.

A frequent visitor to the Dickinson mansion (though she never saw Emily face to face), Mrs. Todd had tried to discover for herself which of those dozens reasons was the answer, but she soon gave up sleuthing for genuine friendship. She had her life's reward for doing so. Shortly after Emily's death, the sister of "the myth" came to her with several little packets of hand-sewn manuscripts which she found in Emily's desk. Once reading those manuscripts Mabel Loomis Todd's fate was sealed. She spent the balance of her own lifetime in bringing Emily Dickinson's genius before the public, combatting every step along the way the legend threatening to obscure that genius. Emily had tried society and the world and "found them lacking," she repeatedly told the public. "She was not an invalid, and she lived in seclusion from no love-disappointment. Her life was the normal blossoming of a nature introspective to a high degree, whose best thought could not exist in pretense." But myths die hard. As Emily herself said,

> *The truth must dazzle gradually*
> *Or every man be blind.*

It was Emily Dickinson's tragedy to be the isolated artist in an environment that never comprehended her genius, but it is her triumph that her art survives to throw its light upon times in many ways remarkably similar to our own—with the difference that now at least, and at last, she can be understood.

At year's end, December 10, 1830, Emily Elizabeth Dickinson was born, entering a world in the throes of violence and change, a nation even then dividing against itself. Emily was but a month old when William Lloyd Garrison's mighty *Liberator* appeared in Boston pledging relentless, to-the-death struggle to free the slaves. That same year, not far from Boston in the little village of Concord, a restless young clergyman named Ralph Waldo Emerson sat meditating in his study on the needs to liberate not alone the bodies of enslaved men, but the minds of all men whatever their degree in life. Emily was not quite six years old when Emerson's *Nature* appeared, a simple title for a revolutionary book which young New England rebels quickly adopted as ideological basis behind their fervor to think and act self-reliantly, to put individual conscience above established laws of church and state. Much farther away than Concord, the brilliant young Englishman, Charles Darwin, had set sail on the voyage of the *Beagle* in 1831, laying the groundwork for still another kind of revolution in thought, the tides of which would sweep Emily Dickinson's world.

Nowhere in America was there greater momentum for revolutionary change than in her own New England. Yet, for the moment in the frozen quiet of her native Amherst, where the church stood close by to the schoolhouse, where fenced-in farms and orchards were serviced by a cluster of small shops—the drapers, the blacksmiths, the inn—village life was just as it had been since the days when the first Puritan settlers (Nathaniel Dickinson among them) made their way up the Connecticut River into western Massachusetts. Three times daily Amherst bells rang out over the valley—for waking, for noon, for curfew at nine. And twice more than that on the Sabbath for Meeting. The bells were music on the wind to Emily and her older brother, Austin; to the elders they were symbols of order. In other college communities in New England dissent was rising, but in Amherst village orthodoxy and authority were still unchallenged. Or so it seemed.

In the early 1830s, if any one man represented authority in Amherst, it was Emily's paternal grandfather, the Honorable Samuel Fowler Dickinson, under whose roof she and her family lived. This austere New England squire wore many hats: church deacon, college treasurer, bank trustee, Hampshire County lawyer, Whig politician, Member of the General Court (the state legislature). A mixture of Yankee pride, native ambition, and strong Calvinist convictions motivated his energy. Standing rocklike behind all the Puritan verities, he led the good fight for temperance, for law and order, for schools, for a clean, prospering village. "To the New England mind," said Henry Adams, "roads, schools, clothes, and a clean face were a connected part of the law of order or divine system. Bad roads meant bad morals." Grandfather Dickinson was New England through and through. To him and to his tireless colleague, Noah Webster, Amherst owed its two most widely known institutions—Amherst Academy established as a secondary school in 1812; Amherst College, founded primarily for the training of young men to Calvinist ministry in 1821. Emily Dickinson might have had little more than a cursory education had it not been for this grandfather who, in making his plea for an academy before the assembled farmers at Hampshire County's annual cattle show, had reminded them that they must educate their daughters as well as their sons. Said he, "the female mind, so sensitive, so susceptible of improvement, should not be neglected. God hath designed nothing in vain."

Although Samuel Fowler Dickinson was progressive-minded in many ways, the fast-moving 1830s soon outrode him. Even while Amherst College was turning out its annual flock of unbearded preachers (growing beards had become an affectation among the more radical minded young men up at Harvard) "the newness," as it was called in Boston, came creeping into the village. Rankling on the subject of slavery set neighbor against neighbor. Feuds in the church led the congregation to quarreling with each new hastily hired, hastily fired minister. Hampshire County newspapers warned of rising juvenile rowdyism, reported in alarm a riot on the campgrounds with police confronting hostile, rock throwing youths. Worse, in the words of one angry headline—"The rum-lovers are angry, elect anti-temperance officers throughout!" One morning the Honorable Samuel Fowler Dickinson awoke to find himself toppled out of office.

Emily was still an infant when her grandfather, whom she barely got to know, suddenly left Amherst village, answering the call of the Reverend Lyman Beecher to bring order and religious education to the wilderness towns of Ohio. The rigors of his western adventure proved too much for the old man. Far from the New England home of his ancestors, he died, a victim of the new times. But his son, Edward, Emily's lawyer father, had caught the fallen banner in Amherst and soon held all the old titles, including that of bursar of the college. A tall, spare, humorless man, even more able than his father before him, Squire Edward Dickinson counted himself truly representative of his times, trying to preserve the best of the past, to accept the challenge of the new without upsetting the balance of order. Moderation in all things was his theme. As "authority" in both local and state affairs, even his children stood in awe of him.

The impending birth of a third child into the Dickinson household in March 1833, precipitated Emily's first adventure beyond the confines of home. Suddenly, and without in the least understanding why, the little girl, not yet three, was whisked up by an aunt and carried off to her maternal grandparents' farm in Monson, Massachusetts. The long sleigh ride to Monson must have had momentary excitement for Emily, but once arriving at her destination where all seemed strange, with no older brother to keep her company in the dark room where she was put to sleep at night, excitement turned to homesickness. Mistaking a quiet child for a contented one, her aunt wrote to assure her family that Emily "is very good & but little trouble. She has learned to play on the piano, she calls it *the moosic*."

A second report following hard upon this one was not nearly so complimentary. Twice on Sabbath Aunt Norcross took auburn-haired, hazel-eyed Emily to an unheated little country church for worship. Something in this atmosphere either frightened her or sorely oppressed her spirit. Refusing to sit still, she cried out so often during service that, as her aunt dutifully reported, it finally became necessary to slap the child into submission. This was the first, but destined not to be the last slap young Emily Dickinson would receive for rebellion inside a Calvinist Church.

For three long months Emily remained at the Monson farm. When she returned home it was to a greatly changed household. Her mother was now too busy with care of the new baby, Lavinia (or Vinnie, as the youngest sister was always called). Her father, who often used to carry her out to the orchard, thinking massive doses of fresh air beneficial to her reputedly weak lungs, no longer carried her anywhere. He was too busy leading what her mother mournfully called "the public life," which carried him for weeks at a time to Boston, and sometimes as far away as New York and Washington. Left to their own devices, she and brother Austin, who was only a year older, would wander about the cheerless house clinging to one another for consolation and company.

In later years Emily would often refer with bitterness to what she thought had been neglect by her parents. Yet out of neglect came compensations. She early learned to depend on her own initiative and imagination, early developed that independence of thought so indispensible to creativity. And sharing so intimately a boy's view of things tended to toughen her spirit.

Austin Dickinson was a stubborn boy,* blunt tongued with truth. Emily adored and emulated him. What she had with him in the years before Vinnie was old enough to share their companionship was childhood's secret joys—its daring of danger, its hiding places, its impassioned moments in the face of terror and beauty. Though the social mores that dictated so many restrictions for nineteenth-century girls seldom allowed Emily to be a happy child, she dearly loved childhood and like so many other New Englanders of her day was to romanticize and idealize it all the days of her life. Her poems abound in nostalgia, even for the long winter months of the mountain-enclosed village when

> *Glass was the street! In tinsel peril*
> *Tree and traveller stood;*
> *Filled was the air with merry venture,*
> *Hearty with boys the road.*
>
> *Shot the lithe sleds like shod vibrations*
> *Emphasized and gone!*
> *It is the past's supreme italic*
> *Makes the present mean.*

Instinctive response to nature, bold inquiry after truth, insatiable thirst for reading, these Emily had in common with Austin. As they were growing up, brother and sister were keen observers of their village environment, tending to be more critical than approving. The grown-up world seemed to them stiff and foreign, full of pomposity and solemnity, the elders putting higher priority on how to die than how to live. Sabbath day, Emily and Austin often observed, had strange contradictions, for

---

* Austin Dickinson was so stubborn as a man that when he told his wife if anybody put a stone over *his* grave when he died, he'd get up and move somewhere else, she believed him. To this day the headstone lies a little apart from where he lies in Amherst Cemetery.

even while birds would be singing gay hallelujas out in the fields, in church it was Death, always Death, with his metallic face staring from the altar, grinning from the doorway, drumming in the fearful news

> *That awful day will surely come*
> *The appointed hour makes haste,*
> *When I must stand before my Judge*
> *And pass the solemn test.*

A hymn "depressing enough in plain print, when sung to accompaniment appalling," said Austin. This and similar verses from Watts hymnal Emerson had heard in his childhood, as had Hawthorne, Thoreau, James Russell Lowell, Mark Twain, Abe Lincoln—each in his own way to react to the pall of fear and death that hung over their lives as children. Obsession with death was an affliction common not only to New Englanders but to all nineteenth-century Americans. From a practical, as well as a doctrinal point of view, the church felt justified in keeping death a central theme even for the youngest child. Statistics, they thought, vindicated them. In Massachusetts alone, more than two-fifths of all children died before they were twelve years old; diphtheria, tuberculosis, "brain fever," malaria—these but a few of the killers against which no defense had yet been found. Extolling the virtues of the "other world" made it easier for a child to die, easier for a parent to give over an ailing infant "to the angels." But so much talk of death and the afterlife frightened fun-loving, earth-loving children like Emily and Austin Dickinson. To be told in church that an "angry God" kept watch upon their immortal souls and had selected some to suffer the everlasting fires of hell was particularly tormenting.†

If Emily and Austin had only a negative impression of church, the first school to which they were exposed fared little better. Miss Nelson's (so-called for it was held in that lady's house) was more notable for discipline than for education. The penalty for talking out of turn was to have a corncob stuffed between one's teeth. The penalty for not "staying still" was to be shut up in a dark closet, a punishment Emily

† Of her religious training in Amherst, Susan Gilbert Dickinson wrote: "I sat through many hours of the Sabbath in a deadly, monotonous Bible class under Deacon Luke Sweetser's [Emily's uncle] leadership, who never by a word or smile lent a relaxed beam of hope to the simplicities of the new testament . . . he weighted down our youthful spirits every Sunday morning with his picture of ourselves as rebellious sinners in the hands of an avenging God, with possible death before another dawn staring us full in the face."

Dickinson apparently once fell victim to. Authority, though, little knew
the quality of the bird it sought to tame:

> *Still! Could themselves have peeped*
> *And seen my brain go round!*

Growing ever more reticent in this suppressive outside world, Emily
saved all her natural mirth and mental energy for her playmate brother.
It never occurred to the clinging little sister that Austin's world could
not always be her own. "Young females should be accustomed very
early in life to a certain degree of restraint," warned Hannah More, whose
book, *Essays on Various Subjects Principally designed for Young Ladies,*
was looked upon by middle-class New England parents as the "bible" for
proper rearing of daughters. "The natural cast of character, and the moral
distinction of the sexes should not be disregarded even in childhood. That
bold, independent, enterprising spirit, which is so much admired in boys
should not, when it happens to discover itself in the other sex be
encouraged, but suppressed." By the time Emily's preoccupied parents
discovered her independent spirit, suppression only intensified her determination to be free. She was sometimes put into the closet at home too.

Any portrait of Emily Dickinson drawn against Hannah More's
Essays, will at once reveal what it cost a girl of her social class to be
a rebel in her time. Emily's dream of becoming a poet would be met
by Miss More's insistence that it was pretentious for women to "assume
a strength of intellect requisite to penetrate into the abstruser walks of
literature." Her delight, as she grew older, in talking philosophy in the
company of her brother and his friends, would be frowned upon, for
Miss More warned that this was a man's field, and most unladylike for
a woman to engage in. As for religious dissent the direst warning of all:
social ostracism while alive, hellfire in the life to come.

One pleasure Emily particularly enjoyed as a girl was to wander
freely in the fields and woods. Society was always pulling her back with
unsatisfying explanations. "When much in the woods as a little girl," she
told Colonel Higginson at the start of their correspondence in 1862,
"I was told that the snake would bite me; that I might pick a poisonous
flower, or goblins kidnap me; but I went along and met no one but
angels who were far shyer of me than I could be of them, so I haven't
that confidence in fraud which many exercise." The moment she ran
off to where mushrooms grew in shadow, violets along a brook, and
trees everywhere pointing fingers to the sky:

>*The pretty people in the woods*
>*Receive me cordially.*

Emily's mother was reportedly a timid, neurotic, fearful woman, totally unable to cope with the realities of life, and given to such frequent moods of melancholy that even her neighbors took pains to avoid her. "Plaintive talk as usual from Mrs. D.," one of them recorded in her diary after a morning's visit in the Dickinson parlor. Little wonder that out-of-doors was merrier for Emily than in. Like so many nineteenth-century women oppressed by superstition, ignorance, and discriminatory laws, Mrs. Dickinson had come uneasily into marriage. Her finishing-school education at New Haven had ill prepared her for the large household she was to manage without servants, for child rearing, for making personal sacrifices for an ambitious, worldly man. If Edward Dickinson's neighbors came quickly to the conclusion that he had married the wrong woman, he must often have harbored the same thought as he read his wife's letters sent to him while he was away at Boston serving in the legislature. In them she admitted to fear of the dark, of creaking timbers, of storms, mice, strange noises; fear for her own health, and that of the children, fear even of walking to church alone—all reasons why he should give up the public life, come home and "be of some little assistance to me." Her lonely lamentations so tore at Edward Dickinson's conscience that he finally promised to throw up his political career, but it was a promise he failed to keep.

One peculiar feature of life among the Dickinsons was that the father seemed to count more upon his children to keep their mother happy during his prolonged absences than the other way around. "All good children are obedient to their mothers and do all they can to make them happy," he would urge. "If you do exactly as mother wishes, I shall bring you something when I come home." This promise he did keep, books only, for toys were frowned upon in this strict, Calvinist home. In Noah Webster's little speller used by New England children appeared the warning: "A wise child learns to love his book; but a fool would choose to play with toys." Edward Dickinson's home library was stocked with English classics, as well as a smattering of travel, religious, and natural science books interspersed among legal tomes. To his children he brought little booklets (published by a Boston relative) filled with biblical tales. They liked these well enough because of the lively illustrations, but would have preferred Father at home to any present he could bring. "Emily says she is tired of living without a father," Mrs. Dickinson wrote once to tell her husband.

His homecomings, so eagerly looked forward to by his children, seldom proved as blissful as anticipated. Edward Dickinson was entirely lacking in understanding of a child's emotional needs, and so rigidly structured that his children could never be at ease with him. "Dry, thin, speechless," was the way Thomas Wentworth Higginson described him at first meeting. Yet the interior world of this man fits none of those descriptions. Indeed, if the legend is true, he one day rang the bells of Amherst at an unaccustomed hour, and when the townspeople came running from their homes thinking the millennium upon them, it was simply Edward Dickinson summoning them out to see a spectacular sunset. But according to Emily's report of him, work and duty was the only way of life he understood. His passion for orderliness; his stern adherence to the clock was a torture to his young children, and especially to Emily. Still, in the way of a parent, he was all she had. "When a child, and in trouble, I always ran home to Awe," she said in later years. "He was an awful mother but I liked him better than none." "Father never kissed us good night in his life," Vinnie Dickinson said. "He would have died for us, but he would have died before he would let us know it." Indeed, it was only after he did die—while at work, as usual, on the floor of the legislature in Boston—that Austin's long restrained love for his father was expressed; leaning down to kiss the dead man's cheek, the son said with a ring of bitter regret, "There, Father, I never dared do that while you were living."

Not to give vent to emotion was an intrinsic part of puritan training. Austin himself early learned this from his father. Yet in his own way, Edward Dickinson thought he was conveying normal human warmth to his children. "You were all asleep when I came away, and Mother said she would kiss you all 'good bye' for me," reads one message written when his children were small. Perhaps this message and many more like it, as well as the kiss, were never delivered. Perhaps in her physical and mental suffering, Mrs. Dickinson had little sympathy to spare for anyone other than herself. When her daughter Emily writes of her, "I never had a mother, I suppose a mother is one to whom you hurry when you are troubled," all the bitter hurt is revealed, but beneath lies a lifetime of love and longing.

The kind of marriage shared by this strong father and weak mother left its mark on Emily. Both admiring and resenting the power of her father, sympathizing with and raging against the loneliness and ineptness of her mother, she was never certain she wanted either to grow up or to marry. In Emily's mind, *freedom-power-men* would always be synonymous, and be expressed in her poetry as "the bee." Women, rooted to home by social law, would become, in the language of her art, "thirsty blossoms"— the perilously frail and frustrated flowers of nineteenth-century society. It is not surprising that by age twenty-two, in a society in which marriage loomed as the only acceptable career for a woman of her class, a girl with Emily's intellect should cry out to her adored friend, Susan Gilbert (Austin's sweetheart, later to become his wife), "It [marriage] does so rend me, Susie, the thought of it when it comes, that I tremble lest at some time I too am yielded up." "Sacrificed" was the word commonly used by many of the young women in Emily's circle when referring to their coming marriages.

In 1840 disaster befell Edward Dickinson along with thousands of others who suffered severe financial reverses in an economic panic that hit the country. The chagrined squire was forced to move his family from the mansion into a less pretentious house bordering the cemetery on North Pleasant Street. Barely a day passed in which he was not scheming how to mend his fortune and reclaim the old homestead, but his children quickly learned to love the new one. Luckily so, for here it was they were to spend the next fifteen years, the most important developmental years of Emily Dickinson's life. It was this home which Emily so often referred to as Eden; here, as a romantic young girl, she wrote her first poems. And it was from this house, in 1840, that Emily walked daily to Amherst Academy to begin her formal education. It was a lonely beginning, for Austin had been sent off to Easthampton to school and the separation from him was not easily offset even by vivacious little Vinnie. "We miss you very much," she wrote to him, a few days after he had gone. "There was always such a hurrah where you were." Her letters telling all the news of life in the new house, of Austin's barnyard animals and of village gossip, were written with such original, bubbling humor that Austin thought there was always a hurrah where Emily was too. As a schoolgirl between ages eleven and fifteen, she adored reading romances (especially the forbidden ones), thought valentine week the best in the year, and could sit for hours listening to such chatter as, "Sabra Howe has a ring from Charles *you-know-who*," her informant being one or another of a circle of five soul mates who became her earliest friends at the academy. They would sit on her front doorstep after school in spring

> and the shy little birds would say chirrup, chirrup, in the tall cherry trees, and if our dresses rustled hop frightened away; and there used to be some farmer cutting down a tree in the woods, and you and I sitting there could hear his sharp axe ring

she reminded one of these girls years later. Confessing to one friend that she intended that night to collect as many flowers from her garden as possible so as to save them "from Jack Frost just this time if no more," she added quickly, "I know you will laugh and say, 'how sentimental Emily is.' I am, about *everything.*" Her friends did think her odd, but knew also that she was by far their intellectual superior. One of Emily's professors, D. T. Fiske, later wrote: "I remember her as a very bright but rather delicate and frail looking little girl; an excellent scholar of exemplary deportment, faithful in all school duties but somewhat shy and nervous. Her compositions were strikingly original, and in both thought and style seemed beyond her years, and always attracted much attention in the school, and, I am afraid, excited not a little envy."

Having grown up in a home with books but no toys, in a village with no entertainment except the rhetoric of the lyceum lecturer, or that of the politician stumping at annual Fourth of July or Cattle Show celebrations, Emily's only playthings were words. In later years when she began, as an aspiring artist, to worry over her poems, she would remember how easily, spontaneously, almost disrespectfully she had handled words in her school days, and say to Joseph Lyman, Austin's Easthampton classmate who had become Vinnie's sweetheart and her own close friend:

> We used to think, Joseph, when I was an unsifted girl and you so scholarly, that words were cheap and weak. Now I don't know of anything so mighty. There are those to which I lift my hat when I see them sitting princelike among their peers on the page. Sometimes I write one, and look at his outlines till he glows as no sapphire.

But even as playthings words had had a special glow for Emily. However nervous or shy in Dr. Fiske's presence, or in the presence of notables attending college teas annually held in her own parlor, when she took pen in hand all hesitancy vanished. Emily lived aloud on paper, made words live too, liked to make abstractions such as Time, Death, into lively characters. Her writing in these early schooldays reflected nothing morbid. "Emily Dickinson and Mary Humphrey were the wits of the school and the humorists of the comic column," (referring to the academy's literary magazine, *Forest Leaves*) recalled Noah Webster's granddaughter. But despite Emily's reputation for originality, she once held off writing to Abiah Root, an adored classmate who had recently left the village, because, as she later explained to Abiah, "I thought as all the other girls wrote to you, my letter if I wrote one would seem no smarter than anybody else's and *you know I hate to be common.*" Common she was not, then or ever. Abiah soon enough made that discovery and farsightedly saved all the letters she received from Emily; it is primarily through these that we know what we do of the maturing mind, the trials and heartbreak of Emily Dickinson as an adolescent schoolgirl.

To Amherst Academy came girls from many outlying parts of New England, all seeking the advantages of an institution considered progressive for its day. Its proximity to Amherst College greatly aided the quality of education it was able to provide. From the higher institution came most of its principals over the years, and handsome young tutors to be idolized by romantic girls like Emily Dickinson and her friends. "Oh, I do love Mr. Taylor," Emily rhapsodized in a letter to Abiah. But then Emily loved "dear Miss Adams" too—indeed all her teachers. Often, for expediency, she and her classmates were permitted to leave academy grounds and walk up the hill to sit in on college lectures, usually those on geology, botany, or astronomy. Harriet Martineau, the British writer, had been so impressed on her first visit to America at finding girls attending Amherst College lectures that she made special mention of it in her published memoirs: "We found that the admission of girls to such lectures as they could understand was a practice of some years standing and that no evil resulted from it." No evil indeed. Much of the scientific knowledge displayed in Emily Dickinson's mature poetry was a result of her interest in the earth sciences during Amherst Academy days. As an academy student she boasted of a curriculum that included the classical languages, mental philosophy, history, and rhetoric, but in later years she was to think she had had only the barest beginnings of an education.

In her fourteenth year Emily suffered a severe nervous collapse following the death of Sophia Holland, "a friend near my age & with whom my thoughts and her own were the same . . . after she was laid in her coffin & I felt I could not call her back again, I gave way to a fixed melancholy. I told no one the cause of my grief though it was gnawing at my very heart strings." Taking her out of school, her father sent her, for a change of scene, to stay with relatives in Worcester where, curiously enough, among other new sights in the vicinity, he thought she might enjoy "the lunatic asylum." Looking in on the insane was, indeed, a nineteenth-century pastime, but Emily went instead to a Chinese Museum, struck up acquaintance there with two oriental gentlemen who enthralled her with their account of how, by sheer will power alone, they had conquered the opium habit. "There is something peculiarly fascinating to me in their self-denial," she wrote to her friend Abiah. She does not explain *why* fascinating, but it is interesting to note at what an early age Emily Dickinson began to take an interest in self-denial.

After the death of Sophia Holland, loss of friends, even if due only to geographical separation, became traumatic for Emily. As one of her acquaintances in Amherst said, whatever or whomever Emily Dickinson loved "she loved with all her might." She had a genius for friendship never matched by those upon whom she bestowed her affection; as a result heartbreak often lay at the end of her pursuit of favorites, male or female. Loneliness motivated much of the energy Emily put into finding and holding on to friends. With Austin away at school, and eventually Vinnie, too, Emily was left for long periods of time the single child at home. Contributing to loneliness was the fact that Amherst village had taken on a transient character, the majority of its student and faculty population coming from out of town. At the end of each quarter session always an exodus; at graduation more permanent partings. No word was more familiar than good-by, and it was one which could break the heart of the sentimental girl left behind. A pattern of trying to hold on to school attachments became characteristic of Emily as early as her eleventh year:

> The worst thing old Time has done here is he has walked so fast as to overtake Harriet Merril and carry her to Hartford on last week Saturday. I was so vexed with him for it that I ran after him and made out to get near enough to him to put some salt on his tail when He fled and left me to run home alone.

Running home alone was to be Emily Dickinson's fate so often it would not be many years more before, in part to ease the pain of perpetual loss, she would close the door of home behind her forever. More than one lost love would bring this young poet finally to say,

> *Parting is all we know of Heaven*
> *And all we need of Hell.*

Even more significant to Emily's future than loneliness was the religious dilemma she confronted in her teens. She was too independent-minded to swallow doctrine. For her, knowledge had to come through adventure—argument and counterargument—the great pause of doubt with truth somewhere just beyond, truth teasing, sly, always a jump ahead like "the June bee/Before the schoolboy" as finally the poet Emily Dickinson would say. The origin of the universe, whether or not there was an afterlife, the true nature of God, eternity, and soul—these and other metaphysical questions almost equaled slavery as topics of everyday debate in nineteenth-century society. Emily discussed them long and seriously with her brother and friends, coming finally to the decision that she preferred to linger on in a state of wonderment than to slip comfortably into easy belief.

> *Wonder is not precisely knowing*
> *And not precisely knowing not.*
> *A beautiful but bleak condition*
> *He has not lived who has not felt.*

As church doctrine disdained the world for heaven, reduced man to but "a worm in the dust" and called earth "foul," Emily, who lived in one of the most beautiful spots in all New England, could not reconcile doctrine with reality. Through the snow the crocuses rose, after the snow the lilies, the annual resurrection a signal of heaven on earth. She had too much pride in God and in herself to renounce the world, and that was what religion was asking her to do. "I feel," she told Abiah Root after a great religious revival in Amherst in 1845 had failed to "melt" her into becoming, by church definition, a Christian, "that I have not yet made my peace with God. I am still a stranger to the delightful emotions which fill your heart. I have perfect confidence in God & his promises yet I know not why, I feel that the world holds a predominant place in my affections . . . Pray for me, dear Abiah, that I may yet enter into the Kingdom, that there may be room left for me in the shining courts above." Though her father and brother were not yet Christians, neither having had that "mystic experience of conviction of sin, self-despair, and conversion," they did not suffer, as Emily did, the eye of society upon them for "sin of pride." It was expected that the softer natures of young girls would melt like butter to the call of religion. Of the Revival Emily told Abiah: "Many who felt there was nothing in religion determined to go at once and see if there was anything in it and they were melted at once." That *she* was not, brought upon her such charges as "careless," "enemy to Christ," and as her existence turned ever more bleak the Revival became the first turn of the key leading Emily away from society. Any nineteenth-century girl who would say as she did that "A suspicion like a finger touches my forehead now and then that I am looking oppositely for the site of the kingdom of Heaven," was already destined to become an outsider. The irony of Emily Dickinson's life would be that she who loved God would renounce the church; who loved the world would renounce society; who loved art would renounce fame. But in the bittersweet years of her teens she was not yet willing to renounce anything except hypocrisy.

As graduation neared Emily grew uneasy about her future, self-knowledge telling her she was ill suited for the pattern of life followed by most Amherst girls who usually settled down as clergymen's wives. Still, she liked to indulge in romantic fantasy. Though in one breath she tells Abiah,

> I expect you have a great many prim, starched up young ladies there who, I doubt not are perfect models of propriety and good behavior. If they are, don't let your free spirit be chained by them.

in another she exclaims

> I expect I shall be the belle of Amherst when I reach my 17th year. I don't doubt that I shall have perfect crowds of admirers at that age. Then how I shall delight to make them await my bidding, and with what delight shall I witness their suspense while I make my final decision.

Edward Dickinson expected that when his brilliant eldest daughter ended her school years at the academy, she would take her place in society, performing not only duties as hostess for him, but, in the area of "good works," set an example in the community. To his dismay she showed little sign of acquiescing to either role, preferring to write, to read, and to play the piano. She also had her heart set on having an education equal to that of Austin who had begun his freshman year at Amherst College.

Whether because of Emily's tenacity in seeking her own ends, or because the squire thought by yielding he might be saving her for his own, he did at last decide to send her to South Hadley Seminary for Females (later Mount Holyoke College)—an announcement that almost bowled Emily over. She wrote excitedly to Abiah:

Are you not astonished to hear such news? You cannot imagine how much I am anticipating entering there. I fear I am anticipating too much, and that some freak of fortune may overturn all my airy schemes for future happiness. But it is my nature always to anticipate more than I realize.

The freak of fortune that overturned her future happiness lay in wait in the person of Miss Mary Lyon, renowned educator, currently preceptress at South Hadley who had a missionary's zeal for bringing to Christ rebellious girls like Emily Dickinson.

Upon entering the seminary in the fall of 1847, Emily was appalled to discover that it was not to be her scores in academic subjects which would bring good or bad report of her at home, but the state of her immortal soul. The Revival all over again and this time no escape. At four-thirty each afternoon "impenitents" like herself were made to meet with Miss Lyon for prayers and lectures, the strain of which offset all the pleasure of her other studies. "I am more and more convinced of the exceeding hardness & depravity of the heart as I see how little effect truths presented applied in Miss Lyon's forcible manner has upon those who listen," the school secretary recorded after one such session. By the end of the first quarter the number of impenitents had diminished considerably, but Emily Dickinson was still among the "unsaved." "I hoped I might have some good news to write with regard to her," Emily's cousin-roommate wrote to tell the Monson relatives. "She says she has no particular objection to becoming a Christian and she says she feels bad when she hears of one and another of her friends who are expressing a hope but still she feels no more interest."

Depressed, feeling more and more isolated from her classmates all of whom thought her odd, Emily wrote to Austin: "Home was always dear to me & dearer still the friends around it, but never did it seem so dear as now. . . . I suppose the time flies faster, but to me slowly, very slowly so that I can see His Chariot wheels when they roll along & Himself is often visible." When the school closed for the Christmas break, Emily had no joy of the holiday, her thoughts constantly on her contest with Miss Lyon. "I am not happy," she confessed to Abiah, "and I regret that last term when that golden opportunity was mine, that I did not give up and become a Christian. It is not now too late, so my friends tell me, so my offended conscience whispers, but it is hard for me to give up the world."

The new term proved to be her last. One day Miss Lyon stood before a large school assembly asking, "All those who want to be a Christian rise!" Emily, who dreaded nothing more than all eyes upon her, was the only one to remain in her seat. "They thought it queer I didn't rise," she said long afterward. "I thought a lie would be queerer."

A scholar who could no longer go to school, an innately religious girl who could find no peace of mind in the tenets of Calvinist faith, a young poet unsuited for woman's work either at home or abroad, Emily returned to Amherst and to more troubles than she had ever dreamed of. The world seemed to close in upon her like a trap, offering no place for her to develop her mind or her talent. She found herself burdened down with household tasks (her father either could not or would not hire a servant) that came close to crushing her comic spirit. "Tears are my angels now," she wrote to a new friend, Susan Gilbert, the girl Austin was courting.

> Mother is still an invalid, Father and Austin still clamor for food, and I like a martyr am feeding them. Wouldn't you love to see me in these bonds of great despair, looking around my kitchen, and praying for kind deliverance, declaring "I never was in such plight!" *My* kitchen, I think I called it. God forbid that it was or shall be my own. God keep me from what they call households.

Even when Vinnie came home from school, and Mother was up and about, the tone was much the same. "Nobody loves me here," she wrote to Sue, nor would you love me if you should see me frown and how loud the doors bang whenever I go through; and yet it isn't anger—I don't believe it is, for when nobody sees I brush away big tears with the corner of my apron and then go working on . . . Vinnie sweeps upon the chamber stairs, and Mother is hurrying around with her hair in a silk pocket handkerchief on account of dust. Oh, Susie, it is dismal, and dreary and the sun don't shine. I do think it is wonderful our hearts don't break every day . . .

What usually saved Emily was her restorative sense of humor, for her revolving spirit of light and dark always had love of life fixed at its center. Whatever her troubles, she always managed to rouse herself and sail on—unguided—in the direction she knew she had to go.

> *Adrift! a little boat adrift!*
> *And night is coming down!*
> *Will no one guide a little boat*
> *Unto the nearest town?*

So sailors say. On yesterday
Just as the dusk was brown
One little boat gave up its strife
And gurgled down and down.
So angels say. On yesterday
Just as the dawn was red,
One little boat, o'erspent with gales
Retrimmed its masts—redecked its sails
And shot exultant on!

Often the sea was rough. If it were not the out-of-town relatives arriving
for long stays giving her additional household chores, it was the army
of visitors arriving to see Father the moment the legislature finished
its session. "Our house is crowded daily with the members of this world,"
she complained wearily to Austin who was by now at Harvard studying
law. At intervals she had precious moments of escape with parties of
young people who went "sugaring" in the woods, or took off for the
mountains. But such opportunities were few. Father needed her at
home. "Larceny of time and mind," she called the mundane chores he
required of her. In order to have at least a few hours to herself in which
to read and write she soon resorted to retreat in her own room, locking
the door behind her. Visitors to the Dickinson household counted themselves lucky if they caught but a glimpse of Emily's white skirt sailing
past the stairway railing as she breathlessly made her escape after the
doorbell's ring. "Queer" her neighbors called her, but then queer ones
like to hide. Even in hiding Emily thought privacy hard to come by, for
while writing a poem there would come bells that *could* lure.

To my quick ear the leaves conferred,
The bushes they were bells;
I could not find a privacy
From nature's sentinels.

In cave if I presumed to hide,
The walls began to tell.
Creation seemed a mighty crack
To make me visible.

If it greatly upset Emily's parents because she went running every time
she heard the doorbell ring, they were even more upset by her shying

away from social responsibilities expected of the daughter of the town's leading citizen. Of one of the girls of her circle, Emily wrote:

> She is more of a woman than I am, for I love so to be a child. Abby is holier than me—she goes among the poor, she shuts the eyes of the dying, she will be had in memorial when I am gone and forgotten . . . The shore is safer, but I love to buffet the sea. I can count the bitter wrecks here in these pleasant waters and hear the murmuring winds, but I love the danger.

"*Pleasant waters.*" Emily had at last learned that she was not alone as a dissenter, that others besides herself loved the danger of veering off course to discover new truths. One who aided her in that discovery was a young man by the name of Ben Newton who was studying law in her father's Amherst office. Ben did not think her queer, took an interest in all that she wrote and thought. To idolizing Emily, he became "gentle, yet grave Preceptor"

> . . . teaching me what to read, what authors to admire, what was most grand or beautiful in nature . . .

In her nineteenth year Ben introduced her to the works of Lydia Maria Child, an author whose strong anti-slavery sentiment and independent thought on religion had won her a wide audience in intellectual circles. But the most treasured of his gifts to Emily that year was Emerson's recently published *Poems*. She thought: "This, then, is a book! And there are more of them!" Eagerly she began begging, borrowing books not alone from Ben, but from all Austin's college friends who would join her little conspiracy to get the broader education she craved. These young men were intrigued by Emily's mind and talent (she exchanged poems with them, sent them clever, clandestine messages on transendentalism displaying her reading of Hawthorne, Emerson, and Lowell—moderns the college frowned upon, therefore devoured by the students). George Gould, editor of the Amherst College *Indicator* printed anonymously in the magazine a poem Emily had written for his eyes alone, further enhancing her reputation among the "literati" on the campus. For Emily it was marvelous fun and joy, too, to be part of a bright ring of young men who fed her the latest works of such diverse authors as Donald Grant Mitchell, Oliver Wendell Holmes, Longfellow, the Brontës, De Quincey, Browning, Thomas Moore, Charles Dickens, Carlyle, as well as Hawthorne, Emerson, and Lowell. So swiftly did her mind mature, she felt moved to score, in Moore's *Lallah Rookh*, lines which seemed to fit the new Emily Dickinson, "Whose life, as free from thought as sin/ Slept like a lake till Love threw in His/Talisman, and/Woke the Tide, and spread its trembling circle wide." Love was for all these fellow conspirators—Ben Newton, George Gould, Joseph Lyman, "Tutors" Humphrey, Emmons, and Howland. When Father was off to Boston, one or another of these admirers took her for long walks or rides, on occasion keeping her up past midnight for the excitement of lively argument on philosophical and social questions.

Thus, for one brief moment in her twenty-first year Emily tasted happiness; then, suddenly, it was all over. Suspicious of Ben's attention to her, her father maneuvered him out of his Amherst office. Ben went to Worcester, married within a year, died within another—from tuberculosis. His loss was a terrible blow to Emily who never forgot him. "My Dying Tutor told me that he would like to live till I had been a poet," she was to tell Colonel Higginson ten years later.

Joseph Lyman, too, fled after becoming aware that his love affair with Vinnie was on dangerous ground. He went to the South, occasionally writing to the Dickinson sisters until both his marriage and the Civil War cut off all correspondence. The other young men, being of the world beyond Amherst, moved on after graduation, most to become clergymen—all to forget the lonely, loyal girl they left behind whose letters they failed to answer. Again Emily had occasion to underscore a passage in Moore's exotic ballads—"I knew, I knew it could not last./'Twas bright, 'twas heavenly, but 'tis past!/O ever thus, from childhood's hour,/ I've seen my fondest hopes decay." Then she wrote her own brave-sad little poem:

> Poor little heart,
> Did they forget thee?
> Then dinna care. Then dinna care.
>
> Proud little heart,
> Did they forsake thee?
> Be debonnaire. Be debonnaire.
>
> Frail little heart,
> Could'st credit me? Could'st credit me?
>
> Gay little heart,
> Like morning glory
> Wind and sun wilt thee array.

For both Dickinson girls, whose father was elected to Congress in 1852, life had suddenly become the age-old conflict—a "flinty"-hearted sire censoring their books, friends, and correspondence. According to Vinnie, she and Emily were "watched and guarded for fear some young man might wish to marry one of them." Both girls grew increasingly rebellious and secretive.

"Father was very severe to me," Emily wrote to Austin. "He thought I'd been trifling with you, so he gave me quite a trimming about 'Uncle Tom' and 'Charles Dickens' and these 'Modern Literati' who he says are *nothing* compared to past generations who flourished when *he was a boy* . . . so I'm quite in disgrace at present, but I think of that 'pinnacle' on which you mount when anybody insults you, and that's quite a comfort to me." One night, coming home after curfew, she opened the door to find her mother and Vinnie at the foot of the stairway screaming a warning that Father was so angry he would surely kill her. Squire Dickinson's temper was indeed getting out of hand with all the evidence of rebellion around him. One day Vinnie posted this little note to her brother: "Oh, dear! Father is killing the horse. I wish you'd come quick if you want to see him alive. He is whipping him because he didn't look quite 'humble' enough this morning. Oh, Austin, it makes me so angry to see that noble creature so abused. Emilie is screaming to the top of her voice she's so vexed about it."

Father did succeed in frightening Emily, but never in humbling her. Once when the Monson relatives came to pay one of their interminable visits, Emily sat quietly amused in the parlor listening to the usual woeful talk about the disgraceful morals and manners of modern-day youth. "They [the relatives] agree beautifully with Father on the 'present generation' she reported to Austin. "They decided that they hoped every young man who smoked would take fire. I respectfully intimated that I thought the result would be a vast conflagration, but was instantly put down." Remembering Austin's warning not on any account to let slip at home the fact that he had gone to the theater‡ in Boston, she added: "Grandmother has been here, and you certainly don't think I'd allude to a Hippodrome in the presence of *that* lady. I'd as soon think of popping firecrackers in the presence of Peter the Great!"

‡ Nineteenth-century morality frowned upon theater-going. "I am told that Christians *do* attend theatre," sermonized Amherst-educated Henry Ward Beecher, who was considered more liberal than most New England clergymen. "If you would pervert the taste—go to the theatre. If you would imbibe false views—go to the theatre. If you would put yourself irreconcilably against the spirit of virtue and true religion—go to the theatre."

Something more than a shy, timid little creature wrote those lines—
and these:

> *What soft, cherubic creatures*
> *These gentlewomen are!*
> *One would as soon assault a plush*
> *Or violate a star.*
>
> *Such dimity convictions,*
> *A horror so refined—*
> *Of freckled human nature*
> *Of Deity ashamed!*
>
> *It's such a common glory,*
> *a Fisherman's degree!*
> *Redemption, brittle lady,*
> *Be so ashamed of thee.*

Since a second Revival in Amherst in 1850 when once again Emily
failed to be "melted,"* she had found little peace from cherubic gentle-
women and church deacons. At last the day came when she would go
to church no longer. To one of her favorite cousins, she described how
she now was spending her Sabbath morning: "It is Sunday now, John,
and all have gone to church—the wagons have done passing and I have
come out in the new grass to listen to the anthems." The thought carried
over to a poem.

> *Some keep the sabbath going to church*
> *I keep it staying at home*
> *With a Bobolink for chorister*
> *And an orchard for a dome.*
>
> *Some keep the sabbath in surplice,*
> *I just wear my wings,*
> *And instead of tolling the bell for church*
> *Our little sexton sings.*
>
> *God preaches—a noted Clergyman—*
> *And the sermon is never long,*
> *So instead of getting to heaven at last*
> *I'm going all along.*

* In this Revival both her father and Vinnie officially became Christians. Austin
withheld until 1856, the year of his marriage to Susan Gilbert.

Increasingly uneasy about Emily's dissenting attitudes, the Dickinsons resorted to lecturing her on "good works" as a means of improving her character. Nothing in their way of life appealed to her. "Somehow or other I incline to other things," she said sadly, "and Satan covers them up with flowers and I reach out and pick them. The path of duty looks very ugly indeed—and the place where I want to go more amiable—a great deal—it is so much easier to do wrong than right—so much pleasanter to be evil than good, I don't wonder that good angels weep and bad ones sing."

But alienation is a loneliness. How isolated Emily felt even within the shelter of her family she made plain to Joseph Lyman in one of the most revealing passages she ever wrote concerning life inside the Dickinson mansion.

My father seems to me often the oldest and oddest sort of a foreigner. Sometimes I say something and he stares in a curious sort of bewilderment though I speak a thought quite as old as his daughter. And Vinnie, Joseph, it is so weird and so vastly mysterious, she sleeps by my side, her care is in some sort motherly, for you may not remember that our amiable mother never taught us tayloring and I am amused to remember those clothes, or rather those apologies made up from dry goods with which she covered us in nursery times; so Vinnie is in the matter of raiment greatly necessary to me; and the tie is quite vital; yet if we had come up for the first time from two wells where we had hitherto been bred her astonishment would not be greater at some things I say.

But regardless of all that it cost her in loneliness and isolation, Emily was determined now to make the whole of her life exemplify Emerson's wisdom as expressed in "Self-Reliance" and "Spiritual Laws."

Nothing can bring you peace but yourself.

• • •

Nothing can bring you peace but the triumph of principles.

• • •

Live no longer to the expectation of these deceived and deceiving people with whom we converse. Say to them, O father, O mother, O wife, O brother, O friend, I have lived with you after appearances hitherto. Hence forward I obey no law less than the eternal law. . . . I appeal from your customs. I must be myself . . . I will seek my own. I do this not selfishly but humbly and truly. It is alike your interest and mine, and all men's, however long we have dwelt in lies, to live in truth.

To Joseph she said stoutly, "My Country is Truth."

A traumatic break in Emily's relationship with her father occurred in 1855 when he announced in triumph the reclaiming of his Main Street mansion. Agonized by the thought of separating from her childhood "Eden"—the home she now clung to as sanctuary from a hostile world, Emily interpreted her father's pride in returning to the home of *his* childhood as being for status' sake only, as wanting to be part of a crass materialistic society. "They say home is where the heart is," she wrote bitterly, "I think it is where the house is, & the adjacent buildings." In the contest between them she saw her father's mental world as being all facts and figures, all prose and no poetry. He, on the other hand, charged her with being both impractical and old-fashioned. It was this that kept them pulling always in opposite directions, the two dwellings being an obvious symbol of the difference in their natures. As time neared for leaving Pleasant Street, Emily played dangerously with thought of suicide. But better sense prevailed and she managed to pull herself through the long-remembered ordeal of moving day. "My effects were brought in a band box, and the 'deathless me' on foot. I took at the time a memorandum of my several senses, and also of my hat and coat, and my best shoes—but was lost in the melee and I am out with lantern looking for myself."

Though Main Street was not and never would be Pleasant Street, Emily soon made a new Eden for herself inside this statelier mansion. In the absence of men and women of her village willing to take her on her own terms, she settled for the company of her favorite books, and Carlo, a large Newfoundland dog bought for her by her father. Daily she transcribed her reveries into verse. "By my window have I for scenery/ Just a sea with a stem" says one of her poems, her great delight being to watch there the jays or squirrels "whose giddy peninsula/May be easier reached this way." From this same window she looked east morning after morning, coming from her writing table to watch the sunrise—at last to tell of it in her own uncommon way:

> *I'll tell you how the Sun rose—*
> *A ribbon at a time!*
> *The steeples swam in amethyst,*
> *The news, like squirrels, ran.*
> *The hills untied their bonnets,*
> *The bobolinks begun—*
> *Then I said softly to myself—*

> *"That must have been the sun!"*
> *But how he set, I know not.*
> *There seemed a purple stile*
> *That little yellow boys and girls*
> *Were climbing all the while,*
> *Till, when they reached the other side,*
> *A Dominie in gray*
> *Put gently up the evening bars*
> *And led the flock away.*

There being a servant now to do the bulk of the housework, Emily divided her time between her writing desk and her garden. She called hers a "simple and stern life" much in the same sense that Thoreau thought of his life as simple, spartan—requiring little of worldly goods or fashions for happiness, placing highest priority on friends, nature, poetry. Indeed, in every sense, Emily was the soul-sister of Thoreau. Impractical the world called them both, but ironically, in those giddy, affluent prewar years of the 1850s, the idealism of Emily Dickinson and Henry Thoreau led them to live the most practical life of all—stripped of non-essentials, close to home, close to nature, living in a one-to-one relationship with their fellow man and the spirit they called God. There were those who called Thoreau a madman, and in Emerson's sense, no doubt he was.

> Behold there in the wood the fine madman! He is a palace of sweet sounds and sights; He dilates; he is twice a man; he walks with arms akimbo; he soliloquizes; he accosts the grass and trees; he feels the blood of the violet, the clover and the lily in his veins; and he talks with the brook that wets his foot.

There were those who called Emily Dickinson mad, too, to which she made quick reply:

> *Much madness is divinest sense*
> *To a discerning eye.*
> *Much sense the starkest madness.*
> *'Tis the majority*
> *In this, as all prevails.*
> *Assent and you are sane,*
> *Demur, you're straightway dangerous*
> *And handled with a chain.*

Like Thoreau Emily had ability to make her own company in solitude, saying,

> *The soul that hath a guest*
> *Doth seldom go abroad.*
> *Diviner crowd at home*
> *Obliterate the need.*

And like him, too, she fashioned on her own terms an ecstatic religion to replace oppressive doctrines.

> *I dwell in possibility,*
> *A fairer house than prose,*
> *More numerous of windows,*
> *Superior for doors.*
>
> *Of chambers as the cedars,*
> *Impregnable of eye,*
> *And for an everlasting roof*
> *The gambrels of the sky.*
>
> *Of visitors—the fairest,*
> *For occupation—this:*
> *The spreading wide my narrow hands*
> *To gather paradise.*

"A paradise at hand is worth two in the bush," she would slyly advise all her correspondents. Adventure for Emily in that paradise was the same as Thoreau's challenge to himself and all the youth of his day: "Explore your higher latitudes, nay be a Columbus to whole new continents and worlds within you, opening new channels, not of trade, but of thought." She tried constantly to woo Austin into that adventure, but the realities of her brother's life kept him going on "in trade" and into the church too. In 1856 he married Sue Gilbert, moved into a beautiful new house which his father had built for them next door to the Dickinson mansion. Thus Austin was at least within the hedges of Emily's private world; it was his children who in later years would stand under her window to catch the magic basket she let down for them on a string. Austin, like his forebears, became a prominent Amherst lawyer, took over as college bursar after his father died, completing three generations in that post. But he along with his two spinster sisters seemed to Amherstians a trio of eccentrics with their bluntness, their stubborn integrity, secretiveness, and stern pride.

When people first began to note Emily's recluse habits, gossip started linking her name with that of a cousin who, because of the blood tie, it was said her father had not permitted her to marry. There may indeed have been someone over whom she and her father quarreled, or whose early death hastened the total seclusion in which she finally shrouded herself. In any case, as early as her twenty-first year, Emily had begun to turn down invitations to leave Amherst.

"I'm growing selfish in my dear home, but I do love it so, and when some pleasant friend invites me to pass a week with her, I look at my father & mother and Vinnie and all my friends, and I say—no, can't leave them, what if they die when I'm gone." Shortly after the move to Main Street, her "no" became firmer, her reason more complex.

> You asked me to come and see you, I must speak of that. I thank you, Abiah, but I don't go from home unless emergency leads me by the hand and then I do it obstinately, and draw back if I can. Should I ever leave home, which is improbable, I will, with much delight, accept your invitation . . . I'm so *old-fashioned*, darling, that all your friends would stare. Think of it seriously, Abiah, do you think it my *duty* to leave?

that accented "duty" telling its own tale.

What emergency it was that finally did lead her to Washington—the first and last trip she ever made outside of her native New England— is not clear, though it was probably out of compassion for her father whose defeat in the elections of 1854 at the hands of the powerful Know-Nothing party had, momentarily, brought his political career to a standstill. Not having obliged him by attending when he had his debut in Congress, she was there as he said his last good-by. It is this brief journey that gave to Emily a new and influential friend, and gave to legend the romance it now attributes to her.

After three weeks in Washington, Emily and Vinnie went to Philadelphia to visit friends formerly of Amherst. In Emily's words, "we have wandered together in many new ways—seen much that is fair, and heard much that is wonderful." In the latter category were the sermons of the Reverend Charles Wadsworth, who held a nationwide reputation for rhetoric of intense poetic power. Apparently Emily was granted a private interview with this man who became the first clergyman willing to reprieve the hell-fire sentence hanging over her head.

Emily's profound gratitude to "My Philadelphia" (as she clandestinely refers to him in her correspondence) was made evident in her lifelong interest in him and his family (Wadsworth was married, father of two children). That it was to him she turned seeking spiritual guidance in times of crisis during the following years—as when blindness threatened in the 1860s, or when her father died in 1874—there is no doubt. But there is little hard evidence that it was for unrequited love of him she renounced all but the spiritual pleasures of life. Nor is it safe to assume that the famous "love" poems of Emily Dickinson are either love poems in the ordinary sense, or are autobiographical. "When I state myself as the representative of the verse," she was to warn Colonel Higginson, "it does not mean me, but a supposed person."

Supposed or not, it was always the poem that mattered most to Emily and that ought to matter most to us. She used the personal tone for immediacy, to convey universal emotions—love, pain, fear, wonderment—to put philosophical questions, to argue religion ("the flood subject"), or the human condition even with Deity himself. The power of Emily Dickinson's mind and excruciatingly sensitive heart are intrinsic to her work, but poetry, as Emily well understood, had to have its own power apart from its creator. With marvelous economy of word she could convey the richness a soul acquires when it shuns the pomp, the false, to rediscover—in simplicity—true values; and richness may come from what one learns of truth and love whether from man, a woman, or a book.

> The soul selects her own society
> Then shuts the door;
> On her divine majority
> Obtrude no more.
>
> Unmoved she notes the chariot pausing
> At her low gate;
> Unmoved an emperor be kneeling
> Upon her mat.
>
> I've known her from an ample nation
> Choose one
> Then close the valves of her attention
> Like stone.

What matters a century later is not whom Emily Dickinson loved but that her enormous capacity to love took in so many—women as well as men—each contributing to the intellectual and emotional tensions of a life out of which was forged a powerful and unique art. After her return from Philadelphia, save for two extended stays in Cambridge in the early 1860s during which she underwent treatment for failing vision, Emily never again went beyond her father's gate. Having found a philosophy and an occupation to enrich her life, having Austin, Sue, and Vinnie close by, the balance of her days on earth might have been blissfully content had not a terror come with news that struck like lightning—the news that she was in danger of going blind. To be without eyes, to be without books—that for Emily was death. What such loss meant to her comes through in a wonderfully vivid account she gave to Joseph Lyman of being denied reading, presumably at an earlier period when she was suffering a nervous breakdown.

> Some years ago I had a woe, the only one that ever made me tremble. It was a shutting out of all the dearest ones of time, the strongest friends of the soul—Books. The medical man said avaunt ye tormentors, he also said "down, thought, & plunge into her soul." He might as well have said, "Eyes be blind," "heart be still." So I had eight months of Siberia.
> Well do I remember the music of the welcome home. It was at his office. He whistled up the fox hounds. He clapped and said "Sesame". How my blood bounded! Shakespear was the first; Anthony & Cleopatra where Enobarbus laments the amorous lapse of his master. Here is the ring of it:
>> heart that in the scuffles of
>> great fights hath burst the
>> buckle on his breast
> then I thought why clasp any hand but this. Give me ever to drink of this wine. Going home I flew to the shelves and devoured of luscious passages. I thought I should tear the leaves out as I turned them. Then I settled down to a willingness for all the rest to go but William Shakespear. Why need we, Joseph, read anything else but him.

What the nature of the disease,† or the full extent of damage to Emily's eyes is not yet known. But there is some evidence, including a radical change in her handwriting and innumerable references in letters and poems, to indicate that whatever vision returned after two operations was minimal. Joseph Lyman, who served briefly with the Confederate forces before being taken prisoner and then released, apparently saw Emily when he stopped over in Cambridge on his way home to Easthampton. As though for the opening of a play or story, he later wrote this description of an obviously visually handicapped girl, titling it

---

† Bright's disease, of which Emily eventually died, may well have been responsible for this early eye damage.

EMILY

A library dimly lighted, three mignonettes on a little stand. Enter a spirit clad in white, figure so draped as to be misty; face moist, translucent alabaster, forehead firm as of statuary marble. Eyes once bright hazel now melted & fused so as to be two dreamy wells of expression, eyes that see no forms but glance swiftly & at once to the core of all things—hands small, firm, deft but utterly emancipated from clasping of perishable things.

Why Emily should wish to hide from her neighbors any physical handicap seems more mysterious than her reputed clandestine romance. But the Dickinsons were proud people, and Emily the proudest of them all. In the "polar privacy" of her solitude, she at first faltered, then, with steel nerve—as when a child shut up in a closet—determined to make adventure even of darkness. How she fared is conveyed in many poems telling the various ways of seeing—through memory, faith, above all *soul.*

> *Before I got my eye put out*
> *I liked as well to see*
> *As other creatures that have eyes*
> *And know no other way.*
>
> *But were it told to me today*
> *That I might have the sky*
> *For mine, I tell you that my heart*
> *Would split for size of me.*
>
> *The meadows mine,*
> *The mountains mine,*
> *All forests, stintless stars—*
> *As much of noon as I could take*
> *Between my finite eyes,*
>
> *The motions of the dipping birds,*
> *The morning's amber road*
> *For mine to look at when I liked—*
> *The news would strike me dead!*
>
> *So safer guess with just my soul*
> *Upon the window pane*
> *Where other creatures put their eyes*
> *Incautious of the sun.*

Poetry helped Emily to survive. Often, when her spirit sagged, she would be reminded by her beloved sister-in-law, Susan Dickinson, that Emily Dickinson, *Poet*, must live. Sue had long been convinced that Emily had no uncommon gift, had once risked losing Emily's friendship by sending out a poem to be published without the author's knowledge. "Robbed of me" was the way Emily put it. In her philosophy, poetry, being "of the spirit" was not for sale. "Gold may be bought, purple may be bought, but there never was a sale of the spirit," she said. "If I could make you and Austin proud of me someday a long way off 'twould give me taller feet," she told Sue, and Sue knew Emily's meaning— when she was no longer within range of witnesses or applause, for, as in one of her poems, if birds could do their singing at dawn when

> *Their witnesses were not—*
> *Except occasional man*
> *In homely industry arrayed*
> *To overtake the morn;*
>
> *Nor was it for applause*
> *That I could ascertain,*
> *But independent ecstasy*
> *Of deity and men*

why, then, should not Emily do the same. "In music there is a major and a minor," she said. "May there not also be a private?"

That she had promise of being a poet worthy of publication Emily already knew. Once, back in 1850, she had been astonished to find a valentine verse of hers written only for the eyes of young William Howland "betrayed" and appearing in the poetry column of the Springfield *Daily Republican* whose editors appended the following to the anonymous poem: "The hand that wrote the following amusing medley to a gentleman friend of ours as 'a valentine' is capable of writing very fine things, and there is certainly no presumption in entertaining a private wish that a correspondence more direct than this may be established between it and the *Republican*." Emily had come forward with no more poems, but a correspondence did begin between her and the two distinguished owner-editors of that newspaper, Josiah Gilbert Holland, poet-novelist whose sunnier religion helped brighten Emily's life; and Sam Bowles, one of the most influential newspaper men of his time, whom Emily hero-worshiped, indeed looked up to almost as a father-figure though he was but three years her senior. But neither of these men had since been able to persuade her to publish either for money or for glory. Emily was not, however, averse to seeking a teacher-critic, always hoped there might be someone willing to estimate her work and help her to achieve mastery in the art form she took so seriously. Fortunately, at this critical juncture of her life when failing vision made it seem there was little left to live for, Sue called her attention to an article in the *Atlantic Monthly* titled "Letter to a Young Contributor" in which Thomas Wentworth Higginson presumed to give advice to would-be poets on the art "they presume to practice." The article proved a turning point for Emily, a fateful day for American literature.

On April 16, 1862, a tall, handsome young man, a former clergyman who had won notoriety in New England as a revolutionary abolitionist, whose alliance with John Brown had led him into the struggle for a free Kansas (he also led an expedition hoping to free John Brown after his capture); who now was about to become colonel of the first all-black regiment of the Civil War, took from his post-office box in Worcester, Massachusetts, what he thought to be a most curious letter.

> Mr. Higginson, are you too deeply occupied to say if my verse is alive? The mind is so near itself it cannot see distinctly, and I have none to ask. Should you think it breathed, and had you the leisure to tell me, I should feel quick gratitude.
>
> If I make the mistake, that you dared to tell me would give me sincere honor toward you. I enclose my name, asking you, if you please sir, to tell me what is true. That you will not betray me it is needless to ask since honor is its own pawn.

Hundreds of "effusions," Colonel Higginson later said, he had received in response to the *Atlantic* article, but none that struck his interest like those he received from "E. Dickinson" of Amherst. Such "alive" and "breathing" verse he had never before read anywhere. She sent only four poems: "I'll tell you how the sun rose," "Safe in their Alabaster Chambers," "We play at paste till qualified for pearl," and, said Higginson, "then came one which I have always classed among the most exquisite of her productions, with a singular felicity of phrase and an aerial lift that bear the ear upward with the bee it races."

> *The nearest dream recedes unrealized.*
> *The heaven we chase*
> *Like the June bee before the school boy*
> *Invites the race,*
> *Stoops to an easy clover,*
> *Dips, evades, teases, deploys,*

Then to the royal clouds
Lifts his light pinnace
Heedless of the boy
Staring bewildered at the mocking sky,
Homesick for steadfast honey.
Ah, the bee flies not
That brews that rare variety!

The handwriting, said Higginson, was so peculiar "it seemed as if the writer might have taken her first lessons by studying the famous fossil bird tracks in the museum of that college town." Of punctuation there was little, and the syntax of all four poems had him scanning for connecting lines somewhat as if climbing mountain rock to reach the peak of meaning. "But, after all," he said to himself, "when a thought takes one's breath away, a lesson on grammar seems an impertinence."

Excitedly, he wrote asking the unknown E. Dickinson (an action she was later to tell him saved her life) particulars of her history. The answer which came back to him only served to pique his curiosity the more.

You asked how old I was? I made no verse but one or two, until this winter, sir.

I had a terror since September, I could tell to none; and so I sing as the boy does of the burying ground, because I am afraid.

You inquire my books. For poets, I have Keats, and Mr. & Mrs. Browning. For prose, Mr. Ruskin, Sir Thomas Browne, and the Revelations. I went to school, but in your manner of the phrase had no education. When a little girl, I had a friend who taught me Immortality,‡ but venturing too near himself, he never returned. Soon after, my tutor died, and for several years my lexicon was my only companion. Then I found one more, but he was not contented I be his scholar, so he left the land.*

You ask of my companions. Hills, sir, and the sundown, and a dog large as myself that my father bought me. They are better than beings because they know, but do not tell; and the noise in the pool at noon excels my piano.

I have a brother and sister; my mother does not care for thought, and father too busy with his briefs to notice what we do. He buys

‡ Emily Brontë's poem "Immortality" probably given to her by Ben Newton. Emily's reference to herself as "little girl" means the innocent child she was in her "unsifted" teens.

* It is commonly believed this refers to Charles Wadsworth who took a pulpit in San Francisco—in Emily's original way of using language "left the land" does not necessarily mean overseas.

me many books, but begs me not to read them, because he fears they joggle the mind. They are religious, except me, and address an eclipse every morning whom they call their "Father."

But I fear my story fatigues you. I would like to learn. Could you tell me how to grow, or is it unconveyed, like melody, or witchcraft?

You speak of Mr. Whitman. I never read his book, but was told that it was disgraceful.†

I read Miss Prescott's Circumstance, but it followed me in the dark, so I avoided her.‡

Two editors of journals came to my father's house this winter, and asked me for my mind, and when I asked them "why" they said I was penurious, and they would use it for the world.

I could not weigh myself, myself. My size felt small to me. I read your chapters in the *Atlantic* and experienced honor for you. I was sure you would not reject a confiding question.

Is this, sir, what you asked me to tell you?

It was and it was not. But as the wealth of correspondence he was to have with her over the next twenty years would teach Colonel Higginson, he had to be satisfied with Emily Dickinson as she was. No amount of gentle persuasion could woo her out of her stubborn individuality in verse, prose, or life style. His request for her photograph evoked this now famous reply:

Could you believe me without? I had no portrait now, but am small, like the wren; and my hair is bold, like the chestnut burr, and my eyes, like the sherry in the glass that the guest leaves. Would this do just as well?

The response that most astonished him came when he suggested that, for a while at least, she delay to publish.

I smile when you suggest that I delay "to publish" that being foreign to my thought as Firmament to Fin. If fame belonged to me, I could not escape her—if she did not, the longest day would pass me on the chase—and the approbation of my Dog would forsake me then. My barefoot rank is better. . . .

The Colonel was perplexed, not only by her lack of ambition to be published, but, as her poems continued to flow, by the obscurity of their meaning which her unusual style by no means helped make clearer for him. Never a straight line kind of person, Emily refused to be a

† Walt Whitman's *Leaves of Grass* had been published in 1855.
‡ Harriet Prescott, a young protégée of Higginson's. Her short story "In a Cellar" had appeared in the *Atlantic* in 1861 winning for her overnight fame among the literary elite of New England.

straight line kind of poet. "Tell him I only said the syntax and left the verb and pronoun out," she once wrote to Austin as a comic injunction aimed at her father who had expressed puzzlement over some passages in her letters which he so conscientiously perused for "secrets." Colonel Higginson would have profited by the same advice while working his way through the strange and beautiful language of his "bizarre poetess." An even better guide in trying to decipher both content and form would have been Emerson. "Poetry," said Emerson "is not Devil's wine, but God's—the air should suffice for inspiration, and he [the poet] should be tipsy with water . . . the poet speaks adequately when he speaks somewhat wildly with the intellect inebriated by nectar." Thoreau, at Walden, having tried the formula, exclaimed, "Who does not prefer to be intoxicated by the air he breathes!" Not to be outdone, Emily Dickinson confirmed the recipe, both for poetry and an ecstatic existence.

> *I taste a liquor never brewed*
> *From tankards scooped in pearl.*
> *Not all the vats upon the Rhine*
> *Yield such an alcohol!*
>
> *Inebriate of Air am I,*
> *And debauchee of dew,*
> *Reeling through endless summer days*
> *From inns of molten blue.*
>
> *When "landlords" turn the drunk Bee*
> *Out of the foxglove's door,*
> *When butterflies renounce their "drams"*
> *I shall but drink the more,*
>
> *Till seraphs swing their snowy hats*
> *And saints to windows run*
> *To see the little tippler*
> *Leaning against the sun.*

Some of Emily Dickinson's poems were written in that field where she "went to church," some in the "bed of pain" where she endured physical and mental ordeals, all constituting her diary, her evidence of being, her search for self and God, her discovery of God in Self. In creating a poem she tried to achieve such spontaneous style as would belie the painstaking hand of the struggling artist at work. "The art of composition," Thoreau wrote, "is as simple as the discharge of a bullet from a rifle, and its masterpieces imply an infinitely greater force behind." It was that greater force Emily was constantly seeking, adopting the metaphor of gun and bullet for clearer understanding of the dynamics of her experience and her art. In pleading with Higginson to allow her to be his scholar, she told him that she was always in need of masters because "I had no monarch in my life and cannot rule myself, and when I try to organize, my little force explodes and leaves me bare and charred." Need of masters had, at varying times, put her at the feet of Ben Newton, Joseph Lyman, Sam Bowles, Dr. Holland, Charles Wadsworth—perhaps others whose names are still to come to light—finally to Higginson himself; but as it gradually became clear to Emily that Higginson was quailing before the originality of her language, style and thought, she came back to the power of Emerson's "Self-Reliance," her own hand upon the loaded emotions and talent of Emily Dickinson. It gave rise to one of her most—riddle-like poems which says in part:

> My life had stood a loaded gun
> In corners till a day
> The owner passed, identified,
> And carried me away.
>
> And now we roam in sovereign woods,
> And now we hunt the doe,
> And everytime I speak for Him
> The mountains straight reply.
>
> And I do smile, such cordial light
> Upon the valley glow.
> It is as a Vesuvian face
> Had let his pleasure through.

Her imagination was her coach, her train, her "evanescent wheel" taking her to spice isles or snowy alps—wherever she wanted to go. "It takes but a moment of imagination to place us anywhere," she told correspondents trying to woo her into their world by descriptions of travels abroad. "It would not seem worthwhile to stay where it is stale."

Nothing was ever stale in her world. To join her, whether she is observing a circus parade beneath her window, the pace of a worm in her garden, the approach of wind or rain, sunrise or moonrise, is to be in on a great event. "Do you look out tonight?" she asks one correspondent,

"The moon rides through the town like a topaz girl." Observing spring's arrival always evoked more than ordinary response. "A color stands abroad on solitary hills that science cannot overtake but human nature feels . . . it almost *speaks* to me." At summer's end she listens to an insect choir her neighbors are too accustomed to to hear: "Pathetic from the grass/A minor nation celebrates its unobtrusive mass." Unobtrusive Emily means to be, but she is always on stage with her celebrations. That is one of the fine ironies in the life of this recluse poet. She was the bird soaring freely, she was the cricket on the hearth, she was the apparition "in white"—but always singing. From childhood on she had reached for that in nature which could be translated into sound—the living voice speaking through an inner, seared impression, capturing the deepest of emotion into a simple poem. But she learned that words came easy, poetry did not; nature, for all its closeness, was never to be easily captured. "Nature," she said, "is what we *know* yet have no art to say, so impotent our wisdom is to her *simplicity*." Her aim was not to be a nature poet but a poet of nature without and within, linking man and the elements all in one grand design.

"Our private theater is ourselves," Henry James once wrote. Emily Dickinson drew amply from her own theater, but living and writing in times of rebellion and war, a war that was making for many sorrows, hers was often the central mood as of a Rachel crying for her children.

> I can wade grief,
> Whole pools of it,
> I'm used to that;
> But the least push of joy
> Breaks up my feet.

Experiencing a storm can be terrifying to man and beast alike, whether it be deluge created by the elements, or by the bloodiest of civil wars.

> There came a wind like a bugle;
> It quivered through the grass,
> And a green chill upon the heat
> So ominous did pass
> We barred the windows and the doors
> As from an emerald ghost.
> The doom's electric moccasin
> That very instant passed
> On a strange mob of panting trees,

> And fences fled away,
> And rivers where the houses ran
> those looked, that lived, that day.
> The bell within the steeple wild
> The flying tidings told.
> How much can come
> And much can go,
> And yet abide the world.

From the windows of her world, Emily looked out upon the picturesque little village over which her father and others like him held so tight a rein on morals and manners, and often it seemed to her a slumbering volcano. Underneath all the dusting, scrubbing, and pride of respectability, combustible materials simmered, now and then sparking up with frightening intensity: A mob of students angrily pelts the doors and windows of the house of an offending professor; a young man rides off with his girl to a neighboring town, comes back next day to a tar and feathering party; indignant citizens gather in a body, march down to the railroad station to turn back by force a "foreigner" come to claim the hand of a wealthy Amherst girl; an unknown firebug periodically lights up the night sky with a terrifying and costly blaze, while Emily Dickinson, in her white gown, watches and trembles for the children living outside the gate of Eden.

> Volcanoes be in Sicily,
> And South America
> I judge from my geography.
> Volcanoes nearer here
> A lava step at any time.

In the early days of her solitude she would say

> I never hear the word "escape"
> Without a quicker blood,
> A sudden expectation,
> A flying attitude!
>
> I never hear of prisons abroad
> By soldiers battered down,
> But I tug childish at my bars
> Only to fail again.

Now, though, her own "real life" seemed superior enough, and having mastered self and loneliness there were no more bars. Free she was and free she determined to remain.

The Life that tied too tight escapes,
Will ever after run
With a prudential look behind;
And spectres of the rein,
The horse that scents the living grass
And sees the pastures smile,
Will be retaken with a shot
If he is caught at all.

Experimenting, often writing the same poem in many ways, or, as she put it, "Playing with paste till qualified for pearl," Emily soon had hundreds of poems to lock away inside the cubicle of her desk. In writing them she took cue from Emerson to leave off fancy frills, to use instead the healthy natural speech of the American language as distinct from classical English. "The poet," Emerson said, "shall not his brain encumber/With the coil of rhythm and number/But leaving rule and pale forethought/. . . aye climb high/For his rhyme." And that, too, Emily did.

A narrow fellow in the grass
Occasionally rides;
You may have met him,—did you not?
His notice sudden is.

The grass divides as with a comb,
A spotted shaft is seen;
And then it closes at your feet
And opens further on.

He likes a boggy acre,
A floor too cool for corn.
Yet when a child, and barefoot,
I more than once, at morn,
Have passed, I thought, a whip-lash
Unbraiding in the sun,
When stooping to secure it,
It wrinkled and was gone.

Several of nature's people
I know and they know me.
I feel for them a transport
Of cordiality.

But never met this fellow,
Attended or alone,
Without a tighter breathing
And zero at the bone.

"What portfolios of verse you must have," wrote Amherst-born Helen Hunt Jackson after being put on Emily's trail by Colonel Higginson, who had long since changed his mind about advising his "half-cracked poetess" to publish. "It is a cruel wrong to your day & generation that you will not give them light. I do not think we have a right to withold from the world a word or a thought any more than a deed which might help a single soul." Mrs. Jackson, soon to become renowned for her novel *Ramona*, published her own poems and essays under the pseudonym "H. H." Adventurous, courageous, she was one of the first women to explore the far West as a reporter. Her prose was vigorous, colorful, and much admired by her childhood playmate, Emily Dickinson. But in their continuing correspondence, her tactic of pressing Emily to publish in the name of *duty* was doomed from the start.

In 1878, however, whether acquired by fair means or foul, one of Emily's poems, titled "Success" did find its way into *A Masque of Poets*, a book in which Mrs. Jackson had an interest. The novelty of the little volume was that readers were to guess the name of the authors of the uncredited poems. It was a feather in Emily Dickinson's cap when many critics assigned Emerson as the author of her poem, but she would not allow herself to be unmasked even then. She was still keeping fast to that which had prompted Thoreau at Walden to say:

If the day and the night are such that you greet them with joy, and life emits a fragrance like flowers and sweet-scented herbs, is more elastic, more starry, more immortal—that is your success.

In these last years of her life, spending her days writing letters that read like poems and poems that read like letters, Emily sent abroad messages of such contentedness she made her days seem enviable to friends out in the turmoil of the postwar world. To those still pitying her shut-in life she said, wryly: "Maybe Eden ain't so lonesome as New England used to be." To those who wondered how she spent the long hours of a nunlike existence, she said, in all the ways she knew, that life was full:

There is always one thing to be grateful for, that one is one's self and not somebody else.

I find ecstasy in living, the mere sense of living is joy enough.

We turn not older with the years, but newer everyday.

Those that are worthy of Life are of miracle, for life is a miracle, and death as harmless as a bee except to those who run.

She was not running, indeed was looking forward to the last of life's adventures as Bright's Disease in 1884, began to sap her strength. "Dying is a wild night and a long road," she wrote to one of her cousins. On May 15, 1886, with Austin and Vinnie at her bedside, she arrived at the end of that long road. Then Vinnie went out into the neighborhood to announce "the great event," telling it the way Emily wanted it told— that somewhere now on the other side there was a little tippler leaning against the sun.

"The funeral, if so ghastly a name could apply to anything so poetical as the service was the most beautiful thing I ever saw," Mabel Loomis Todd wrote home to her Washington family. "Several clergymen were there. Colonel Higginson came up from Cambridge to read Emily Brontë's poem "Immortality." Then President Sylee [of Amherst College] and the other honorary pall bearers took out the dainty white casket into the sunshine where it was lifted by the arms of six or eight Irish workmen, all of whom have worked about the place or been servants in the family for years, and all of whom Emily saw and talked with occasionally up to the last. They carried it through the fields full of buttercups, while the friends who chose followed on irregularly through the ferny footpaths to the little cemetery."

That little cemetery was destined not to be an ending for its occupant, for Vinnie now unearthed the poems "of spirit" and Emily was on her way to immortality. The little gold and white volume of her poems, published November 1890 with Mrs. Todd and Colonel Higginson at the helm, astonished all those in Amherst who had never known what it was that kept Emily Dickinson so busy behind her father's gate. For many of her fellow New Englanders, Emily Dickinson was, for the first time, coming to life. The rector of Trinity Church, Boston, who on occasion had summered in Amherst, wrote:

Who could have imagined, never having known her, or for that matter, having known her, that all unknown to the thousands who have
passed her silent house eager only not to miss a train, there was a
mind and imagination that could tell them more of nature and the
mysteries of life than the combined wisdom of the college . . .
There is a keen condemnation and in some sort, a shame upon us,
upon me at least, & others, that we should have been so insensitive
as not to have felt, through silence and invisibleness, the presence of
one who was reading the inner life of bee, grass, and sky, the secret
of the most passionate lives of men & women. My God! What a
bloodless tragedy must have been enacted behind those doors—what
an innocent hedge . . . I testify that she did not live in vain.

Emily made for lively copy everywhere. The Boston *Herald*, while
certain that "Madder rhymes one has seldom seen," yet assured its readers
that there was in Emily Dickinson's poems "a fascination, a power, a
vision . . . that draws you back . . . again and again." The poet Robert
Bridges, inclined to shrug off Colonel Higginson's latest protégée, said
Emily's love poems were "saved from being absurd only by sincerity."
Oddly enough, the Colonel himself was reserving judgment, admitting
in print that he did not know "what place ought to be assigned in
literature to what is so remarkable, yet so elusive of criticism." "The bee
himself did not evade the schoolboy more than she evaded me," he
said, "and even to this day . . . I stand somewhat bewildered." One
who was not bewildered was William Dean Howells, distinguished novelist
and editor, who reviewed Emily Dickinson's *Poems* for *Harper's New
Monthly*, a magazine Emily had read enthusiastically over the years.
"Terribly unsparing many of these strange poems are," Howells said,
"but true as the grave and certain as mortality. They are each a com-
pressed whole, a sharply finished point . . . the author spared no pains
in the perfect expression of her ideals. Occasionally the outside of the
poem is left so rough, so crude that the art seems to have faltered.
But there is apparent on reflection the fact that the artist meant just
this harsh exterior to remain. If nothing else had come out of our life
but this strange poetry, we should feel that in the work of Emily
Dickinson, America—or New England, rather—had made a distinctive
addition to the literature of the world and cannot be left out of any
record of it."

Not all the millions of words of criticism written then or since
(and they continue to flow, Dickinson now being included in all the

scholars' volumes) can add or detract from Emily's own brief comment
on that which determines the value of a poem.

> *The poets light but lamps—*
> *Themselves go out.*
> *The wicks they stimulate*
> *If vital light*
> *Inhere as do the suns,*
> *Each age a lens*
> *Disseminating their Circumference.*

For this poet as for Shelley who called poetry "at once the center
and circumference of knowledge," the vital light she made illumines
more than an age—it illumines for all the world to see the free spirit
that was Emily Dickinson.

Edwin Arlington Robinson
(1869–1935)

"... a light of my own. ..."

"I was born awkward," Edwin Arlington Robinson said of himself at age twenty-five. "I was always a fossil and I suppose I always shall be one . . . experience is continually reminding me of it."

Physically, too, he felt uncomfortable, with a tall, lean, stoop-shouldered body, long arms, long legs, all moving as if he took up too much space and somehow had to squeeze out of the way quickly before he was noticed even by himself. He looked and felt older than his years—owlishly solemn in a pair of large, rimless spectacles and plagued by pain in a once abscessed ear. But the awkwardness of which he spoke ran deeper than this. He was, he thought, a man born out of season, an idealist in the America of 1894 which had no time for ideals, a poet in a world in which money was everything and poets a kind of clumsy deformity shaming the family setting.

> *Miniver Cheevy, child of scorn*
> *Grew lean while he assailed the seasons;*
> *He wept that he was ever born,*
> *And he had reasons.*

Only when he was at work on a poem, going at it silently like any other earnest craftsman did he know where and what he was. As soon as he emerged, squinting into the light, he had no sense of how, socially, to be comfortable in public. Stifled by small talk, embarrassed by sophomoric intellectualizing, he learned to set up a dense fog of tobacco smoke behind which to hide and hope to be left alone. Lacking a talent to make merry except in the company of one or two close friends or with children, he was awkward even in handling his enormous

sense of humor which carried with it a laughter that sputtered upward
in short, jerky, cackling sounds, coming never richly or easily, but as if,
like whistling in a classroom, it were against the rules, a sin against
gentility. Gentle he was and trained in all the gentlemanly amenities,
but he avoided "society" in favor of a corner chair in a downtown tavern
where other offbeats like himself dreamed and struck kingly postures in
their fantasy worlds. Living in a time of fierce competitiveness and
roughshod commercial dealings, his eye and his heart dealt primarily in
the tragedies of failures, understanding the suffering of others even more
than his own. Compassion summed him up, and that kind of excruciating
sensitivity denoting a man who seems to wear his skin inside out. In
the small New England town where he grew up, he was markedly
different from his fellows, a "puzzlement" to his elders. Sadly and early
the young poet came to the conclusion—

> *. . . this is the end of life, I suppose*
> *To do what we can for ourselves and others;*
> *But men who find tragedy writ in a rose*
> *May forget sometimes there are sons and mothers—*

> *Fathers and daughters of love and hate,*
> *Scattered like hell-spawn down from Heaven,*
> *to teach mankind to struggle and wait*
> *Till life be over and death forgiven.*

In his youth what saved Edwin Arlington Robinson was not so much
his sense of humor as his sense of destiny—an absolute and stubborn
certainty that whether in season or out, he had been born to a purpose—
that he would be a poet and live in literature to say of his times and
his world what needed to be said—how all men have humanity in
common, the least and the greatest bound by common frailties and
common dreams. To see himself through, he made four lines of a Hartley
Coleridge sonnet his motto: "*Let me not deem that I was made in vain/
Or that my being was an accident/ Which Fate, in working its sublime
intent,/ Not wished to be, to hinder would not deign.*" And so believing
he learned in time to accept himself for what he was: "Can you imagine
me jumping for joy—or for anything else, unless it be a hornet's nest?"

> I often wonder whether I should be happier if I had the power or gift
> of making friends with everybody. I suppose it stands to reason that
> I should, but if I were given the opportunity of changing my nature,

I am afraid my vanity would keep me as I am. . . . As you know, I seldom laugh. The smoothest part of my face is around my mouth, where the only wrinkles of youth rightly belong. My wrinkles are in my forehead and I have been more than once reminded of the fact. That, I fancy, is because I think more than some people, and do my laughing in my grey matter instead of upon my face. Real solid laughter is almost a physical impossibility with me. When it occurs it almost frightens me. I grin upon the slightest provocation, however, but my grins are not the sort that makes friends . . . there is nothing contagious about them . . .

Like Emerson he did not have to travel too far afield to perceive the tragicomic elements of existence; he was his own theater almost from the moment the curtain raised upon his life.

The year was 1869, the season summer, and Mary Elizabeth Robinson was vacationing in South Harpswell, Maine, looking properly ladylike and frail in the afternoon sunlight as she displayed her six-month-old baby son for a group of gushing ladies to admire. Brightly dressed in their summer finery, making a pretty picture under the trees, the ladies heard with amazement that the young mother had not yet chosen a name for her child. How could she, they asked, let the darling little boy go so long without any definite identity? Mary herself wasn't quite sure. She had married Edward Robinson in 1855, though fifteen years his junior, and when their first son was born two years later, had not hesitated a moment in choosing *his* name—Dean; nor, in 1865 was there any hesitation in selecting one for her second son, Herman. Perhaps when this thirdling arrived, still another boy, she had been both surprised and disappointed. Her husband, no longer a young man, could hardly be a companionable father to this child. Even young Dean, twelve years older than the baby, would probably be a stranger to him by the time the child was in knee breeches. Still it did not adequately explain why the baby was being denied a name. Never mind, said the ladies, they'd fit him up with one themselves. On little slips of paper each wrote down her suggestion and dropped it into Mary's overturned bonnet. With no hesitancy whatsoever the young mother dipped in to bring forth the winning name—Edwin. Appropriate enough since the father's name was Edward. But oughtn't the child to have a middle name— something all his own and more poetic? The ladies solved this too. She whose choice had so happily named the boy Edwin hailed from Arlington, Massachusetts. Thus, on a lazy summer afternoon in South Harpswell

did a child destined to grow up a New England poet become Edwin
Arlington Robinson.

Back in Head Tide, Maine, the pretty little hamlet where Edwin
was born, his busy father, a "local potentate" was glad the matter of
a name was solved—and in his favor. Edward Robinson thought it a
grand thing to have three handsome young sons. With the war over
and the country fairly booming with reconstruction, business was looking
up for him too. He had begun life as a shipwright; now he owned a
general store and was buying and selling timber on the side. Soon he
would be able to afford a bigger house for his family, and increase his
holdings by speculating in western lands. With three sons to inherit
his wealth, carry on his business, he saw himself the head of a dynasty.
As for his pretty Mary, she made a storybook portrait surrounded by
adoring husband and sons. A former schoolteacher, she wrote verses and
was "accomplished" on the piano. She boasted as ancestors Thomas
Dudley, who had been a governer of the Massachusetts Bay Colony,
and Dudley's famous daughter, Anne Bradstreet, New England's first
poet. "I am obnoxious to each carping tongue who says my hand a
needle better fits," Anne had long ago declared. Mary Robinson too,
preferred poetry to needles. Edward liked a jolly song, could tolerate an
evening in which she recited rhymes, but he was through and through a
practical man. His ancestor, Gain Robinson, a Scottish carpenter living
in the north of Ireland, had migrated to New England at the time
George the First was on the English throne, and ever since the Robinsons
of New England had known how to apply brawn and brain to survive.
Mary put great stake in education and gentility; he in work and the
dollar. He hoped all three of his sons would emulate him, become
robust, successful businessmen.

In July 1863, the summer of the battle of Gettysburg, Edward
Robinson had moved from the family homestead at Alna to Head Tide.
His new neighbors had taken to him at once as an enterprising man,
liking him well enough to consider naming him for the legislature
in Augusta. "The Duke of Puddlecock" they called him (Puddlecock
being an adjacent hamlet), but Edward didn't mind the title's sly reference to his sense of self-importance. He was famous in his own way for
a wry sense of humor. One day a customer walked into his general
store in Head Tide to find him—though alone—busily talking away to
himself. "Why do you talk to yourself, Mr. Robinson?" the puzzled

customer asked. "Because now and then I like to talk to somebody that's got some sense," the old man shot back.

When Edwin was a year old, the "Duke of Puddlecock" achieved his ambition to move from Head Tide to that bigger house in the not-too-distant town of Gardiner, Maine, where instead of sheepcote, sawmill, blacksmith shop, and rural appleblossom-lilac bush setting, there was the commercial Kennebec River jammed up with salable ice in winter, millbound logs in summer. This industrious little town, fast losing its outlying woods, boasted a population of some four thousand souls. It had paved streets, a park, civic square, corner drugstores, brick schools, white churches, and a prosperous bank—the latter now the business residence of Edward Robinson, speculator, trustee. In Gardiner this self-made man with his picture-book American family seemed assured of his happy-ever-after reward; unfortunately, the story was to turn out otherwise.

On Lincoln Street stood his handsome, clapboard house among the elms, backed up by an imposing barn beyond which his acreage ended alongside a picturesque stream. Within the fenced grounds, the child, Edwin, played alone, his brothers being away at school. He liked to watch farm wagons and buggies heading down to Dresden Street, to see strange gentlemen hitching horses to the posts before entering their houses across the road. These were his sounds and sights of the outside world. When the bell sounded from the Episcopal spire, making its Sunday-meeting call or nightly curfew at nine, he, like every other boy in Gardiner knew its history: Paul Revere had cast that bell. It was the rhythm and music of the bell, however, not its history that entranced Edwin. According to family memoirs, he early showed a feeling for music, especially enjoying family gatherings about the piano at evening when his father, that "mighty stranger"—whom he so seldom got to be with—boomed out a favorite Civil War marching song. Sometimes, down by the stream where the waterwheel turned, lonely 'Win Robinson would make up his own songs, understanding nothing of that golden edged success which kept his father so occupied, and which was gradually turning his town away from waterwheels and other country ways to fit the pattern of the new American progress.

Business was a foreign place to Edwin's mother too. She seems not to have understood that her husband's move from Head Tide was symbolic of the times—of the way people in New England were moving as the century progressed—toward the towns away from rural tranquillity;

or that she was a remnant of a decaying New England culture, sheltering under her roof a new generation born into an age that was going to be much too preoccupied with problems of mass production to value the genteel manners and ideals she was trying to instill in her young sons. When the Gardiner-Family-Robinson grouped around the piano in their Lincoln Street mansion they were a study in nineteenth-century styles, even their songs of love and heroes, their marches and hymns having little to do with the whirlwind of the fast approaching twentieth century. The youngest child, who would go deepest into that century, would sense as time went on that he belonged neither to the past nor the future. His graceful, lovely mother who wore white kid gloves when she dressed up, and black velvets and Malta lace, put him into a Lord Fauntleroy suit to be shown off to company. He was her darling, well-mannered little boy, though too shy to speak to strangers. Having no company of his own, he would sit in his small rocker while his mother entertained and, to his own inner rhythm, moved the chair gently back and forth. Visitors thought him an odd, unimaginative child. They did not know that even at age four one can have an inner life all one's own.

As he grew older Edwin was not emulating his outgoing father, but his first true hero, big brother Dean, who at sixteen was introspective, an incurable romantic, and an insatiable bookworm. He loved Dean the more because Dean was often in trouble at home, his idealistic world clashing with Father's more practical one. Vaguely Edwin understood that much of the dissension had to do with Dean wanting to go to Bowdoin College and what he would study if he got there.

There was no quarreling about Edwin's schooling. At the age of five he, for the first time, stepped outside of his mother's protection into an alien world among a noisy, cliquish child gang which met every day somewhat informally in a neighbor's house called "private school." From the first day he had trouble, was painfully awkward in making approaches to the children who, when he told them his name was 'Win, insisted on calling him Pin because it rhymed, and then, for the year's duration Pinny. There seemed a wide schism between the gentle culture of his home and this rough and tumble place. Many years later Edwin Arlington Robinson was to say that he knew as early as that—age five—he was never going to be able to elbow his way through the "trough of Life."

He began to seek cover-ups and escapes, finding them as he grew older in two seemingly opposing directions. At home he was Dean all over again—nose buried in a book, or hankering after Dean's clarinet; away from home, either alone or with a single companion, he liked to explore places of fun and danger in Gardiner. He had developed a keen sense of observation, and along with it (reserved only for the company of chums) a peculiar kind of humor which could see irony in almost everything. Living in a town that offered ample opportunity for a boy's adventures, his activities veered from a race down to the wharf to watch paddle wheelers, to log-walking, or swimming in the river; a hike through the woods for berrypicking or tree-climbing. Following curiosity's inclination, he would also often wander onto sidestreets and alleyways where boys could experiment with tobacco and watch "fallen" men and women come and go. Sensing drama in them, Edwin's imaginative world began to be peopled with some of these strange, sad figures haunting Gardiner's streets. Any odd person—miser, drunk, hermit—the one who was different, or who lived in a state of separateness from ordinary people—had the compassionate eye of this boy upon them long before he ever put them down as portraits in stories or poems. Though his first try at writing was to be in story form, it was poetry he really was ambitious to write. As a very young child he had discovered in Bryant's *Library of Poetry and Song* Edgar Allan Poe's "The Raven," and the drama and language of this poem had greatly excited his imagination. In and out of books he early appreciated the effectiveness of language. In the house of two neighborhood children, Gus and Alice Jordan, whose father was a sea captain, tales of adventure abounded told in words somewhat less genteel than those used in his own parlor. During the happy, carefree hours he occasionally spent in listening and play-acting in the Jordan home, 'Win Robinson enlarged and enriched his vocabulary. No one had to tell this boy that his most famous ancestor was a poet for him to begin to build a poet's vocabulary. The instinct was already there.

Mary Robinson soon began to realize that like Dean, her youngest son was different from other boys. The middle son, Herman, was outgoing, popular, "a chip off the old block" people said; of the three boys he was his father's favorite and seemed most likely to succeed in the world. Edwin showed no particular inclination to do anything except wander about on the streets, read, or sit alone dreaming. He much preferred books to people. As his father frowned upon the idea of any son of his becoming a scholar, Mrs. Robinson worried about Edwin's future—what *could* such a boy do to earn a living? In later years Edwin

Arlington Robinson was to say "I could never have done anything but write poetry." In his youth it took a long time before he dared confide his aspiration; Dean's example had taught him that it was best to keep to himself those things most sacred to his inner life.

Innately honest, gentle, unquarrelsome, and filled with intense love of family, the pain of being slighted, teased, or misunderstood by Dean or Herman would plunge young Edwin into darkest melancholy. Yet he never failed in loyalty to his brothers, allying himself to them in all causes, theirs, not his. Whatever the family quarrel, it was always he who found or tried to find the way to draw together those he loved. In the end he was to come face to face at home with a true New England drama in which faith and love would be sharply tested, and the sad disintegration of an American family become a young poet's tragic inheritance. In the early years he thought the strength of his love could heal all wounds but his own.

With compassion as well as self-interest Edwin silently watched as his brother Dean was being forced to confront reality. Still bookish and idealistic at age twenty, Dean, throughout his undergraduate years at Bowdoin had kept up a running argument with his father that a college degree ought not to be evaluated in terms only of dollars and cents. Mr. Robinson, who had made his way up in the business world without benefit of an education, insisted that he was not paying for pure scholarship, that Dean must choose a profession guaranteed to bring in a good living. Poets, dreamers, idealists could not, he said, exist in the real world. Dean had finally compromised by taking up medicine in the belief that it at least was a humanitarian profession. His father stubbornly refused, however, to see him through to advanced studies in medical research. In 1881 Dean graduated cum laude from Bowdoin and went directly into practice. He seemed not fated for happiness. A Gardiner girl to whom he had become engaged before he went off to work as a city physician in Camden, Maine, died while he was away. In mounting despair and frustration at a life already turned sour, the young doctor tried to lose himself in his work. He contracted neuralgia from over exposure while making night calls in Maine's icy winter weather, and to ease the pain began treating himself to doses of morphine. By 1890 Mr. Robinson's storybook house on Lincoln Avenue would be hiding its first disgrace and failure. The debate between dollars and ideals had claimed a victim whose suffering young Edwin Arlington Robinson beheld with mingled pity and terror.

While Dean's star descended, Herman's was rising. Most popular boy in Gardiner High School, upon his graduation Herman went immediately to work in his father's bank as an assistant cashier. Carefully schooled in all the tricks of the trade—deals, loans, investments—by age twenty he became western representative for the bank, so successful in matters of finance that all of his family's financial affairs were being entrusted to him. By age twenty-four Herman was publicized nationally as "a young man who from early boyhood has been connected with the financial interest of the country." In silk hat and fashionable coat, a handsome figure of a man (his father's pride and joy), he traveled west and east dealing in real estate and staggering sums running high into millions. Edward Robinson felt it safe to retire.

The sad experience with Dean prompted the father to see to it that Edwin, at high school, took no courses leading toward college. He set Herman up as example, saying the sensible thing to do was to plunge straightaway into the business world. "Long Robinson" the boy was being called now. He had shot up suddenly and was anguished by being too much noticed for his awkward posture. That his facial features had extraordinary beauty and sensitivity didn't help him to feel better about himself. He showed little interest in formal studies, gave his teachers and everyone else the impression that he was "born lazy." His closest associates at school were readers, thinkers, like himself; unlike him they were being directed toward college by their parents. With his mind already dead-set against going into business of any kind, Long Robinson faced the unhappy prospect not only of being left behind by his friends, but—unless he could quickly prove himself a poet—ending up like other Gardiner misfits with no place to go except down the street.

This problem troubled Robinson more than anyone around him at the time realized. He was never one to brood aloud about his personal difficulties. His mother knew now and sympathized with his poetic leaning but would say nothing to encourage it thinking it boded ill for his future. It made her particularly uneasy to see him taking up with Dr. Alanson Tucker Schumann, a man much older than himself and one of Gardiner's "characters." Apparently rich enough not to continue the practice of medicine, Dr. Schumann had abandoned it for three non-medical hobbies: writing poetry, swearing, and drinking. He was, nevertheless, a respected charter member of the Gardiner Poetry Society. To Long Robinson genial Dr. Schumann was a guide and counselor—al-

most a lifesaver in a town where few could understand that a boy of
fifteen was already seriously committed to an art. As the doctor's protégé,
he became the Poetry Society's youngest member, but never allowed
his youth to let lesser talents than his own sway his course. "He was
very determined," the society's secretary remembered years later. "He had
his own notions, he was one of those persons whom you cannot influence
ever, he went his own way."

In his high school years, the young poet experimented with ballads,
villanelles, blank verse, developing as early as his sophomore year the
idea of recording for posterity in-depth portraits of certain local personages
whose lives were dramatic exposures of broken dreams. The "Tilbury
Town" he was one day to make famous was real enough for him as
he wandered from day to day on the streets of Gardiner observing the
"down and outs," the lost and the damned. He saw these people not
for how they had ended up, but for how they must have begun, dreamers
—like Dean, like himself—having to cope with a world that was too strong
for their fragility, that left them no where to go for solace except into
fantasy. Reading Shakespeare, he asked himself why it was that, in most
literature, society's tragic heroes were always of the aristocracy—kings
and princes. Were there none, then, among ordinary people? Did not
Gardiner's cast of commonplace characters deserve a poet to point up
their dreams of glory, their fatal flaws, and downfalls? He read the
English poets, Milton, Browning, Wordsworth—and decided not to imi-
tate. He had a light of his own. And a land of his own.

He was living in times when economic panics like that of '77
overnight had swept once powerful men into the dust; when men were
torn between puritanical ideals deeply imbued and the temptation of gold;
when towns like Gardiner were filling up with New England workmen
already beginning to lose the adeptness of their forefathers to eke a
living out of their own land by individual labor. It seemed to him
Hamlet suffered "outrageous fortune" no more than did a tradesman's
son who spent his days wandering in the alleyways of a New England
manufacturing town looking for causes that destroyed his happiness and
that of his family.

Many years later, describing Captain Craig wandering "patch-clad
through the streets" Edwin Arlington Robinson, in his famous poem of
that name, went on to say "A few . . . found somehow the spark in
him." More likely there were not "a few" but only one who found that
spark; a boy shy in the presence of girls, tongue-tied in the presence of

the ladies of the Poetry Society, blundering at school, overshadowed at home but able to communicate with suffering humanity—stranger and brother alike. That odd boy—Long Robinson—was perfectly comfortable "on paper," at ease when composing a familiar world and peopling it with the funny, the sad, the colorful relics of society for whom he *could* find his voice. Unknown then to "Tilbury Town" its artist was working secretly in a small garretlike room in a house that no longer sang rowdy marches and valentine-and-lace love songs.

> *Life was a dream of heaven for us once*
> *And has the dream gone by?*

Yes, for Dean was fighting the furies upstairs, and Herman already showing signs of the alcohol addiction that soon was to be his ruin. The young poet looking on, knowing he too would be one of the off-beat characters he had to draw, determined he was also the child he had to save.

> *. . . neither parted roads nor cent per cent*
> *May starve quite out the child that lives in us—*
> *The Child that is the Man, the Mystery,*
> *The Phoenix of the World.*

Already in possession of his subject when he graduated from high school in 1888, Long Robinson was granted one last summer to spend before having to face up to the realities of a commercial world. As if to flaunt beauty in his eyes as a last piece of mockery before youth's dreams were snatched from him, that summer at Booth Bay Harbor was an idyllic one by the sea where for the first time he saw the face and spirit of love—Emma Shepherd. Even her name was a poem to him. She was twenty-three, he eighteen. Emma was not only beautiful, she had the grace to listen patiently while he read to her his poems, the wisdom to recognize something in them and in his character too, that was special and rare. Long Robinson's feeling for Emma Shepherd was also rare. He loved her "not for her face, but for something fairer— something diviner."

> *I love the spirit—the human something*
> *that seemed to chime with my own condition,*
> *And make soul music . . .*

For a few marvelous days he had Emma all to himself. They sat talking together on the rocks, walked along the beach, he too shy to say anything of the emotion filling his heart. Then suddenly walks and talks came to an end. A newcomer was taking up all of her attention, a man "with news of nations in his talk/And something royal in his walk"— none other than his brother, Herman. A brief whirlwind courtship on the rocks by the sea and Herman succeeded in winning Emma Shepherd's yes to a proposal of marriage. It has been said by one of Robinson's biographers that that "yes" left to the poet a lifelong anguish. If so, the tension of this first loss was not without benefit, for it furnished the emotional climate out of which art is so often deepened and enriched.

In the fall Long Robinson returned to "Tilbury Town" and began to live with himself as he would always be—a lonely outsider, committed only to becoming a better poet in order to draw the kind of world that was shutting him out. That first winter he worked on the Kennebec River as a timekeeper for ice harvesters; rising at dawn, he would walk to work before the rest of the town was awake hearing his own footsteps sound loud on the lonely sidewalks as he went steadily downhill. Spirits and ghosts kept him company, speaking their way into the poetry he was harvesting to river and back. There was drama enough for many ballads: an ailing old man (his father) with all glories behind him, senile, barely aware that Herman's rash speculations in the market were dwindling the family fortune, spending his time now rocking on the front porch or in the parlor, seeing flitting images everywhere to confirm his belief in spiritualism; Brother Dean discovering in Emma Shepherd when Herman brought her home for bride, beauty he could never possess; and himself—Long Robinson—a shadowy figure in the window-seat at night, playing a sad clarinet—*Abide with Me*—scaring the cat and himself too, then taking up his pen to see if he couldn't do better with a more familiar instrument as he scratched away at a sonnet.

There were days when Robinson thought he ought to leave Gardiner, find a college somewhere that would take him in. But his father's condition and Dean's left him the single man at home to help his mother take care of things. Herman was off in the West somewhere, once again investing family savings—perilously, as it turned out. From time to time Dean, desperate for money, would go off to weigh ice down at Smith-town. So, for the youngest son, college had to be postponed. But that sonnet he had been working on got into print. "Thalia" it was called,

published in the Gardiner *Reporter Monthly* March 3, 1890, settling
once and for all Edwin Arlington Robinson's stubborn sense of destiny:

> I realized finally . . . that I was doomed, or elected, or sentenced for
> life to the writing of poetry. . . . I kept the grisly secret to my-
> self. . . . My father died two years later without suspecting it. Before
> the family fortune went to smash, I could see it going and could see
> myself setting out alone on what was inevitably to be a long and
> foggy voyage.

A voyage which took him nowhere, physically, the next two years except
around the house and around the "farm" (orchard and kitchen-garden
in which he did most of the work), and down the street with Dr.
Schumann to tavern or confabs with other addicts to the muse. He seemed
to lack any ambition to see a life away from Gardiner now, *homeness*
sinking into him doubly—as a necessity because everything in the family
was "going to smash," and (as for Hawthorne and Emily Dickinson
before him) as the best place for obscure, struggling poets to work.
There were lines from Longfellow's "Song" which he now and then
quoted to himself (in those days it was not fashionable to "put down"
Longfellow): "Stay, stay at home, my heart, and rest;/ Home-keeping
hearts are happiest." But not once in those anguishing years could he
truthfully say that he was able, in the words of Edna St. Vincent Millay,
to put aside despair to drink happiness like bread. Whenever he heard
about a former classmate at Gardiner High reaching the pinnacle of
some profession, he bored down deeper into his shell so as not to hear
tales that by implication meant *he* could be crowned king of *unsuccess*.
The only friends he cared about were no longer in Gardiner—away
at college, or married. Lonelier than he had ever been in his life, he
reminded them that "a letter from a friend is an event in my life."
Once, out of compassion, a friend hinted that trying to depend on
income from anonymous poems and waiting for recognition as a poet
especially in the age in which they were living was perilous. Yes, "dollars
are convenient things to have," Robinson mused, "but this diabolical
dirty race that men are running after them disgusts me. I shall probably
outgrow this idea, but until I do I shall labor quite contented under
the delusion that there is something to life outside of business. Business
be damned."

Queer duck, that Robinson. Over his head in ideals, reading Thoreau
and agreeing that most men live lives of quiet desperation—even poets.
When money got too scarce, he took temporary work on the river and

"a devilish cold job it is, too." So cold it almost got him to cursing the literary ambition which made him suffer through that "hell." "Poetry," he said bitterly, "is a good thing provided a man is warm enough."

When he wasn't writing, he occupied himself with reading: Omar Khayam's quatrains, Keats, Bret Harte (he convinced himself that "Outcasts of Poker Flat" was the best short story in the language); and Carlyle's *Sartor Resartus*, becoming "soaked with its fiery philosophy." Kipling was already a favorite poet from whom he learned much to aid him in the unadorned style he was attempting in his own work, but it was not until now that he discovered Thomas Hardy, that great giant of poetry and prose who also was singing the tragedy of the commonplace and the common man. *The Mayor of Casterbridge* (as later *Jude the Obscure*) was a revelation to him. "I never would have supposed," he said, "that a writer of such power could achieve so little popularity." While it was discouraging to learn that so distinguished a writer as Hardy was struggling to get noticed, Hardy's method of recording the lives of his Dorset neighbors and placing them within the boundaries of a geographical area only faintly disguised as "Wessex" inspired Edwin Arlington Robinson of Maine to keep on re-creating his familiar surroundings in Gardiner as "Tilbury Town"—in making poetry of the commonplace. As the months rolled on his notebooks swelled with poems, some of them sailing out and staying overlong at magazines, or getting printed "for nothing." Meanwhile "Tilbury Town" neighbors were looking askance at him as if noticing for the first time he wasn't "getting anywhere" not "doing anything," at least nothing that they could see.

> . . . occasionally someone says, "Well, now, Robinson, what do you intend to do?" This makes me mad. I cannot tell what I shall do . . . I thought I might go to Harvard in the fall for a year or two, but as I am not sure of it I do not say so when these pleasant people question me . . . I suppose it does look a little queer to see me practically doing nothing at my age [he was now twenty-two] but at present there is no getting out of it. Someone must be at home to run the place . . . I try to console myself with Blackmore's lines: "The more we have in hand to count/The less we have to hope for." There is a good deal in that if you will stop to moralize a little; but the devil of it is, while we are moralizing someone else gets what we hope for. This is a sad world . . . where the underdog gets his neck chewed.

He had a fierce pride, almost as great as his ambition. Brooding about his "failure thus far to accomplish anything or to be anybody in the world," he would say, "Until I feel that I am independent, 'a man among men' I shall not have much peace. My pride is almost unnatural and sometimes I wonder if it is not killing me by inches." But as he was to say in his poem, "Matthias at the Door":

> *All things that are worth having are perilous,*
> *And have their resident devil, respectively.*
> *. . . there's love, pride, art,*
> *Humility, ambition, pride and glory,*
> *The kingdom itself, which may come out all right,*
> *And truth. They are all very perilous,*
> *And Admirable, so long as there is in them*
> *Passion that knows itself—which, if not hushed,*
> *Is a wise music.*

And so, continuing to make his "wise music" because he believed so passionately in himself, he kept on at his snail-like life in which he was also general handyman for his family. "My time is now pretty well taken up with farming, and I am raising a giant harvest of cucumbers, cauliflowers, onions and God knows what more in the prolific garden of my mind. That is the only garden in which I have not succeeded in raising anything thus far in my life, but I have hopes that I may plant a seed before long that will take root and bring forth something." As fall approached, this "horny-handed son of toil," as he called himself, was wheeling wood ("and the worst kind of wood at that . . . full of splinters and conducive to all sorts of swear words") and reaping in a harvest of apples from the orchard. ("I never could find any poetry in gathering apples. It is the worst work I know of except washing dishes and listening to a debate.") No longer as patient as formerly, he often got into "grouches" and "doubts" and began to wonder if the six hens he owned weren't wiser than he. "They are saying something down there behind the barn that I can't understand, and for some reason they are making me think of the whole scheme of life and of its final outcome. A man is more than a hen, but a hen knows something of which a man knows nothing. I'll bet they know more about the weather than all men and women in the world."

Paddling down-street even through the rain to get a plug of tobacco, he was becoming daily more attuned to the gallery of characters accompanying him indoors and out. He thought he had found a style of verse suitable for their lives and their environment somewhat after Thoreau's description of poetry as "healthy speech." His poems must

never ring false, must come alive with man's true voice. He must catch
the ironic laughter, the pity and pain. Joy, too, if it was to be found.

What he *had* found was his method. As if on to a small stage, he
the creator, the poet, brought out his cast of characters, sometimes in
pairs, sometimes starkly alone to say in a few lines a great deal about
the human condition, a great deal about the place and time that en-
compassed his moment for making a mark upon it. As in "Amaryllis":

> *Once, when I wandered in the woods alone,*
> *An old man tottered up to me and said,*
> *"Come, friend, and see the grave that I have made*
> *for Amaryllis." There was in the tone*
> *Of his complaint such quaver and such moan*
> *That I took pity on him and obeyed,*
> *And long stood looking where his hands had laid*
> *An ancient woman, shrunk to skin and bone.*
>
> *Far out beyond the forest I could hear*
> *The calling of loud progress, and the bold*
> *Incessant scream of commerce ringing clear;*
> *But though the trumpets of the world were glad,*
> *It made me lonely and it made me sad*
> *To think that Amaryllis had grown old.*

For this poem Robinson discarded the precise rhyme structure as
then so commonly used in poetry sold to the magazines. His sonnet
had to have the same kind of power as that world beyond the forest
where "loud progress" was the order of the day. The old was dying,
the new was here. The reality must be faced even if it made the poet
lonely and sad. There were lots of towns like Gardiner in America.
"Tilbury Town" was not the only one with people mourning lost values,
with streets harboring the lost and the damned, with once proud houses
graying and falling into decay. But *this* Tilbury Town was the one the
poet knew best, he was its "Watchman" as Hawthorne had been the
Watchman of Salem. He knew its miser who had "eyes like little dollars
in the dark":

> *Year after year he shambled through the town,*
> *A loveless exile moving with a staff;*
> *And oftentimes there crept into his ears*
> *A sound of alien pity, touched with tears,—*
> *And then (and only then) did Aaron laugh.*

Knew its "Richard Cory" who "glittered when he walked . . . rich, yes, richer than a king" yet went "one calm summer night . . . and put a bullet through his head." And best of all knew "Old King Cole" whose "two disastrous heirs . . . made music more than ever three did."

The more Robinson worked in his method the more he felt it was right for Gardiner—Gardiner with its misty mornings and shadowy exits and entrances; its pathways to respectable gardens enclosed by neat fences, to trade streets where the bank was morning's hope and evening's disappointment, to sidestreet shabby hotels and ill-lit bars, to a river captured for industry, turned for profit; also to the woods lying just beyond where a shaft of inviting light on wilder paths inward offered cool escape. The Gardiner which had schooled him and neglected him was now become his poetic kingdom for lovers and clowns, wisemen and fools, for Flammonde, "the Prince of Castaways" and Damaris and Annandale—

But as time went on, instinct told Robinson he ought to get a distance away from his subject, at least for a while; ought to try himself in a broader world of intellect.

> The truth is, I have lived in Gardiner for nearly twenty two years and, metaphorically speaking, hardly been out of the yard. Now this is not right; the process tends to widen one's thought, or rather sympathies, to an unwholesome extent . . . Solitude (in the broad sense of the word) tends to magnify one's ideas of individuality; it sharpens his sympathy for failure where fate has been abused . . . in short, this living alone is bad business; and I have had more than my share of it.

There was ample excuse for going to Boston. An overzealous teacher had once cuffed him on the ear when he was a boy, and recurring pain indicated now the need of examination and treatment. But it required a tremendous leap forward in courage for him to knock at the gate of Harvard College while there. He had once written to a former high school friend lucky enough to be a collegian, ". . . keep on with your pedagogic work and go through college if you can, and sometime when you are strolling around the campus after twilight, alone . . . you may think of the fellow down east who never seemed to amount to much in school (or anywhere else) but who was prone to believe that he was not altogether a nincompoop." It was hard now, after all this time, to visualize himself strolling around any campus, but as Harvard surprised him by accepting him as a special student, all he could say was, "I expect it will seem rather odd at first, but I trust I shall get used to the new life in a few weeks."

Like Robert Frost after him, Robinson did not take too well to formal academic subjects. Unable to concentrate on anything more than his own creations, he submitted poems so different in style and approach from those usually printed in college publications that not many found favor with the editors-in-chief. But they did win him entree to campus literary fellows whose bull sessions made college life almost bearable. Harvard, he said, was "a great place to set a man's thoughts going." By the end of the first year, however, he was so homesick even his pipe, he told a friend "tasted lonesome." To make matters worse, an operation on the bad ear not only interrupted his studies but didn't succeed in relieving the pain which played havoc with his nerves. To solace himself he tried large doses of French novels and Massachusetts whiskey, but nothing seemed to aid his grades or his longing for familiar old Gardiner. By summer 1893 the poet was ready to pack up and go home. His two years at Harvard had not been altogether a waste, however. "I have seen things that I could not possibly see at any other place and have a different conception of what is good and bad in life" he conceded. As for poetry, it was obvious that Gardiner, not Boston or Harvard College was the landscape and the teacher he needed.

But to go home to live with his mother at age twenty-four and continue on in the same old pattern as before also had its problems. Once again the neighbors had cause to gape from their windows and wonder what that youngest Robinson—the one who had been to Harvard College—was good for. Some even ventured to offer advice as to opportunities the business world presented for an educated man. The impractical young poet was hard-put to explain why he wasn't good at making money like everyone else. "One of my greatest misfortunes," said the woeful Robinson, "is the total inability to admire the so-called successful men who are pointed out to poor devils like me as examples to follow and revere. If Merchant A and Barrister B are put here as 'examples to mortals' I am afraid that I shall always stand in the shadows as one of Omar's broken pots." An unbroken faith that he would yet prove himself to be somebody was all that kept him going.

Daily he wrote and rewrote his poems, working four hours a day and often satisfied only after a fourth or fifth version was completed. Throughout 1894 he was sending out poems at a fast and furious pace but still not making an impression or money. It was, he said later, a hard apprenticeship, and so quiet in his writer's underground world that even "the expectation of a returned manuscript is better than no excitement at all." To his mother, to himself, and to all his critics looking on, it seemed likely that he would be living from hand to mouth all the days of his life. Yet he refused to lose hope or give up.

> One peculiar thing in my make-up is that I don't seem to have any capacity for discouragement. I have done a few things which I know are worthwhile and that is a great deal to be sure of. If printed lines are good for anything they are bound to be picked up some time; and then, if some poor devil of a man or woman feels any better or any stronger for anything that I have said, I shall have no fault to find with the scheme or anything in it. I am inclined to be a trifle solemn in my verses, but I intend that there shall always be at least a suggestion of something wiser than hatred and something better than despair.

Which was not to say that his pride didn't suffer while he waited for success. From year to year his cry was similar to the one in 1896. "You don't know what it is to be twenty-six years old, and still a little child as far as a prospect of worldly independence goes." In all the annals of New England authorship, not even Hawthorne's or Robert Frost's seem comparable to the heartache of Edwin Arlington Robinson stubbornly refusing to be anything but a poet. After reading *The Marble Faun* and learning that it had cost Hawthorne five years of work to write it, Robinson pointed out that it was the kind of labor "of which the modern inkspiller has no conception. When I leave Hawthorne for my own poor, patient manuscript," he said, "I feel very foolish indeed, but I get over that and go pegging away, sometimes a page at a time without any trouble, sometimes spending an hour over a dozen words."

The "poor, patient manuscript" to which he referred he had begun in the spring of 1894 as "some ninety lines of a queer poem" titled "The Night Before." A tragic monologue written in unrhymed tetrameters, it was to grow into his first major work. Its plot was founded on what he called a system of "opposites," that is, "creating a fictitious life in direct opposition to a real life which I know." "To show that men and women are individuals" was his major intention with a minor injunction running through it "not to thump a man too hard when he is down." This statement written while the work was still in progress in 1895 serves well as an introduction to most of Edwin Arlington Robinson's poetry. Poem after poem during the years that followed, whether short or long, would have in it something of

> *I tell you, Domine*
> *There are times in the lives of us poor devils*
> *When heaven and hell get mixed.*

In 1896 his own life was a prime example. At the very moment when one of his uncles agreed to finance privately the publication of "The Night Before" including other poems selected for the poet's first volume, tragedy struck. His mother, Mary Robinson, fell victim to the "Black Death" as diphtheria was commonly called in those days. So fearful of contagion was the community that no one would come near the stricken woman except her three sons. Even after her death the brothers had the heartbreaking task of dressing and burying their dead, for the undertaker refused his services. Embittered by this experience, the poet momentarily came to believe that any world was better than this one. "She has gone ahead and I am glad for her," he said. He had wished her to live to see him a professional poet, but the printed volumes of *The Torrent and The Night Before* arrived too late for him to put into her hands the one gift he had always wanted to give her.

First volumes are almost always on unsure footing, but a first volume self-published and poorly publicized seldom meets with anything but disaster. *The Torrent and The Night Before* was no exception. Three hundred and twelve paper-bound copies printed at a cost of fifty-two dollars soon rested roped and unopened in the room of the author who had not the heart to pay attention to them after his mother's death. Eventually a few found their way into the hands of Robinson's Gardiner and Harvard friends, while others went to selected newspaper and magazine critics to examine. The poet dedicated the book "To any man, woman or critic who will cut the edges of it—I have done the top." But though he had one or two hopeful comments, including a request for his photograph from a Bangor newspaper, on the whole, as he said, his brain child had "fizzled." Locally, however, it had the effect of bringing him the kind of publicity that made the neighbors understand better what he was up to, and also initiated an interest in him on the part of one of Gardiner's most prominent families.

Laura E. Richards, author, and daughter of Julia Ward Howe, lived in a romantic, suburban manor house called "Oaklands," which Robinson had often admired from a distance as a boy. Her husband, Henry, was

Emily Dickinson. This photographic likeness, probably taken in 1847, is the only one that exists.

The Dickinson house in Amherst, Massachusetts.

Edwin Arlington Robinson, at his high school graduation, 1888.

Edwin Arlington Robinson. Portrait by Lilla Cabot Perry, 1916.

Edna St. Vincent Millay, 1914.

Camden, Maine, a jewel by the
sea, where Edna Millay lived as
a girl and wrote "Renascence."

Edna St. Vincent Millay being
escorted to prison for picketing
for Sacco and Vanzetti.

Robert Frost, 1896.

*Robert Frost
at Franconia, New Hampshire,
1915.*

The farmer-poet in Vermont, 1921.

the son of an old-line Gardiner family, owners of a prospering paper mill. The Richards had known Edwin's father through his position at the bank, and Herman too, for that athletic young man had participated as an oarsman in a river crew organized by Henry Richards. But not until now did the youngest of the Robinsons come within close range. In a note reminiscent of one which the Peabody sisters had sent to lure Hawthorne out of *his* nested-in dwelling, Laura Richards, forewarned of Long Robinson's anti-social ways, now tried to tempt him to Oaklands —"Prithee, good Hermit Thrush, come out of thy thicket."

The embarrassed Robinson waited a few days before denying that he was a hermit thrush, then a few more to summon up the courage to sally forth on his first visit to the famous writer and her family. From that time forth, as long as he remained in Gardiner, "Oaklands" became another place for the poet to go when he felt like wandering down the street. Now, with his newly acquired glasses, black umbrella, and polished manners, he looked almost comically another "Duke of Puddlecock." But inwardly he was the same old shy fellow, so uncomfortable among "literati" gatherings at the Richards that he was grateful for the three dogs belonging to the family who one by one, as if recognizing another mute in the parlor, would obligingly "put their heads upon my knees and give my hands something to do." On one occasion he arrived at Oaklands to find himself the sole visitor with none of the elders at home, only the two pretty young daughters of the house. At a loss for conversation, and inwardly terrified at his predicament, he never forgot how one of the family dogs came forward to have its ears scratched, all the while "looking at me in a way that implied, 'Go ahead, you're getting along first rate.'"

But just when it looked as if he might get used to being sociable, his visits to the Richards came to an end. After his mother's death, Herman, Emma and their children came to live in the decaying house on Lincoln street and the poet decided the time had come for him to leave his Gardiner thicket forever. By now most of the family fortune was gone, and Herman wrecked amid his fallen empire. Ironically it was the impractical Edwin who soberly tied up loose financial ends and helped settle his parents' dwindled estate. After a sale of property, there remained to each son a scant few hundred dollars. Hoping to reshape his brother Dean's sad life, the poet encouraged him to use his inheritance to set himself up as a pharmacist.

He helped Dean establish a drug store, and when it seemed well

on the way decided it was time to take off for New York to set up a
new life of his own. To Emma Shepherd Robinson, who through the
years had remained his friend, and who had never stopped believing
him, he said before leaving: "I don't expect to live to be forty; whatever
I do has got to be done soon." To everyone else in Gardiner, and
especially those who had not believed in him, his farewell had a familiar
ring: "The shame I win for singing is all mine,/The gold I miss for
dreaming is all yours."

Approaching thirty, the king of "unsuccess" entered the biggest city
of all with his usual ingenuous self-confidence. "I am thankful that I
cannot *see* a life of failure before me. When I picture it to myself
there is a dim vision of something that renders it impossible for me
to wholly give up the fight." But the dim vision did not grow brighter
for years to come. Half starving in New York, rich only in the few
friends waiting in the wings to help when even his pride had to be put
aside, he at last was forced for mere subsistence to work at something
else besides poetry. He took a job in "hell"—the first subway being
built in New York—earning twenty cents an hour for a ten-hour day.
Meanwhile some prose sketches he had written to ward off hunger were
returned "with curt comment" (his description), while a poem "The
House on the Hill" was accepted, but published without payment by
a small magazine that offered him a year's subscription instead. "Apparently they didn't want to pay for my shoes," Robinson wryly told
a friend. A sonnet addressed to Poe brought him a scant seven dollars
and one giant-sized poem, "Captain Craig" went on a tragicomic journey
from publisher to publisher, getting accepted at last by an editor who
promptly lost it—the only copy in existence. When it was found again
after having languished some months unnoticed in a brothel it landed
back in Robinson's possession with the explanation that the company
had meanwhile lost interest in it. To the resigned author his poor
battered "Captain Craig" seemed as doomed as the original on whom
he had based his tale: "I doubt if ten men in all Tilbury Town had
ever shaken hands with him or called him by his name, or looked at
him so curiously or so unconcernedly as they had looked at ashes."

Yet the inextinguishable faith of Edwin Arlington Robinson, who
would not commit his manuscripts to ashes, held a light to the spirits
of those who cared for him. "A howling optimist" he called himself,
while in the shadows of towering buildings and in the din of turn-of-the-
century uproar he trudged along narrow streets and measured himself

against lesser literary lights then making names for themselves in Gotham. Below ground in the subway he was poet of the damned; above ground he had to wonder if America would ever have a poet-king to sing its turbulent times as Whitman had, or if America cared enough for poetry to crown any king it found. "The age is all right," he said, "material progress is all right, Herbert Spencer is all right, hell is all right. These things are temporal necessities, but they are damned uninteresting to one who can get a glimpse of the real light through the clouds of time . . . what I am after is the courage to see that every man has it in his power to overcome whatever obstacles may be in his way . . . for all my long lean face I never gave up and I never shall give up."

With this Puritan doctrine to warm him as he wandered through Manhattan, he saw better the Maine town of his origin and the influence upon his character of New England verities. In melting-pot New York he could meet at any tavern the by-products of American culture who wandered, as he did, into places of common loneliness to unburden themselves of healthy speech. And understanding them, he could give "the tribute of a tempered ear/To an untempered eloquence."

The poetry Robinson was able to make of this untempered eloquence —though yet unrecognized—was in keeping with the general trend of prose in the early 1900s which, under author-editor William Dean Howell's influence, was abandoning "romantic nonsense" for real life or *réalisme*, as the French called it. Realism, said Howells, "is nothing more and nothing less than the truthful treatment of material." No poet was more adept at truthful treatment than Robinson himself, but what was good for prose didn't seem acceptable yet in poetry. Still, it was inevitable that as more and more novelists responded to the call for realism the day was at hand when poets who believed as Robinson did that "Nothing that God has made is contemptible" would also be recognized as new voices speaking for the times. On another score, too, he was in time for what he hoped to do. The center of power in the publishing business had gradually shifted from Boston to New York. Books were "booming" and pressure groups throughout the country were pushing state laws for free libraries of which, by 1900, there was some 1700. Clever-tongued "Mr. Dooley" quipped that these "were for the dead authors and that live authors stood outside and wished they were dead," but numerous signs pointed to better days ahead. A few poets were being noticed while Robinson impatiently waited his turn: Edwin Markham, William Vaughn Moody, James Whitcomb Riley; and such Victorian poets as Edmund

Clarence Stedman, Bayard Taylor and T. B. Aldrich were still popular. One New England author, hailing from Robinson's own state of Maine was more justifiably noticed—the prose poet Sarah Orne Jewett.

Daughter of a South Berwick doctor, she had published her first story in the *Atlantic Monthly* in 1869, the year of Robinson's birth. It was well received and, on the advice of the editor, William Dean Howells, the twenty-year-old author collected a number of similar stories, all of regional New England to be published in 1877 under the title *Deephaven*. With the declining popularity of novelist Harriet Beecher Stowe, Miss Jewett (she was never to marry) was well on her way to becoming the bright new star on the New England horizon. *The Country of the Pointed Firs* (1896) is still considered by many critics to be the best piece of regional fiction to have come out of nineteenth-century America. It depicts with tenderness and insight a dying generation in Maine, unlike Robinson's work in that it touches upon the retained faith and quaint folkways of old-timers who continued to cling to village coastal life long after "loud progress" had passed them by. Like Robinson, Sarah Orne Jewett's portrait eye and poetic sensibility had compassion for those grown old or neglected. Her Maine characters have the odor of pine and sea; his of city streets and taverns. Their total world traces the dilemma of New England's past, present, and future meeting head on. Some in the region are sturdy and survive; others go out with the tide never to return. Of those who have gone away leaving the shell of their decayed environment behind, Robinson starkly makes us see their "House on the Hill."

> They are all gone away,
>   The house is shut and still,
> There is nothing more to say.
>
> Through broken walls and gray
>   The winds blow bleak and shrill:
> They are all gone away.

while Miss Jewett's *Deephaven* reveals

> . . . that fireless, empty, forsaken house where the winter sun shines in and creeps slowly along the floor; the bitter cold is in and around the house, and the snow has sifted in at every crack; outside it is untrodden by any living creature's footstep. The wind blows and rushes and shakes the loose window-sashes in their frames, while the padlock knocks—knocks against the door.

Her star was blazing while Robinson struggled in obscurity. There is no record that the shock of recognition united them at any point, but the Miss Jewett who helped Willa Cather define *her* regional world would surely have aided Robinson had he entered her orbit. "Write to the human heart, the great consciousness that all humanity goes to make up," had been her advice to Willa Cather. "You can write about life, but never write life itself." This was the subtlety that had transformed her own realistic world into prose art. When Sarah Orne Jewett died in 1909 her rediscovered life in *The Country of the Pointed Firs* was already destined to be temporarily swamped in the flood of new-wave literature, but Edwin Arlington Robinson's Tilbury Town poems would keep Maine alive in a way not too remote from her own.

The turn for him began quietly enough when a Harvard friend advanced him the money to see through the press two more volumes of poems. *The Children of the Night* (1897) and the formerly ill-fated *Captain Craig* (1902) initiated a flurry of favorable response from critics but still not enough to get the author out of frayed clothing. One review in the *Bookman* which described Robinson's poetic world as a "prison house" got his back up a little. The critic was putting him down, he thought "because I don't dance on an illuminated hilltop and sing about the bobolinks and bumblebees." The scene of his poetic world, he said, was *not* a prison house but "a kind of spiritual kindergarten where millions of bewildered infants are trying to spell God with the wrong blocks."

As things turned out it was a reader, not a critic, who succeeded in turning the nation's eyes in Edwin Arlington Robinson's direction. Kermit Roosevelt, son of Theodore, was introduced to *The Children of the Night* through a classmate—one of the Richards boys Robinson had known in Gardiner. Young Roosevelt was so moved by what he read that he solicited his father's aid for the struggling, still hungry poet. In 1905, as President of the United States, Theodore Roosevelt responded by lifting Edwin Arlington Robinson out of the New York subway into the New York Custom House (apparently—as witness Hawthorne and Melville—American Presidents thought custom houses ideal places for authors in distress), but the President told Robinson, "I want you to understand that I expect you to think poetry first and customs second."

The big jump from being "nobody" to President's protégé was almost too much for the astonished Robinson. Overnight, publishers who had once turned him down were scurrying to put his work within covers. Two months after his appointment by the President, Scribner's reprinted *The Children of the Night* and Robinson's long night of neglect was over. He was thirty-six years old.

The honors that continued to pour in upon the poet from that moment until the day of his death in 1935 he took with almost ironic indifference. In his Harvard days he had admitted that "the sight of success awakens a feeling painfully approaching envy, and I am inclined too much to look upon its achievement as a kind of destiny," but once destiny was realized his major satisfaction was expressed in the quiet statement: "It is the triumph of my life to know that I am good for something." As Gardiner's most famous son, it gave him great pride to be able to donate in Dean's name (his brother had died in 1899) a research laboratory to a local hospital. The day was to come when a plaque in his own memory would be placed on the Gardiner Common, but the most treasured relationship the poet had to his hometown was his periodic visits with Emma and her children—three of them—whom he adored and by whom he was adored in return. Ruth, Emma's youngest daughter grew up to buy and maintain in its original condition the Head Tide house in which her uncle had been born.

In 1922 a British collection introduced Edwin Arlington Robinson abroad. That same year Yale University awarded him an Honorary Doctor of Letters degree. *The Man Who Died Twice* took the Pulitzer prize in 1924. Bowdoin College also awarded him an honorary degree in 1926. *Tristram* a true best seller in poetry, won for him another Pulitzer prize in 1927. But the poet had too long walked alone to become, as he said, "swell-headed," or to exchange his small retinue of devoted friends for a more decorative court. He still looked the Duke of Puddle-cock with his high forehead, receding hairline, spotless spectacles, neatly trimmed mustache and walking cane; but those who knew him best found him as unworldly as ever. He had once said that one of the most terrible things in life was to walk alone, to go along "the street and glance into the eyes of passers-by and catch a glimpse of recognition and know that you will never see them again." Now he was content to go unrecognized, for this most honest of men could not abide fawning or flattery, or the kind of social attentions that took him away from his work. He seemed always to be saying: Meet me in my poems; you'll find all you have to know about me there—and something about your-self too.

An anthologist asked him about his "central message." He replied, "I suppose that a part of it might be described as a faint hope of making a few of us understand our fellow creatures a little better, and to realize what a small difference there is, after all, between ourselves as we are, and ourselves, not only as we might have been but would have been if our physical and temperamental make-up (that is, our inheritance) and our environment had been a little different."

Dividing his time between New York in winter and the MacDowell Colony in summer (this haven for artists in Peterborough, New Hampshire, had become his second home since 1913), Robinson's output of sonnets, ballads, dramatic narrative poems did not let up until the year in which King Jasper was published—(1935), which was also the year of his death. Work and friends were his life. Incident and adventure were not. He went once to London, never traveled further west than the Hudson River in his own country. Despite his fame, his contact with other prominent writers of his time was remote—a brief exchange with Robert Frost who admired his work; a moment's meeting with Willa Cather, passing acquaintanceship with a number of poets, artists, and musicians who crossed his path at the MacDowell Colony. Many of the latter attested to his dislike of any fuss being made over him. Once when a newcomer to the colony was introduced to "Mr. Robinson," she spluttered out "Not the Mr. Robinson!" and the poet, with his usual uprising of embarrassment looked away for a moment before replying quietly, "No a Mr. Robinson."

In the last years of his life, Edwin Arlington Robinson, the unaltered idealist, feared that the whole Western world was going to be blown to pieces, foresaw a "played-out world." Ailing and old in the early 1930s, the once "howling optimist," observing the world-wide depression and the threat of war abroad, could only express a hope that "something better will come sometime in spite of human stupidity." In the past he had always been able to see life as his old friend, the genial Dr. Schumann, had taught him to see it, matching the sad with the comical, always finding room for laughter at himself and the universe. It had been that sense of laughter which had seen him through many a bad time. Hadn't he known a man, "Claverling/Who died because he couldn't laugh?" On April 6, 1935, his own laughter played out, and Long Robinson went to join Claverling, with the satisfaction of having left the best of himself behind.

Assessment of Edwin Arlington Robinson as an artist began in

earnest on the day of his death and has not yet let up. A man of
nineteenth-century ideals anticipating the impact of twentieth-century
culture on individualism, he had chosen for his literary canvasses recog-
nizable American figures in strife in modern times. Thus, for his content
even more than for his form, critics generally agreed that he was the
first modern poet of the twentieth century, or, as one literary historian
put it, a poet who "became the first of his generation to understand,
however darkly, the new." Like Hawthorne, whom he admired, Robinson
delved deeply into human character to throw light on paradox and the
capacity for good and evil in the best and worst of men. Concentrating
on the inner life of his characters more than the outer, nevertheless
the outer world is always in evidence, for when tragedy unfolds, the
callousness of modern society emerged as the last straw for a man
doomed to go under. In depicting man's universal struggle to understand
whether his destiny be determined by "The mad Queen spinner" (fate)
or "God—a name/That somehow answers us when we are driven/To feel
and think how little we have to do/With what we are," Robinson succeeded in transcending narrow regional material to explore the whole of
the human condition. He employed myth and Arthurian legend not for
its romance, but to demonstrate in poetic terms how, though times
change outwardly in dress, sophistication of weapons, styles of architecture, human emotions such as love, hate, jealousy, guilt defy time,
remain eternally the same. As Tristram and Iseult unite in love, "Time
was aware of them" says the poet—*all* time so that centuries later
artists like himself identify and compassionately recast the lovers in the
light and dark of Brittany, Cornwall, or New England.

Robinson *was* New England in the same way that Hawthorne was
New England, recognizing the nature of guilt and responsibility, conscious of his land born in a struggle of good and evil, glory and tragedy
walking hand in hand. Thus, in his ballads, sun and dark interfuse,
and strains of Puritan doctrine lock in memory a once proud, and
princely Indian civilization:

> *Dark hills at evening in the west*
> *Where sunset hovers like a sound*
> *Of golden horns that sang to rest*
> *Old bones of warriors underground*

He was a poet who did not believe in "art for art's sake" to the
exclusion of an artist's responsibility to society. But he also said, "I do

not believe that anything is good literature where art is wholly sacrificed to the subject matter," his criticism of much of the literature in the early 1930s. A confirmed individualist, he would not get drawn into movements either in politics or in art. In 1912 he remained aloof from Amy Lowell's imagist free verse camp, refusing to get embroiled in squabbles about innovations in modern poetry. "Robinson stayed content with the old way to be new," said Robert Frost. Speaking for himself, Robinson said: "I don't care a pinfeather what form a poem is written in so long as it makes me sit up." For him the poem was the thing; if the thought were true, a light would shine upon it.

Critics have praised Robinson for making loneliness his theme, not hopelessness; for revitalizing old forms with new content; for his mastery of the genre of the narrative poem, the compression of story. Some have taken him to task for "dry, mechanical tone and feeling," or for too many dark hills and dark souls. Malcolm Cowley said "he gave his characters memorable names, but sometimes forgets to give them faces."

There is no general agreement on where Edwin Arlington Robinson ranks among the nation's poets or whether he will survive as a poet at all. Back in 1897 the Denver *Times*, reviewing his first book, had said "to write verse on a plane with his is a task beyond all save some half dozen of our poets." Today most critics prefer to reserve judgment. But Robinson, who had matched years of half starvation with his declaration that "if anything is worthy of a man's best and hardest effort, that thing is the utterance of what he believes to be the truth," seldom worried about critics. He had begun his career with two essential thoughts: "I can't get over the feeling that I'm going to write a poem some day— a poem that will live even though it kills me," and "what I am after is the courage to see and to believe that every man has it in his power to overcome whatever obstacles may be in his way—even that seeming obstacle we call by the name of death." On both scores he realized his life's dream. For though his name may go in or out of favor while critics debate, Edwin Arlington Robinson is too deeply embedded in the history of American poetry for him ever to be long out of season. His strong simplicity and simple humanity will re-emerge whenever men feel need to get back to essentials. Like Lancelot, of whom he wrote,

> He rode on into the dark, under the stars,
> And there were no more faces. There was nothing.
> But always in the darkness he rode on,
> Alone; and in the darkness came the Light.

Edna St. Vincent Millay
(1892–1950)

"Time cannot break the bird's wing from the bird."

The world knew her as Edna St. Vincent Millay; her friends called her Vincent. But "Sefe," the name her family called her by, a make-believe, elfin name associated with childhood's play and imagery, was the one the poet herself most cherished. It signified joy, love, home, an instantaneous recall of times long past. No matter how high she rose as a poet, she could never escape nostalgia for "Sefe's" world, for childhood, the place where true poetry lies untouched by the palette knife of criticism or conscious striving for art. No matter how far afield fame took her—to New York, Washington, Paris, London, Rome, the Orient—the primary sensations of the child-poet lingered and kept alive in her a desire to go back again to where it had all started; to be herself again in the places and ways that for all imagination and make-believe were most real, most happy.

Rockland. Union. Camden. Maine. New England! Magic names. A young girl walking alone into morning to see the sunrise over a bay: Megunticook! Penobscot! The smell of sea; the sight of bobbing green planks; coast grasses and coast birds; the cries of young voices close by to fishing boats. Singing. Singing—

> O world, I cannot hold thee close enough!
>   Thy winds, thy wide grey skies!
> Thy mists, that roll and rise!
> Thy woods, this autumn day, that ache and sag
> And all but cry with colour!
>   . . . .

Above all a house where nasturtiums grew over the trellis, higher than the porch roof. A house where the door opened upon a road that opened upon a wood that opened upon a poem. A house where, as she once said, quoting her favorite poem by Gerard Manley Hopkins, "All were good to me, God knows, deserving no such thing . . . those kind people a hood all over, as a bevy of eggs the mothering wing." Her house. Her home. Childhood. "The kingdom where nobody dies."

Nostalgia for childhood is common to almost all New England writers, but it sounds peculiarly poignant through the prose and poetry of the Camden poet, born into a family of modest means, February 22, 1892, in Rockland, Maine; who grew up to be something of a princess in the world of American *belles lettres*; who, by her sparkling wit and poetic charm succeeded for more than a decade in making her poetry not only a "best seller" (a miracle in itself) but the *art* of poetry worthy of a nation's attention and admiration. Lyrical in her joy of nature, laughing in her joy of life's adventure, witty in her defiance of love's deceits—sometimes proud, sometimes melancholy, sometimes bittersweet but never defeated—in that guise a whole generation of American youth, gaily breaking ties with Victorian gentility, first adopted her for their own. To them she was a symbol of the mind and heart of New Womanhood advancing bravely and innocently upon the threshold of a sophisticated new century. In white muslin blouse, full-gored skirt reaching just to the tops of her buttoned boots, smart and daring in a boned collar and patent leather belt, flaunting a smile enchanting enough to be captioned "Valentine," a mind intellectual enough to crown her Poetess of the Day, Toast of the Town—such was Edna St. Vincent Millay.

But fame, as the little girl from Maine soon discovered, had its hazards. Determined to be taken seriously for the serious poet she was, she journeyed into womanhood with her artist's handbag slung over her shoulder only to find, as most poets do, that society adds to the burden, and conflict between art and reality is a battle not made easier because one happens to be a woman. The voice of the adolescent girl singing her love of life gradually changed over the years to sound a more disheartened, even tragic, tone as knowledge increased and travels in a broader world than New England failed to sustain her first shining illusions. Like the birds which were her intimates, Edna Millay made flights from season to season always hoping to recover that "first fine careless rapture" left behind somewhere on a New England hill. But hers was a human restlessness and a human fate; unlike the birds, she never really found her way home.

Once upon a time the story could begin—for it has that kind of quality—there were three beautiful young girls, Edna, Norma, and Kathleen Millay, living with their mother not far from the sea in the jewel-like town of Camden, Maine. With the ups and downs of fortune at the turn of the century, the Millays had had to move from one town to another, one house to another, always struggling to make ends meet; but by virtue of their industriousness, family unity, and a remarkable flair for laughing at adversity, their poverty was never dire enough to detract from normal childhood joys. Having for reasons of incompatibility separated from her husband, Cora Millay went out to work as a practical nurse to support herself and her daughters. Frail in appearance, but large of heart, tireless in energy and abounding in good humor and imagination, Mrs. Millay was determined to ornament what might otherwise have been a drab existence for herself and her children by filling their lives with the best in classical music and literature, at the same time encouraging any imaginative efforts in which her daughters wished to engage. Independence of thought, fair play, the right to privacy were also encouraged. But it was love that ruled this household where each cherished the other, where books were prized because ideas were never considered expendable or too costly.

Often it was necessary for Mrs. Millay to go out of town for a few days on a nursing case, but life proceeded with eight-year-old Edna trusted to extend a mothering wing over her two younger sisters, Norma and Kathleen. Edna St. Vincent she had been named—fine for a poet, solemn sounding for a slim, tomboyish, auburn-haired little girl who one instant was scrambling up an apple tree, the next half woman with apron and broom. "Sefe" abandoned Edna whenever she had a mind to and turned a vividly creative imagination upon homely duties, drawing into her net of fancy and magic her two adoring helpers who became, in turn, "Hunk" and "Wump" as they all kept house until mother came home. At age eight Sefe Millay was not a master of spelling or punctuation, but she diligently kept her mother posted on homefront news:

> I am getting along all right and so is Norma and Kathleen's cold is better now I went to practice and a boy called me a little chamipion and I asked him what he ment and he said because I was the best singer and I thanked him . . .

By the time she was ten the "best singer" had conquered commas and periods and gotten enough words under control to enable her to compose a business letter to Harper & Brothers asking for a subscription to *Harper's Young People*. At this tender age she was composing poems, too, recording them carefully into a ten-cent copybook to have ready for her mother's approval. Approval she received, for Mrs. Millay from the outset thought Edna's verses quite remarkable. That the child one saw dashing off to play with friends in the carefree role of Sefe was the same serious-minded little girl who could catch in a poem so sensitively and so freshly the quality of her surrounding world made the mother suspect genius in her daughter.

Traces of a double nature remained with Edna Millay as she matured to adolescence. Sometimes she was gamin, sometimes as ladylike as any other girl in town, but whether gamin or lady she always made an impression. At high school her friends adored her for her capacity for fun and humor, respected her for her capacity for leadership, self-discipline, and hard work. She was one moment that sparkling, carrot-haired girl who could make a crowded streetcar resound with singing as it carried its load of students to a Rockland Picnic; next, the tireless, demanding, editor-in-chief of the *Megunticook*, Camden High's literary magazine, striving to make it the best in the state. Often the *Megunticook* had to rely on poems and stories by the Millay sisters, Edna's poems particularly catching the attention of school authorities.

Much more significant for her, however, was the attention she received from the editors of *St. Nicholas Magazine*, a national periodical that published and awarded prizes for poetry written by its young readers. Even before reaching high school, she had had the pleasure of seeing her poems in print in *St. Nicholas*, and often starred for a prize. With "Forest Trees," written and published when she was fourteen, it became clear to the *St. Nicholas* editors that the author of the poem had a skill far beyond her years. "The Land of Romance" was chosen to be reprinted in *Current Literature*, a magazine for adults with the editorial comment that it was nothing short of phenomenal. Thus Edna had reason in these early years to believe in herself as a poet. When, at her graduation from Camden High, the faculty awarded her a prize for an essay in verse titled "La Joie de Vivre," both the honor and the poem's title seemed prophetic of a charmed future.

The year was 1909, a time when careers for women outside of the home were only just beginning to be looked upon with some degree of tolerance, when a college education was undreamed of by any except the daughters of well-to-do families. At seventeen, unable to afford college, and with no thought at all of marriage, Edna St. Vincent Millay had a summer free to ponder her future both as a woman and a poet. With her mother's blessing she used the prize money she had received for "La Joie de Vivre" to take time away from family chores, but even while vacationing with relatives at Chelmsford, she did not desert her big-sister role. Almost daily she wrote to Norma and Kathleen letting them share her new experiences in the world beyond Camden. Of her first ride on a roller coaster she gave a wildly exuberant account, little realizing then how that gigantic structure would remain with her as a symbol of the momentous life she lived.

> Did you ever see one? . . . I will try and tell you what it is— You start at the bottom in a bright red plush and gilt car—bright enough to look very pretty as it whirls along the white-washed track . . . The man behind gives you a push, the car slides around a curve and starts to climb—by machinery—a steep straight track to the very top of the whole business— Hang on to your hat! Sit still! Don't stand up!— When you get to the top— Whoosh!—you go down the other side a little way— Whish! up again! hold your breath and down—gasp and you're up—whack! round a corner . . . and all the time screeching and laughing with your hair-pins falling out, your hat over one ear— every now and then catching a glimpse down through the trees of people walking around eating pop-corn and ice cream, and over through the trees the flying horses going at full tilt. Then before you have time to catch your breath the car slides serenely down the track to its starting place and delivers its passengers to the gaping crowd— any side up—with no care whatsoever.

For the next two years, despite a restless certainty that her talent both on the piano and in poetry was superior enough to be the start toward an unusual career, there were no electrical sparks anywhere indicating that Edna St. Vincent Millay was about to take that hold-on-to-your-hat ride. Too old now for her poems to be eligible for *St. Nicholas*, she learned with some disappointment that there were not many other publications in America which accepted poetry—a situation that fellow New Englanders, Robert Frost and Edwin Arlington Robinson, both older and more experienced poets than herself—had already discovered. Thus, still in her teens, with notebooks fast filling up with unpublished

poems, Edna Millay was spending her time alternating between summer
jobs in Camden's seafront hotels and acting as substitute mother at
home when Mrs. Millay was working out of town. But poets tend to
grow impatient with domesticity, and this one was no exception. It is
not hard to sense the frustration behind the brave front she put up
before her mother:

> I am feeling fine now and I have been doing well at home lately.
> I baked the most delicious beans Friday. . . . I shall put up bread
> tonight or tomorrow. Saturday we had baked beans and I had awfully
> good luck with them. I have made pies, cakes, and doughnuts and
> we are living almost wholly from home cooking.

It was fortunate for Edna Millay that she lived in Camden. Its
beauty helped to appease a troubled spirit, its gay resort atmosphere to
take the edge off of dull kitchen chores and too much introspection. She
loved the green-white days, the sparkling nights of summer, the woods,
the bays, the crowds of young people milling along the streets and at
the water's edge. "Oh, I'm having some perfectly great times this summer!" she wrote once to assure her mother. Motorboat rides, overnight
fishing trips, beach parties, outdoor band concerts—all these a natural
part of her New England girlhood. One afternoon in her eighteenth
summer a camera caught her posing along with six other popular Camden
girls in middy blouse and farmer hat, all lying flat on stomach, elbows
on the ground, chin in hand, feet in air. She plunged into the bay
each afternoon determined to learn to swim, and when, finally, with
Kathleen and Norma following her lead, she managed to reach a white
slab stuck as a marker in a barrel of rocks, her sense of accomplishment
was almost overwhelming. "*Seventy five feet! Just plain breast-stroke and
without even turning over to float. What do you think of that? . . . .
Aren't you proud of us?*" The delighted mother was proud enough to
send her girls a bit of extra money which they saved and spent that fall
"just as you would have wanted us to if you had been here. We all
went to see 'The Man on the Box.' Marion Johnquest played in it. . . .
and I wouldn't have missed it for anything."

As was typical of the Millay sisters, at this first play all three became
stagestruck; they were to remain so for the rest of their lives. In or out
of the theater its glamour would be always upon them, for these girls
had innate ability to create real or imaginary drama wherever they went.
Norma, besides writing competent short stories, was destined to work

in the theater as a professional actress and singer; Kathleen, who wrote
poetry, would also dance her way onto a stage; Edna, poet, pianist
(she played well enough to warrant a public concert in Camden), would
also shine as a delightful actress. But for the moment all were simply
local talent, and the oldest of the sisters almost despairing of her dream
ever to rise beyond that category.

Edna St. Vincent Millay's ride on the "steep, straight track to the
very top of the whole business" began, though she was then unaware of
it, one bright spring morning while she stood alone on the summit of
Camden's Mt. Battie looking beyond Penobscot Bay to Mt. Megunticook. A poem suddenly began to form in her mind, the lines flowing in
swiftly, spontaneously one after the other:

> All I could see from where I stood
> Was three long mountains and a wood;
> I turned and looked another way
> And saw three islands in a bay.
> So with my eyes I traced the line
> Of the horizon, thin and fine,
> Straight around till I was come
> Back to where I'd started from
> And all I saw from where I stood
> Was three long mountains and a wood.

To stand alone sensing how the "world stands out on either side/
No wider than the heart is wide"—to reach out and discover that the
sky, for all its distance, looms "no higher than the soul is high" was
no ordinary event. For nineteen-year-old Edna Millay it was a religious,
a transcendental experience, a passionate identity at that moment in
time with the birth-death force in nature, sensing in all parts of her
being the energy of living things. She who so girlishly was one of the
gossiping crowd on a Camden beach, here, on Mt. Battie, was one with
"the gossiping of friendly spheres/The creaking of the tented sky,/The
ticking of Eternity." And in awe at the transformation she thought: "I
know not how such things can be!

> God, I can push the grass apart
> And lay my finger on Thy heart!

Part of the miracle was to feel herself emerging as if from the dormant
state of a cocoon to controlled mastery of wings.

And all at once the heavy night
Fell from my eyes and I could see!
A drenched and dripping apple-tree
A last long line of silver rain,
A sky grown clear and blue again.

"Renaissance," the poem begun so spontaneously that day on the mountaintop, grew into a finished work through Edna's pruning care upon it. The first quiet ten lines developed into a work fourteen stanzas long, a unity of dramatic expression that convinced Cora Millay, when the poem was at last put into her hands, that here, at last, was proof of her daughter's genius. *This* poem, she said, Edna must publish.

The year was 1912—a banner one for American poetry which since the death of Walt Whitman had been suffering a sad decline. It was the year Harriet Monroe founded *Poetry, a Magazine of Verse;* it was the year Mitchell Kennerley announced he would bring out an anthology (*The Lyric Year*) featuring one hundred poems, one each by one hundred contemporary American poets, three of whom would share one thousand dollars in prizes. Ironically it was also the year that an unappreciated and discouraged Robert Frost sailed for England with his trunkful of poems to look for a more receptive audience. And now, suddenly, came this spark of new energy on home ground, this renaissance awakening America to the wealth of talent on its own shores. Poets old and new, some writing in traditional style, others in fresh, modern style, bombarded *Poetry* and *The Lyric Year* with manuscripts. *Poetry* was interested primarily in those poems written in experimental style expressive of modern times. Based in Chicago, this magazine lured over the next few years the *imagists*, the *lyricists*, the *balladeers*, free-versers and blank-versers, letting controversy boom to prominence names like Ezra Pound, T. S. Eliot, Amy Lowell, Vachel Lindsay, Carl Sandburg, Robert Frost, William Carlos Williams, Marianne Moore, Wallace Stevens. But it was *The Lyric Year* that had first chance at seeing the work of the fresh talent from Maine—and it almost thrust genius aside.

"Renaissance" by E. St. Vincent Millay was one among thousands of poems submitted for the anthology. When the jury met to make judgments for or against each poem, "Renaissance" elicited from the reader into whose hands it first fell only scoffing laughter. He read aloud in exaggerated singsong rhythm the poem's opening lines:

> All I could see from where I stood
> Was three long mountains and a wood

and, thinking his point of mediocrity made, tossed E. St. Vincent Millay's manuscript into the wastepaper basket. "Hey, that sounded good," shouted another member of the jury, who then insisted upon hearing more. The manuscript was fished out and another two lines read in much the same deprecating way before being discarded once again. But editor Ferdinard Earle, who also happened to be the donator of the prize money, was still not satisfied. He rescued the poem and read it aloud through to its conclusion. This time, without knowledge of the age or as it turned out, the sex of the author, the jury agreed unanimously that "Renaissance" was a poem of shining power and would be published in the anthology.

To "E. St. Vincent Millay, Esq." the enthusiastic Mr. Earle at once dispatched his congratulations predicting the poem would take first prize. "Dear Sir . . ." his letter began, delighting the young "sir" at the other end of the line who already had become an outspoken feminist. If fuddy-duddy old judges thought only a man capable of writing a fine poem, well—they would learn soon enough the flaming spirit of Camden's Joan of Arc coming pen in hand to conquer the field. Celebrations ran wild in the Millay household with mother and sisters dreaming of all that could be done with that handsome first-prize money. Then came the terrible blow. Mr. Earle's vote was overridden by his colleagues. When, in November 1912, The Lyric Year was published, "Renascence" (now so respelled) was included, all right, but it placed fourth and was not a prize winner at all.

Once beginning to climb, however, a roller coaster cannot be held back. Edna Millay was aboard and going for a ride. It was her poem the public thought should have taken at least one of those three prizes. As a storm of protest broke over the heads of The Lyric Year editors, these three gentlemen were in part dismayed, in part glad that poetry had suddenly become the center of such widespread controversy. Even Orrick Johns, whose poem "Second Avenue" had taken first prize, thought "Renascence" deserved the honor. Many years later, describing his emotions at the time, Johns wrote:

> When the book arrived I realized that it was an unmerited award. The outstanding poem in that book was by Edna St. Vincent Millay, immediately acknowledged by every authoritative critic as such. The award was as much an embarrassment to me as a triumph.

In Camden the fourth-place poet was trying to take all the hullabaloo in stride. Save for the fact that she now had national attention, her life had not essentially changed. She was still dividing her time at home between housework and writing. But hovering in the air was a hint of change. The turn came one evening when she was asked to entertain guests at the Whitehall Inn with some of her original songs. Edna seated herself at the piano and, as always, completely won over her small audience. Then someone asked if she would read aloud the poem that had caused so much public controversy. As she complied, reciting the lines in the soft, rich voice, which in later years was to become so famous, there sat quietly listening Miss Caroline B. Dow, head of the National Training School of the YWCA in New York City. Greatly impressed both by the reader and her poem, Miss Dow set out to learn more about Edna St. Vincent Millay—her work and her personal history. What she learned brought her to the conclusion that this young maker of songs deserved an opportunity to widen her horizons and to build through higher education a more solid classical foundation for her poetry. She paid a visit to the Millay family to propose that under her sponsorship Edna attend Barnard College in New York and there take courses preparatory for a possible scholarship at Vassar.

The suggestion, of course, was enthusiastically accepted. A few weeks later when the Vassar catalogue arrived Edna pored over it, telling her absent mother, "I've had lots of fun looking up names, in that and in the Smith catalogue . . . In Vassar now there are four girls from Persia, two from Syria, two from Japan, one from India, one from Berlin, Germany, and one or two others from 'across the water.' Lots of Maine girls go to Smith. . . . I'd rather go to Vassar" At Miss Dow's request she prepared a list of authors and books she had read, then sent it along with the comment "This list must seem awfully crazy to you. I've really read so much that I hardly know what to pick out." Authors with whom she said she was "well acquainted" included Shakespeare, Dickens, Eliot, Scott, Tennyson, Milton, Wordsworth, Ibsen, Arnold Bennett; in the "slightly acquainted" category fell Bacon, Addison, Ruskin, Macauley, and Thoreau. She had read, she told Miss Dow, all the works of Hawthorne, Barrie, Tolstoi, the Brontës, Scott, George Eliot—everything from *Pilgrims Progress* to Holmes' *Elsie Venner*, from *Pam* and *Pam Decides* to Oliver Goldsmith's *Vicar of Wakefield*. Miss Dow was impressed. The admissions officers at Barnard and Vassar were also impressed.

With all signs looking fair for New York, the Millay sisters busied themselves sewing for Edna as if it were for her trousseau. She must be fashionable, make a big splash in that big pond where, if rumor was true, the whole literary world was waiting to receive her. Stitching away, Edna knew there was much still she had to learn about the ABCs of her art, but trusted the instinct that told her she had "something for the world to hear." She felt ready now, she told a friend "to pierce a way into the world's great heart."

She was not alone in that conviction. With the appearance of "Renascence" in *The Lyric Year*, a whirlwind of correspondence had come blowing down upon the little house in Camden—strangers from all parts of the country writing for autographed copies of the poem; distinguished authors mystified by the depth of feeling expressed in the work asking if E. St. Vincent Millay was really as people said, a slip of a girl from the provinces. Poets wrote to say her style was reminiscent of John Masefield, Coleridge, Blake. "Did you get it [the idea of the poem] from a book?" Poet Authur Davison Ficke asked (he was to become Edna's lifelong friend) and she, with youthful indignation replied: "I see things with my own eyes, just as if they were the first eyes that ever saw, and then I set about to tell, as best I can, just what I see. All of my poems are very real to me and take a great deal out of me. I am possessed of a masterful and often cruel imagination."

To this same new friend, whom she had yet to see in person, Edna wrote a few weeks later: "I'm hoping that college will help me, but if I should come back a suffragette instead of a poet, wouldn't it be dreadful?" On the February night in 1913 when she was at last on her way to New York, sleep was out of the question. Once, in the thick darkness when the train pulled to a noisy stop, she raised the shade of her window "a little so as to peek, and leaned on my elbow and saw a big sign all lighted up on a dark factory." A symbol of the kind of world she was entering now, moving her far from New England sea, woods, and fields. But she was not yet thinking in terms of symbols. Nothing could more indicate the kind of naïve excitement the journey stirred than the words in her first letter home, "Just think, dear mother and girls, I travelled Pullman all the way."

Gaping for the first time at the public library in New York, St. Patrick's Cathedral, warships in the harbor, Edna became increasingly excited. Like any other student she registered for courses at Barnard, but her life outside the college walls was not ordinary. "*Yesterday I got a note from Sara Teasdale inviting me to take tea.*" The Poetry Society

gave a luncheon in her honor at which poet Alfred Noyes shook her hand
and paid his compliments. At Literary Evenings young and old authors
crowded around to get a glimpse of the little girl who had written the
biggest poem of the year. Rumor was true. "Renascence" had made her a
celebrity.

"But I am not being a Bohemian," Edna quickly assured Arthur
Ficke. "I am not so Bohemian by half as when I came." All her bad
habits, "bridge-pad, cigarette-case, and cocktail shaker," she laughingly
told him, she had left at home, while bringing with her "all my good
habits—diary, rubbers, and darning cotton." One day she went to the
International Art Exhibition and stood amazed to see all the fantasia—
not clear, explicit lines like her own, but queer distortions "done by
people they call the Cubists, and especially the one called 'Nude De-
scending the Staircase.'" ("*if you can find the figure, outline it in ink
and send it back to me.*") Clearly this was a world beyond "shining
apple trees." In this environment the new intellectuals were everywhere,
challenging comprehension: Stravinsky's "The Fire Bird"; Schoenberg's
"Pierrot Lunaire"; artists Picasso, Braque, Paul Klee; in literature—Marcel
Proust. It was a relief to get back to one kind of artistry clear to the
whole world. "*O, Mother and girls! Sara Bernhardt in Camille! I'm all
gone to pieces . . . oh, when I can tell you, when I can tell you!*"

Settling down to studies at Barnard, where her intimates called her
Vincent, her sharp, inquisitive mind quickly began to discern the new
trends and to learn to evaluate them. She had an intellectual grasp of
concepts that belied her luminous frailty. Already a professional, she
sold "God's World" to *Forum Magazine* for twenty-five dollars, which
seemed a fortune then. Suddenly the celebrity daughter was able to
send extra money to her mother. ". . . do something to make something
easier for yourself. Shoes, dear, or have your glasses fixed."

This turnabout situation foretold the future. Edna St. Vincent
Millay's name was already on its way to becoming a household word in
America. But the simple, direct, loving relationship that existed between
mother and daughter, sister and sisters remained the same. To her mother
the poet expressed gratitude that went beyond recognition of the usual
sacrifices parents make for their children; whatever stamina she possessed
with which to face the world she felt had come from emulating her
mother's "rock-like courage." Whatever opportunities came to her because
of her success as a poet she felt were due to the opportunities her mother
had given her in her girlhood to express herself in poetry and music.

The trauma of adolescence had been made easier by this mother's understanding of the sensitivities of the young, and most particularly of the
sensibilities of a developing poet. Throughout her life the poet would
say over and over again her thanks, letting it spill out uninhibitedly
at moments that took her back to the early days: "I have been having
an orgy of playing the piano lately, several hours a day—Beethoven,
Bach, and Mozart. It has been wonderful. I seldom put my hands on
the keys without remembering how you taught me to play when I was a
baby, and all the money you paid for my music lessons afterwards. No
one was ever more grateful for anything than I am to you for this
beautiful gift you gave me, mother."

The freedom Vincent Millay had known as a responsible, self-
sufficient girl at home made it hard for her to endure the close supervision of dormitory life at Vassar College in the years 1913–1917. She
was twenty-one when she entered the freshman class, not only older than
her classmates but with a head start on a career. By this time her interests
were no longer compatible with sturdy old subjects like history, geometry,
German, Old English—all of which she predicted she'd "surely flunk"
especially when so many eyes turned upon her expecting genius performance. She resented that nowhere from the campus could she see the
Hudson River as someone had promised—a small thing perhaps to those
who didn't understand the need this particular New Englander had for
sight of the sea. To make matters worse ". . . a man is forbidden as if
he were an apple." She was not altogether happy with this "*pink-and-gray
Alice in Wonderland*" college, her description at that time of Vassar.

Nevertheless the presence of Edna St. Vincent Millay was an elec-
trifying one in the Poughkeepsie environment. She was too vivacious a
personality to sulk, too perfectionist a student to do less than her best.
Her talents for composing, singing, acting, would have lifted her to
stardom on campus even if her name had not already been up in literary
lights. A ready warmth quickly won for her many lasting friends; her wit
enlivened dormitory and classroom. In her sophomore year it was she
who wrote the class marching song and donned costume for pageants
and May-Day celebrations which she helped organize. In 1915 she delighted her classmates with her performance of Marchbanks in George
Bernard Shaw's *Candida*. Other roles followed: Deidre in Synge's *Deidre
of the Sorrows*; Sylvette in *Les Romanesques*, the princess in her own
poetic play, *The Princess Marries the Page*.

But for all that activity and conscientious scholarship she came

close to being denied the right to participate with her class at graduation
exercises. "I have wept gallons all over everybody," she wrote heartbrokenly
to her family. The administration had forbidden her presence at Commencement because

> I was absent-minded and stayed away out of town with three other
> girls one night, forgetting until it was too late that I had . . . lost my
> privileges for staying a couple of days in New York to go to the
> Opera.

It was typical of Edna St. Vincent Millay to laugh, cry, and rebel
all at the same time. "The class is exceedingly indignant, bless 'em," she
went on, "& is busy sending in petitions signed by scores of names, &
letters from representative people, & all that. It will do no good. But
it is a splendid row. I always said, you remember, that I had come in
over the fence & would probably leave the same way.—Well, that's what
I'm doing." It turned out an up-to-the-wire finish. Having packed books
and clothes and gone back to New York City she was given a last
minute reprieve: ". . . the class made such a fuss that they let me come
back and I graduated in my cap and gown along with the rest." It was
with a sigh of relief that she signed this last letter from Poughkeepsie
"Edna St. Vincent Millay, A.B.!"

Four years of classical education which had included a thorough
grounding in languages, including Latin, were both a boon and a deterrent
for the poet who had now reached the ripe old age of twenty-five. Returning to the world of letters at a time when most artists were working strictly
in new forms, Edna St. Vincent Millay, as a result of her training, was
imbued with respect for classical forms in which to enclose her modern
ideas. Grounded in centuries of English poetry and with an innate love
for the language, her touch was that of a perfectionist in form while
the words were immediate and real. With all her New England sensibilities still intact, her sentiment now was that of a perceptive young
woman whose mind and heart were deeply affected by the mores of the
"gay twenties," the speed of a decade heading for dizzy collapse. The
bold and witty poems of Edna St. Vincent Millay delighted readers of
all ages and both sexes despite "new" critics who at best were merely
tolerating the poet's feminine viewpoint. In four years she had come a
long way from the adolescent poet of 1912 of whom Harriet Monroe in
Poetry said "she sings freely and musically in a big world. Almost we
hear a thrush at dawn discovering the ever-renewing splendor of the
morning . . ."

Now, living in the milieu of an accepting peer group in the Green-wich Village of the 1920s, Edna St. Vincent Millay was singing of city streets and "People that build their houses inland" and love:

> I know what my heart is like
>   Since your love died:
> It is like a hollow ledge
> Holding a little pool
>   Left there by the tide . . .

People quoted such lines, reading them superficially, visualizing the poet-in-fashion, for it *was* fashionable then to strip away the sentimentality that surrounded Victorian concepts of love and daringly to expose the real. Whether in the lyrical mood of a Millay, or in the satirical mood of a Dorothy Parker, Love was "in," as always, but with the heart cleverly on guard for disillusion. What went unnoticed by the public, by critics, by reporters who followed after Edna St. Vincent Millay looking for bits of scandal and gossip that would corroborate her "bohemian" reputation, was that she was not bohemian, not really up to date in the popular sense either as a woman or an artist. She was in most ways conservative, never a faddist, but seeking truth above all. She was deeply in earnest in all that she did, passionately convinced of women's rights, passionately dedicated to the highest standards in the art she practiced. Throughout these New York years as a stunning celebrity in a star-oriented society, she was all the while suffering from overblown publicity, and from a deep sense of exile. Few knew the real—the shy Edna St. Vincent Millay who wrote

> No matter what I say,
>   All that I really love
> Is the rain that flattens on the bay,
>   And the eel-grass in the cove;
> The jingle-shells that lie and bleach
>   At the tide-line, and the trace
> Of higher tides along the beach:
>   Nothing in this place.

She who had always "climbed the wave at morning,/Shook the sand from my shoes at night," was conscious now of how treacherously she was "caught beneath great buildings,/Stricken with noise, confused with light."

Why, then, did she not return to New England? A moment's in-

decision after leaving Vassar as to whether to go home or remain in
New York had been decided in favor of the latter partly because New
York was the literary center of America, partly because, with Kathleen
now at Vassar, Norma wanted—and deserved, Edna thought—to try her
luck on the stage in New York. "You're the most talented one of us
all," she had written to Norma, going on to say how by sharing a Green-
wich Village apartment and working they'd all get rich "in a few months,
of course." The dream did not seem too far fetched. She was continuing
to sell individual poems to magazines, and editing now her first volume,
which Mitchell Kennerley was to publish under the title *Renascence*.
Another source of income was public readings of her poems, increasingly
popular events at which she made a striking, theatrical appearance in
long, trailing dresses.

There was a lot of fun, a lot of glamour, but little money for two
pretty young sisters sharing one apartment in Greenwich Village. Poetry,
Edna discovered, could not be counted on for a living, so to the hours
of literary labor essential to the completion of her first volume, she added
hours of auditions for acting parts in plays. It came as something of a
shock to her and to her sisters that acting in off-broadway groups—the
Washington Square or the Provincetown Players—though a glorious
business, earned little, if any money. Playwright Floyd Dell, one of the
many during those Village years to be won over by the spiritual and
physical beauty of Edna St. Vincent Millay, has recorded the poet's first
contact with the Provincetown Players:

> When the Provincetown Players were starting their venture and a
> play of mine was to be given, I remember how in response to a call
> for some girl to play the ingenue part, a slender little girl with red-
> gold hair came to the greenroom over the stable and read the lines
> of Annabelle in "The Angel Intrudes." She looked her frivolous part
> to perfection and read the lines so winningly that she was at once
> engaged at a salary of nothing at all . . . She left her name and
> address as she was departing, and when she was gone we read the
> name and were puzzled, for it was "Edna Millay." We wondered if
> she could possibly be Edna St. Vincent Millay, author of that
> beautiful and astonishing poem, Renascence!
> And indeed she was. Having just been graduated from Vassar she
> had come to New York to seek fame not as a poet, but as an actress:
> for who could expect to make a living at writing poetry? She acted in
> several plays at our theater and put on some of her own, including the
> tremendously impressive "Aria da Capo." But the stage, as it turned
> out, could offer even more meager rewards than poetry, and so Edna

Millay turned back to her first Muse, fortunately for American litera-
ture. She lived one icebound, dreadful winter in a tiny room on
Waverly Place a few doors from the house where Poe wrote "Ligeia."
The house she lived in may one day be known as the place where
"She is Overheard Singing" and "Oh, think not I am faithful to a
vow!" were written.

Dell erred in saying she "sought fame not as a poet." Poetry was
then and ever her first love; for it alone, as always, she was burning
candles at both ends.

In 1917 *Renascence* came off the press, a slim little volume that
immediately established more firmly her reputation as a fine lyric poet.
It was followed in short order by *A Few Figs from Thistles* (1920),
Second April (1921), and *The Harp-Weaver and Other Poems* (1923)
for which she won the Pulitzer prize for poetry. Prior to this event she
had won an award of $1000 for a single poem titled, significantly enough,
"Bean Stalk," which ecstatically announced just what rung Edna St.
Vincent Millay had reached on the climb to fame and how much higher
she intended to go:

> *Ho, Giant! This is I!*
> *I have built me a bean-stalk into your sky!*
> *La, but it's lovely, up so high!*

and, gaily with never a thought to falling or failing:

> *Here my knee, there my foot,*
> *Up and up, from shoot to shoot*
> . . . .
> *Far and out above . . .*
> *. . . the city I was born in*
> . . . .
> *What a wind! What a morning!*

In that fair morning *Vanity Fair* magazine devoted a whole page
to poems by Edna St. Vincent Millay and carried a photograph "that
looks about as much like me as it does Arnold Bennett." Up so high,
she gave a sparkling new appearance—bobbed red hair, "sweetest new
evening gown you ever saw, and shoes with straps across them, and
embroidery up the front."

But to those who knew what a perfectionist she was the newest
fashions were no cover up for the hard-working woman always striving

for a higher quality of performance. In 1921, even while *Vanity Fair* was heralding her, no one was more conscious than the poet herself that the greatest danger she faced was to allow honor and fame to intrude upon her artistic growth. She knew it was time both in her personal and professional life to pause and take stock of direction.

When it begins to get a little easy or one begins to write in certain forms almost from habit, it's time to stop for a while.

Making the hard decision not to write another poem for at least a year, Edna Millay booked passage in January 1921 on the *Rochambeau* for Paris, her first trip abroad. To be alone, she told her mother, was what she required, solitude being the nurse necessary for renewal of spirit. Huddled small in her great white Hudson Bay blanket aboard ship, it thrilled the poet to be at last upon the sea so intimately connected with her childhood visions. On the eighth night out when lights were sighted in the distance and she heard someone say "those are lighthouses on the coast of Cornwall—we are just now between Cornwall and Brittany" she was equally thrilled to see so close by shores familiar to her in childhood through literary and musical legend. The following day, at sunset, the steward pointed to a "distant, shadowy grey bluff on starboard bow,—saying, 'la terre de France!' " And a few hours later Edna St. Vincent Millay's new life in the Old World had begun.

Aloneness in Paris was in itself an experience, rewarding in freedom to move and see again at her own pace, with her own eyes, materials in nature and the human condition that are the innersprings of poetry. From one end of Paris to the other, mile upon mile she walked ". . . until I can't lift a foot" she wrote the family. At night, alone in her hotel, she restrained temptation to write poetry, worked instead on her articles for *Vanity Fair* (published under her "prose-name"—Nancy Boyd). As a means of bread and butter, a short story could bring in $400 as compared to $25 for a poem in a magazine. She also wrote a play promised to Vassar, titled at first *Snow White and Red Rose* later renamed *The Lamp and the Bell*. Written to be played out of doors "as spectacularly as possible" in Elizabethan drama style, this play was produced successfully a few months later in Poughkeepsie, but the poet did not, in future years, think highly of it. The early 1920s were seeing Eugene O'Neill's great plays introduced by the same Provincetown Players who in 1919 had produced her own *Aria da Capo* with Norma Millay playing the role of Columbine, and Norma's future husband, Charles

Ellis (who also designed the set) as one of the shepherds. In the author's eyes *Aria da Capo* was "a peach—one of the best things I've ever done" and she never changed her mind about it. Three years before her death in 1950, in typical, honest, self-critical appraisal of her work, she was to say that she thought none of her plays worth preserving except this one.

By the end of spring Edna's solitary life had begun to pay creative dividends, but she was growing increasingly lonely for her family. When news came one day that not only had her mother sold a short story ("Chore-boy"), but in the spirit of modern times had bobbed her hair, the homesick poet wrote back to say that like the "Ancient Mariner who had a tale in his heart to unfold" she was madly "button-holing" waiters, porters, flowergirls—anybody in and about the hotel who would listen, saying, "Someday you must meet my mother." A plan was hatched then to bring the hard-working Cora Millay to Paris, but on more sober calculations, it had to be postponed for lack of money. Bitterly disappointed, Edna wrote, "Almost all people love their mothers but I have never met anybody in my life, I think, who loved his mother as much as I love you."

Separated by distance and time from all that was familiar, Edna Millay became the displaced person living on memory of the past. Reflecting back on the happiness of a girlhood symbolized for her by the vision of three sisters harmonizing around the parlor piano joined by their mother's "rich, deep, absolutely certain and right basso note," she could find consolation only in the knowledge of that continuing harmony. If the price of fame was loneliness, or unhappiness in her search for ways to unite the life of a woman with that of an artist, at least there was someone at home who thoroughly understood her. "The reason I am a poet is entirely because you wanted me to be and intended I should be, even from the very first," her letter to her mother went on. "You brought me up on the traditions of poetry and everything I did you encouraged. I cannot remember once in my life when you suggested that I should put it aside for something else. Some parents of children that are 'different' have so much to reproach themselves with. But not you."

Too restless to remain longer in Paris, the poet decided to go to Rome. But from Rome she soon moved on again, living now in Austria, now in Albania, Yugoslavia, Spain. These flights from country to country were in part symptomatic of her inability to come to terms with herself in regard to marriage. Both of her sisters had recently married, apparently happily resolving the conflict between career and domestic responsibility; but she, now approaching thirty, still feared giving up her independence lest it interfere with the disciplines of a poet's life. Her capacity for love was tremendous; many nooks and crannies of her heart were stored with memories of loves left behind. Was there *one* among them who could understand a poet's need for freedom? In her troubled wanderings, arguing the pros and cons of marriage, she often felt like the little girl in her own poem "A Very Little Sphinx":

> *Come along in then, little girl!*
> *Or else stay out!*
> *But in the open door she stands,*
> *And bites her lip and twists her hands,*
> *And stares upon me, trouble-eyed:*
> *"Mother," she says, "I can't decide!*
> *I can't decide."*

One morning while crossing on horseback through a narrow mountain pass to reach the Albanian city of Elbasan, Edna noticed along the trail some small lavender flowers which the guide informed her were called "lulet." ". . . they were like no flowers I had ever seen . . . I could not bear to pass them without looking at them more closely," but it was too dangerous to dismount. Ten days later, having left Elbasan behind, she was traveling by carriage in the direction of Cattero on a road ten-thousand feet above sea level regretting that she had not once held in her fingers "the beautiful, strange Albanian lulet." Suddenly as her carriage approached at slow speed a small group of people standing along one side of the road, one among them—a child she thought—tossed something in to her through the open window: "a small, carefully-tied fresh nosegay of lavender flowers, my 'lulet.'" This delightful incident seemed to her a good omen, and perhaps it was. Shortly thereafter a change of fortune made it possible for her to bring her mother to Europe.

It was a gay April-in-Paris reunion, after which mother and daughter journeyed on to England, found a little thatched house in the village of Dorset (Thomas Hardy's birthtown), where they settled down for a much needed rest. There, for the first time, Edna St. Vincent Millay heard the English lark, "little brown birds that make their nests in ploughed ground, and when they're not on the ground they're way up in the air; they have never been known to alight in a tree even for a moment. When they sing they leave the ground suddenly and rise right straight up in the air, and then usually they just stand still in one place fluttering their wings all the time and sing the most wonderful, joyous, rippling, trilling drunken songs, sometimes singing longer than three minutes without stopping, way up in the sky, a tiny black speck, or out of sight altogether. There's nothing in the world like it . . ." She had always loved birds, studying their habits, maintaining feeding stations for them wherever she could. One of her friends, author Vincent Sheean, thought the affinity between bird and woman almost mystical, was convinced that birds knew the poet and followed her wherever she went.

"On First Having Heard the Skylark" included in the volume *The Buck in the Snow* (1929), celebrates the moment in Dorset when skylark and poet first found one another.

Not knowing he rose from earth, not having seen him rise
Not knowing the fallow furrow was his home,
And that high wing, untouchable, untainted,
A wing of earth, with the warm loam
Closely acquainted,
I shuddered at his cry and caught my heart.
Relentless out of heaven his sweet crying like a crystal dart
Was launched against me. Scanning the empty sky
I stood with thrown-back head until the world reeled.
Still, still he sped his unappeasable shafts
        against my breast without a shield.
He cried forever from his unseen throat
Between me and the sun.
He would not end his singing, he would not have done.
"Serene, and pitiless note, whence, whence, are you?"
I cried. "Alas, these arrows, how fast they fall!
Ay, me, beset by angels in unequal fight,
Alone high on the shaven down surprised, and not a tree in sight!"

Beset by angels in unequal fight. Emily Dickinson, too, had felt that way listening to the ease of a bird's singing. The hardest moments in a poet's life are when "dry periods" occur, when, after high creativity there suddenly comes an arid season as if the mind is at war with thought and thought's agent—language. At such times Edna St. Vincent Millay found it difficult to be with people, necessary to retreat even from close friends until the flow of song returned. Sometimes her self-imposed hibernation was misinterpreted as aloofness, but she had to accept this as being an inescapable part of her destiny.

For a New Englander living in old England there were, in Hardy's Dorset, many echoes and outlines reminiscent of home—dunes like those at Truro, scrubby hawthorn trees and prickly gorse bushes. And flocks of sheep grazing on a hillside. One day Edna saw "Two little twin bullocks in a meadow, tiny ones, just exactly alike, with about six inches of white on the end of each tail and their mother licked first one and then the other . . ." Reciting it for her sisters, she knew she was at peace with herself again, almost ready to end her exile.

Before leaving West England, she yearned to visit Thomas Hardy, but she was much too shy to intrude upon "Max Gate," as the author's estate was called. Had he known of her presence in Dorset, the aged poet-novelist, who had not many more years to live, would surely have sought her out. It was Thomas Hardy's publicly stated opinion that there were only two great institutions in America: recessional architecture and Edna St. Vincent Millay.

Edna also was too shy to seek out a meeting with another English poet who admired her work, A. E. Housman, author of "A Shropshire Lad." She did, at a careful distance, one day chase "his retreating tall, thin grey figure and cotton umbrella for about half a mile through the streets of Cambridge till he turned in at Trinity College and was lost in the gloom. . . . they say nobody ever sees him, he goes along like a shadow and is lost before he's found."

But never mind—she had found herself. To prove it she went home to take the Pulitzer prize for poetry in 1923. About this same time America saw her in another role: joining ranks with those who protested the arrest and subsequent conviction of Sacco and Vanzetti, two immigrant anarchists accused of a hold-up murder of which she and thousands more like her thought them innocent. (Her militant participation in this struggle for justice was to result, in 1927, in her own arrest and a brief few hours in jail.) The Sacco-Vanzetti case began a lifelong interest in political and social causes that profoundly influenced the direction of Edna St. Vincent Millay's artistic endeavors. Equally significant was her marriage in 1923 to Dutch-Irish Eugen Jan Boissevain, a man of great personal charm and understanding, who enthusiastically agreed with his poet-wife that her life ought not to be dulled by routine domestic activities. "When we got married," he is said to have told a reporter, "I gave up my business. Anyone can buy and sell coffee. Vincent is more important than I am."

He bought a large, old-fashioned house set high in secluded woodland in Austerlitz, New York, which they had fun remodeling, calling it "Steepletop" after a flower found in abundance in their fields. Here, while Edna worked at poetry in her own little cubby above the garage, Eugen happily took on assorted chores—farmer, secretary, keeper-of-the-keys, and general watchdog over his wife's health and privacy. "If I let her struggle with problems of order and routine, she doesn't write," he said. "That will not do! I look after everything. It is a ridiculous idea that the woman must be the one to direct the household."

During the next years Steepletop proved a true haven, as did their own Ragged Island, a deeply isolated retreat in Maine where they spent their summers. Neither her humor nor her passionate love of life had diminished, but to the poet's dismay she discovered that the public was reluctant to accept her for the socially conscious artist she had become. A reading tour through the Middle West shortly after her marriage had showed her how difficult it was to live down the early legend that established Edna St. Vincent Millay as a witty, Bohemian young woman, daringly modern in her life and her verse. Audiences, she complained to Eugen, come "to see what I look like, and bet with each other as to how many of my naughty poems I would dare to read . . ."

Thus, at the peak of fame, the mistress of Steepletop preferred to live quietly among the varied species of birdlife that came daily to her feeder, to have for company the dog, Altair, the cat, Smoky, lambs, calves and friendly white pines on the ridges. It was recreation enough to ride downhill with Eugen for the mail, to swim in the brook, and now and then help harvest berries to be sold at market.

In 1926 she collaborated with composer Deems Taylor, writing the libretto for his opera *The King's Henchman*, which had a triumphant premier performance in February 1927. But six months later all thought of personal triumph was put aside in a last minute fight to save the lives of Sacco and Vanzetti who, after four years of excruciating suffering, were to be executed. In a passionate appeal to the governor of Massachusetts, the poet wrote: "I cry to you with a million voices: answer our doubt—exert the clemency which your high office affords. There is need in Massachusetts of a great man tonight. It is not yet too late for you to be that man." Clemency was not granted and there were those, like Edna St. Vincent Millay, who would always think that the "gay twenties" did not end with the stock market crash of 1929, but a few minutes after midnight, August 23, 1927 when Nicola Sacco and Bartolomeo Vanzetti were electrocuted. "Justice Denied in Massachusetts," "Hangman's Oak," "Wine from These Grapes," and "To Those Without Pity," all were written by the poet to memorialize the tragedy.

Clearly this was a different kind of poetry than the public was used to from the lyric pen of Edna St. Vincent Millay. In starkest sincerity she was conveying anguish that went beyond the personal to a nation's responsibility to justice and the rights of man. Her mood had become pessimistic:

The sun that warmed our stooping backs and withered the weed
  uprooted—
We shall not feel it again.
We shall die in darkness, and be buried in the rain.

Such doleful conclusion as "we sit without hope" from "Hangman's Oak" shocked many of the legend makers. As if betraying their "little girl from Maine" *this* Edna St. Vincent Millay seemed no longer to be embracing the world or gaily "shocking the bourgeoisie" but sitting in judgment. To the poet it was precisely her passionate love of life that made it difficult for her to remain silent or indifferent to injustice. Nor did the historical realities of the next two decades—the "hungry thirties," the "war years" forties with the introduction of atomic weapons —allow time or breath for change of mood. Had history been different, what direction her poetry would have taken during those years no one can say. But as it was she could not, in good conscience, turn her back on a troubled nation and a convulsive world. Like many other American artists in those controversial times, she put aside what critics refer to as "pure" art and directed her talents to "what I am trying to help save"— democracy and the world itself. Admittedly written and published in urgent haste as fascism threatened to engulf Europe, many of the politically oriented poems appearing in *Wine from These Grapes* (1934); *Huntsman, What Quarry?* (1939); *Make Bright the Arrows* (1940) fell short, by critical standards of her past performance as a poet. Caught midair by critics on one side, and disappointed readers on the other, the bird's wings were beginning to show signs of strain. Was "a poet's free and heavenly mind," as Shelley put it, justified in dedicating itself to a cause? Edna St. Vincent Millay assured herself that in this case it was. On June 10, 1942, the Nazis razed the village of Lidice, murdering every adult male, driving the entire population of women and children into concentration camps. At the request of the War Writers Board she wrote a long narrative poem titled *The Murder of Lidice*, which when broadcast by radio in the United States and Europe so moved Dr. Eduard Benes, President of the Republic of Czechoslovakia, that he wrote to tell her how much it meant to him and his people. Others wrote to praise, but warned that she was too fine a poet to be writing propaganda—she was sacrificing her reputation. She replied: "I have one thing to give in the service of my country . . . my reputation as a poet . . . the dearest thing in life I possess which might possibly be of help has already gone over the top." And went on to add,

> Have you the slightest conception of what this reputation means to me who have been building it carefully for more than twenty years, taking a long time, months, sometimes as long as several years before permitting a poem to be published because I felt that in one line of it, one syllable was not as close to perfection as I might be able to make it?

Aside from her editors at Harpers, few knew what it cost Edna St. Vincent Millay during the war years to do anything less than "perfection."

The loss of her mother ("the presence of that absence is everywhere") and of other dear friends closely associated with *Renascence* years added to her burden. At war's end the poet verged on collapse. And, as in other troubled times, she reminisced again and again about childhood —"meseems it never rained in those days—."

> I wish I could see a gooseberry bush again; and an orchard, a very small one, of quince trees; and a russet apple tree. If ever I see a russet apple tree, I shall climb it. And with a book in my hand. Or, if I find that I must use both hands now when I climb an apple tree, then with a book in my mouth, like Fido bringing home the newspaper. And I shall sit in the tree for hours, hidden by the leaves, reading *Hero and Leander*, or *As You Like It*, or the *Essay of Man* . . .

Often, at Steepletop, after a long night of work at her desk, she would go to bed at dawn, fall into a restless sleep and then—

. . . Memories return.
You awake in wonder, you awake at half-past four,
Wondering what wonder is in store.
You reach for your clothes in the dark and pull them on, you
*   have no time*
Even to wash your face, you have to climb Megunticook.

You run through the sleeping town; you do not arouse
Even a dog, you are so young and so light on your feet.
What a way to live, what a way . . .
No breakfast, not even hungry. An apple, though,
In the pocket.
And the only people you meet are store-windows.

The path up the mountain is stony and in places steep,
And here it is really dark—wonderful, wonderful,
Wonderful—the smell of bark
And rotten leaves and dew! And nobody awake
In all the world but you!—
Who lie on a high cliff until your elbows ache,
To see the sun come up over Penobscot Bay.

On August 30, 1949, Eugen Jan Boissevain died. The poet's in-
domitable courage saw her through a terrible winter alone in Austerlitz,
but as signs of spring began to show on the land Eugen had tended
so well, her loss became harder to bear. Encountering the first dandelion,
she stood and stared at it with a kind of horror—"and then I felt
ashamed of myself and sorry for the dandelion. And suddenly, without
my doing anything about it at all, my face just crumpled up and cried."

Among her friends, Edna St. Vincent Millay was famous for a
quality of humor that seemed imperishable even in times of deepest
distress. Her letters sparkled with a sense of laughter that was contagious.
Neighbors who marveled at her ability to cope now with the care of a
large estate, with aloneness (there was not even a telephone), and still,
as she said, "work seventy-two hours a day at Steepletop" despite her
own frail health, could well believe she had inherited her mother's rock-
like courage. Living in a world that had recently known the horrors of
Hitler's gas chambers, the horror of the bomb which decimated Hiroshima,
Edna St. Vincent Millay did not think it right for a poet to stare
dumbly at life out of personal bereavement. A Thanksgiving poem

was promised and delivered to a national magazine. And there were promises to her publishers to fulfill. New editions of her works were still coming off the press; her mail piled high. Solitude and work filled her life.

Time was a subject much on the poet's mind as she and the century reached the halfway mark. In her Vassar years she had been so confident that "Love shall fold like a cloak/Round the shuddering earth/ Till the sound of its woe cease." And when The War to End All Wars had failed in that promise, even then she had continued to believe that "with men just as they are—sinful and loving" it is possible "to secure a human peace that might endure." Now the Atomic Age had her fearful the world itself might not endure. *Epitaph for the Race of Man*, of which one critic said, "I know of nothing in American literature to compare in scope and grandeur of intellectual grasp . . . brief though it is, this is the only poem in the language since Milton that can be compared in mental boldness with Dante and Lucretius . . ." mourns for *Man*

> *Who when his destiny was high*
> *Strode like the sun into the middle sky*
> *And shone an hour, and who so bright as he*
> *And like the sun went down into the sea*
> *Leaving no spark to be remembered by.*

With her Puritan New England spirit, Edna St. Vincent Millay had existed on a certainty that those who nobly engaged the contest of life would thereby make immortal their "adventurous will." Now, a romanticist turned realist, she was bowing to the cumulative power of man's most ingenious weapon, seeing it as too devastating a foe even for the bravest of individual wills. In 1950 the roller-coaster ride downhill seemed to be carrying not one but millions of breathless young girls with hairpins flying, delivering its passengers any side up with no care whatsoever.

On October 19, 1950, Edna St. Vincent Millay's aching and ailing heart gave out. She died swiftly and alone halfway up a staircase at Steepletop. ". . . It is 5:30, and I have been working all night. I am going to bed. Goodmorning—." These last words, left on her desk for the cleaning woman to see, pay eloquent testimony to the poet's dedication to work. And, despite the pessimism of her later poems, no more appropriate word than "goodmorning" could have been the last from one whose life, since childhood, had been spent running to meet the sunrise, running to greet the day.

One of Edna St. Vincent Millay's earliest critics wrote of her that she had come upon the world of literature "heedless and lovely as a fieldfare . . . a barefoot poet doomed yet redeemed under the shadow of Eternity." While poets like Ezra Pound, T. S. Eliot, Wallace Stevens, E. E. Cummings, Edwin Arlington Robinson, Robert Frost were shaping their visions into strong bows aimed at giant targets, she came center stage "expressing the surprise of youth over the universe, the emotion of youth encountering inexplicable infinities." Then, as her "romantic pilgrimage through an over-sophisticated civilization" progressed, criticism too became more sophisticated and little by little an uncomfortable silence began to shroud the name that had been so loved and honored by three generations of readers.

In the years since her death it has been said of Millay by one downgrading critic that "it was not as a craftsman nor as an influence, but as the creator of her own legend that she was most alive to us," and by another (either out of ignorance of the facts or some personal bias), that she "had not sufficient education to allow her to use effectively her poetic endowment." Critic Rolfe Humphries, though conceding that there were moments of unevenness in her work, nevertheless insisted that she could "and did write so memorably that her language was on every tongue," that "she was a fine lyric poet, also, in the classical sense, a fine elegiac poet." Willing to pay tribute to her "unshaken dedication to her art" but saying it "suffered in the attempt to express her maturer convictions . . . under the weight of an active social consciousness," one critic wished she had held on to "her immense capacity for delight in the world of nature which she observed so lovingly and accurately," while another attested to her "hard, alert, logical mind" her "large accurate knowledge about everything relating to her art."

Today there are some histories of American literature that obscure Edna St. Vincent Millay altogether. Yet Deems Taylor who had worked closely with her on *The King's Henchman* said what her editors had long since come to know: "She was ruthlessly self-critical, and would agonize for days over a single, imperfect line. Even so, in a writing career of thirty-four years she turned out six plays, an opera libretto, and eleven volumes containing about five hundred poems, including upwards of one hundred and seventy sonnets, many of which,

in the opinion of one reader at least, are the finest since those of Keats."
And critic Edmund Wilson writing in *Nation* magazine, April 19, 1952,
was willing to register what he declared to be an "unfashionable opinion"
—that she was "one of the few poets writing in English in our time
who have attained to anything like the stature of great literary figures
in an age in which prose predominated. In giving supreme expression
to profoundly felt personal experience," Wilson concluded, "she was
able to identify herself with more general human experience and stand
forth as a spokesman for the human spirit, announcing its predicaments,
its vicissitudes, but as a master of human expression by the splendor
of expression itself, putting herself beyond common embarrassments, common oppressions, and panics."

After the poet's death her sister, Norma Millay, worked tirelessly
to collect the yet unpublished poems and bring them before the public.
When, in 1954, *Mine the Harvest* appeared, Robert Hillyer, in his review,
said of the book: "The clear sayings, the sure and unpretentious metrical
technique, the singing lines, bring the poet back from death in the full
stature of her genius."

For Edna St. Vincent Millay, who had so hoped to leave "a spark
to be remembered by," her own compassionate lines written "To a Young
Poet" of her acquaintance are perhaps her best epitaph:

> *Time cannot break the bird's wing from the bird.*
> *Bird and wing together*
> *Go down, one feather.*
>
> *No thing that ever flew,*
> *Not the lark, not you,*
> *Can die as others do.*

Robert Frost
(1874–1963)

"Anything more than the truth would have seemed too weak."

One day in 1894 poet-critic Maurice Thompson, while casually reading through the magazine *Independent*, was suddenly jolted sharp to attention by a short poem titled "My Butterfly." Curious about Robert Lee Frost, under whose name the poem appeared, he wrote to William Hayes Ward, editor of the *Independent*, inquiring the history of the poet. In reply Ward described Frost as a twenty-year-old millhand from Lawrence, Massachusetts, who through correspondence had told him that though "My Butterfly" was his first published poem he was ambitiously hopeful it would not be his last. To Ward the compassionate Thompson replied:

> "My Butterfly" has some secret of genius between the lines, an appeal to sympathy lying deep in one's sources of tenderness. . . . I thought of the probable disappointment in store for young Frost all his life long. If I had a chance to say my say to him I should tell him to forget that he ever read a poem and to never pen another rhyme. . . . If Frost has good health tell him to learn a trade or profession and carry a slingshot in his pocket for (the muse).

Of the heartaches suffered by poets Thompson knew only too well. In the closing years of the nineteenth century the order of the day was not poetry but build and boom, prepare for the great new century lying just ahead. The boldness it took to face the commercial world with nothing to sell but a poem meant enduring the mockery of realists, the scorn of disbelievers, the pity of fellow poets who had been there before and lost. But Thompson did not know the quality of the young man in whose interest he penned those discouraging words. *Tell him to forget that he ever read a poem and to never pen another rhyme. Tell him to learn a trade or profession and carry a slingshot in his pocket for the muse.* Robert Lee Frost had heard the same—or a variation—many times before from family, teachers, friends. What they, Thompson, and everybody else would have to learn was that this particular poet kept a slingshot handy all right, not to be aimed at the muse but at whoever or whatever threatened to come between him and his burning ambition to "do something about the present state of literature in America." Since the ferment which had inspired such a wide variety of literary expression in the years prior to the Civil War was gone; since Walt Whitman, the "Good Gray Poet," no longer was on hand "to soar to sing the idea of all" a new voice was needed, and was it not an omen of sorts that Whitman had died March 26, 1892, on *his*, Robert Lee Frost's, eighteenth birthday?

Dreaming himself into Whitman's position, the young poet made a pledge never to let talk of poverty or anything else keep him from his goal. He would continue doing any kind of menial work as long as it was understood by those presuming to advise him that he was merely biding time while waiting for the "real thing" to happen. The real thing for Robert Lee Frost was a life lived solely by and for poetry. "I undertake a future," he wrote to the *Independent* on receipt of its check of $15 for "My Butterfly."

I cannot believe that poem was merely a chance. I will surpass it. I still find myself young enough to hate and abhor giving up what I have once really set my heart on.

Hating to give up whatever he had set his heart on was a characteristic to be reckoned with in Robert Frost.

> *Once in a California Sierra*
> *I was swooped down upon when I was small,*
> *And measured, but not taken after all,*
> *By a great eagle bird in all its terror.*
>
> *Such auspices are very hard to read.*
> *My parents when I ran to them averred*
> *I was rejected by the royal bird*
> *As one who would not make a Ganymede.*

> *Not find a barkeep unto Jove in me?*
> *I have remained resentful to this day*
> *When any but myself presumed to say*
> *That there was anything I couldn't be.*

When editor William Hayes Ward reluctantly rejected the next group of poems submitted to him by the young New Englander, he was stunned to receive this brash reply: "To betray myself utterly, such an one am I that even in my failures I find all the promise I require to justify the astonishing magnitude of my ambition." Ward's response to Frost was to urge him to slow down a little, learn to spell, get on with his education if he truly wanted to be a poet; above all not to count so much on the future he was undertaking as to neglect, meanwhile, honest manual labor. This seemed to get the young poet's back up a bit. In a series of pencil-scrawled communications he let his friend at the *Independent* know just who and what he was dealing with in Robert Lee Frost:

> I have sold newspapers on the streets of San Francisco and worked in the mills and on the farms of New England. My pride is peculiar.
>
> I am often entirely discouraged. But I assure you, sometime, money or no money, I shall prove myself able to do everything *but* spell.
>
> My natural attitude is one of enthusiasm verging on egotism and thus I always confuse myself trying to be modest.

And, finally, in one splendid outburst of confidence:

> I am learning to spell. I am writing better poetry. It is only a matter of time now when I shall throw off the mask and declare for literateur [sic] mean it poverty or riches.

To be twenty and poor might be a terrible lot, but to be twenty and a poet—that for young Robert Frost was glory.

A glory that had its price. Over the long years Frost would more than once have cause to brood and wonder if he had not forsaken too much for the "fun of writing a few poems." "The real thing that you do is a lonely thing," he would finally be moved to say. To a clamoring public who heard and honored this poet through almost half a century he seemed anything but lonely. Writing, teaching, lecturing, "barding" his way from campus to campus across the country and saying to all he met by way of introduction, "What's a poem for if not to share?" he seemed, indeed to be leading a charmed life. So ingenuously warm and cheerful was his simple invitation—

> *I'm going out to clean the pasture spring;*
> *I'll only stop to rake the leaves away*
> *(And wait to watch the water clear, I may):*
> *I shan't be gone long.— You come too.*
>
> *I'm going out to fetch the little calf*
> *That's standing by the mother. It's so young*
> *It totters when she licks it with her tongue.*
> *I shan't be gone long.— You come too.*

that thousands upon thousands of his countrymen tripped happily along after him as if he were a New England Pied Piper come to save them from the noise and confusion of the modern world. Only on arrival in the pasture did they discover that it was not only the tottering calf the poet wanted to show them, but something deeper inside the heart of their country and inside themselves.

What Robert Frost was not willing to show were the scars on the heart of a lonely poet. Whenever he was asked, as often he was, how closely "the figure a poem makes" resembled the figure of the man who made it, which event or emotion in his personal life had evoked a particular poem, he was always careful to protect both the poem and his privacy. "I have written to keep the over-curious out of the secret places of my mind," he said, knowing full well that from first to last his poetry abounds in secrets. But he knew, too, that a good poem, once shared, has its own beginning and must find its own end in the recipient leaving the poet himself to go his own way into other shadows and sunlights up another lonely road.

The image he projected to the world was that of a casual, folksy, witty man, easy to know, "simplicity itself" as one reporter who made the trek to his farmhouse door described him. The image was deceptive; neither he nor his poems are simple. He did not, as so many believe, enjoy "peace, contentment, and the perfectly balanced solidarity of the inner man." The real Robert Frost knew his star would not have been so visible except for the depth of darkness against which it finally came to shine. He laughed up his sleeve at the legend makers, wondered they could not see, even without signal from him, that his life in all its parts symbolized the struggle of the creative artist to survive in America, that he was a man tirelessly exploring contradictions within himself and society while striving to keep his balance between illusion and reality. Knowing all the roads he might have taken and why he chose the one he did, he wondered, too, how long it would take before someone besides himself saw his life as much West as East, saw that he walked with devils as well as angels, and that he had no easy answers—not for politics, religion, love—anything.

To really discover the man behind the poems requires backing off from New England farmhouse doors, from pasture, orchard, barn—requires going back into time, into childhood, and further back still, to those in his family who had loved and dreamed of glory before him. Even then there is no guarantee of discovering all that made the miracle of the brash young man who began his career by saying "I undertake a future." But having been himself a daring sort, this poet never tried to stop anyone from *trying* to catch the real Robert Frost. One safeguard he knew he had, having learned it in his own circuitous pursuit of ultimate truth.

> *We dance round in a ring and suppose,*
> *But the Secret sits in the middle and knows.*

Before the birth of Robert Frost there lived a proud, ambitious temperamental young man by the name of William Prescott Frost, Jr., whose forebears had been New England all the way. William—destined to become the father of Robert—came to maturity in the decade after the Civil War, a time in America's history sometimes referred to as "the terrible seventies." Like so many other restless young Americans of that day, William sorely disappointed his middle-class parents by abandoning their comfortable world to try to fulfill his own dreams. Having taken for bride a woman older than himself of whom they highly disapproved, he headed West in 1873—made a "record stride—or stretch" from New England to California, setting the stage for a drama he little suspected would one day have his son making the journey back the other way.

Speed was the mood of the country in the 1860s. The rails that could carry William Frost west in ten days had been non-existent before the Civil War when an overland and sea journey to San Francisco meant four exhausting weeks of travel. Bret Harte, hailing the dramatic meeting of two railroad engines in 1869, one out of Sacramento, one out of Omaha "facing on a single track, half a world behind each back," had enthusiastically recognized the moment as the birth of modern America. The birth of Robert Lee Frost in San Francisco March 26, 1874, which was to have some significance for modern literature, went unheralded except by his struggling young parents. To the baby's paternal grandparents back East in Massachusetts, he was a New England child born in a foreign place; to his proud father he was symbol of independence. "These two years have brought many changes to me," William wrote finally to inform his parents.

> They have changed me from a country school master to a City Editor. They have brought me a wife and a baby now seven months old. . . . My present expectation is that California will continue to be my home for some time to come. The climate I think agrees with me excellently. We are all well, particularly the little boy who, in fact, has never seen a really sick day in his short life. I know you will say he could not be mistaken for anybody but his Papa's own boy.

Even that last assurance probably did little to allay the anxiety of the grandparents. It was in 1874 that Lieutenant Colonel George A. Custer, slowly making his way down through the Dakota hills, stumbled unexpectedly upon a hoard of gold and a trap of death. Gold and death had long since become symbols for the American West. Newspapers in the East thrived on stories depicting not only continuing troubles with the Indians, but greed, lawlessness, and violence on the part of newcomers to the territory as they staked their claims in dust they prayed was gold. Even in the more sophisticated cities such as San Francisco, there was said to be a breakdown of law and order; featured articles in the press told of gambling, riots, duels, murders, suicides, kidnapings, scandals involving public officials and respected financeers. The West seemed made to order for a city editor, but, in the opinion of Robert's grandparents, hardly the place to rear a *New England* child.

Robert's Scottish-born mother, a former schoolteacher, was only too aware of the pitfalls of living in a city like San Francisco. She could do little to hold back her active young husband from plunging into the thick of its daily excitement and temptations, but she did what she could to try to protect her son from whatever dangers she thought lurked on the streets. Robert was not easy to manage, however. He grew into a jaunty, red-headed, strong-willed boy who resisted her efforts to make him bookish. It was the real-life drama going on outdoors he preferred. Escaping her hold on him he would run out onto the crowded sidewalks where he could see sailors, miners, cattlemen, Irish, Chinese, Mexican, Texan, rich and poor, mingling and vying with one another in a mixture of tongues, attitudes, and dress. Though forbidden to stay out after dark, he too often yielded to temptation to wander further afield than allowed him to get back home in time. For this kind of delinquency he fell victim to severe punishment, especially when it was his father who found him and hauled him in off the street. Later he would understand that the Scottish-Presbyterian background of his mother, and the deep-rooted New England Calvinism of his father had been a double dose of Puritanism standing guard over him; at the time he felt these punishments a savage injustice.

Punishment seems never to have succeeded in making a model boy of Robert. He learned to be skillful at avoiding any kind of imposed disciplines meant to keep him from seeing and learning for himself what life was all about.

> The first school I went to was in San Francisco along about fifteen years after the Civil War. I cried myself out of that one in one day. . . . I didn't get back again for two years. I've been jumping school ever since.

What really kept him out of school was not the crying he quickly abandoned as a weakling's way, but taking advantage of infirmity. As his father suffered from weak lungs—a condition his mother feared would lead to tuberculosis—it prompted her to become anxious whenever there was a sound of coughing in the house. Robert Lee Frost slyly coughed his way out of a formal education on a gamble that he would fare better if his schoolteacher mother tutored him at home. This she did regularly in the beginning, but as the struggle to hold her home together began to absorb more and more of her time, lessons grew increasingly haphazard. By the time Robert reached his seventh year, the life begun so confidently in California by his parents was slowly coming to disaster.

Robert Frost would never think it worthwhile talking about the kind of man or poet that he, a California boy, had become without harking back to the romance and tragedy of his father. Born in New Hampshire, but raised in Lawrence, Massachusetts, William Prescott Frost, Jr., whose father acted as overseer in the Pacific Cotton Mill, had thrived in his boyhood on stories of his New England ancestors, many of whom had been heroes active in New England history as far back as 1632. His vision of himself tended to be based on legends of these ancestors, for one of whom he had been named—that same William Prescott famed in American history for having commanded his troops "Don't shoot until you see the whites of their eyes." Apparently with similar glory in mind, eleven-year-old William Prescott Frost, Jr., at the outbreak of the Civil War, had tried to run off to enlist, not in the Union army as might be suspected, but with Robert E. Lee's Confederate forces. His plan had been quickly thwarted by his parents who did nothing, however, to cool his ardor for Lee or the South's cause. Their copperhead sympathies, of which they made no secret, were dictated by the fact that their own and the prosperity of the town depended on a continuing flow of southern cotton into northern mills. Political passions did not cool after 1865. At the conclusion of the war, when young William Frost made application to enter West Point Military Academy, his entrance was blocked by Republican politicians in Massachusetts who would not forgive the copperhead past of his family. Nor did William forget or forgive their thwarting of his long-standing ambition to train to become a career officer; indeed it so embittered him as to motivate much of the course of his future life. Accepted at Harvard at age seventeen, he did well in his studies, finding that he had a flair for journalistic-style writing. His parents pressed him to study law, live close by to them in Lawrence, and marry a local girl of whom they were fond. But by the time William graduated Phi Beta Kappa from Harvard in 1872, he had ideas of his own. Feeling hemmed in both by prejudicial politics in Massachusetts and the restrictive mores of his conventional-minded parents, he wanted no more of New England.

In setting his sights for California, he dreamed of finding work there as a journalist and thought there might even be opportunity for a young man of his stripe to work his way up in the Democratic party. William P. Frost had some scores to settle and was out to prove to the world he was as good a man as any. In need of money for his journey, he took a job as a teacher in a small country school in Lewistown, Pennsylvania, intending to stay no longer than was necessary to get him started in his new life in the West. But one day a Scottish woman by the name of Isabelle Moodie arrived to assist him in his teaching duties, and on the spot twenty-one-year-old William fell "dead in love" with the twenty-eight-year-old Miss Moodie. Within six weeks he was declaring to her (and to his disapproving parents) that despite the difference in their ages, backgrounds, and natures, he, for one, was not afraid of taking "a step in the dark." His philosophy, he told Belle Moodie, was the same as that of the seventeenth-century Scottish nobleman-soldier, James Graham, whose poem he quoted to her:

> He *either fears his fate too much,*
> Or *his deserts are small,*
> Who *dares not put it to the touch*
> To *win or lose it all.*

Belle (William would call her by no other name) at first let her head rule over her heart and resisted the tempestuous young man, but finally she was totally won over by his youthful ardor and determination. Against the wishes of his parents they were married. A few days later, anxious to get to California, William impulsively threw up his head-mastership, and after seeing Belle safely in the hands of her Ohio relatives, proceeded on his way to San Francisco where within a week of his arrival he astonished everyone but himself by selling an article to the *Bulletin,* one of the most influential newspapers in the city. On the strength of this one success, he sent for his bride. "Home is now to me the sweetest thing in life, and home is anywhere in the wide world where you are . . . my heart and my judgment cry aloud to you, come, come, come, I entreat you to come—now." Heedless of the protest of her now anxious relatives who felt it too soon to risk living in that far away place where William had barely begun to be established, Belle pinned her meagre savings securely to her underskirt and set out for adventure with the man whose aim in life was to dare to win it all. Many years later when it came her son's turn to live a similar star-crossed romance, he would write a poem celebrating his own risky escapade into marriage, but for which the impoverished lover of 1873 might as easily have stood for models:

> They *leave us so to the way we took,*
>   As *two in whom they were proved mistaken,*
> That *we sit sometimes in the wayside nook,*
> With *mischievous, vagrant, seraphic look,*
>   And *try if we cannot feel forsaken.*

For the earlier pair of lovers the "seraphic" bliss was not to last long. Survival in California in the 1870s, with or without love, was no easy matter. Thousands upon thousands of Americans were filling up the West the year William Frost, friendless and jobless, arrived there, not only because it offered living space and opportunity, but because at the moment five "bonanza" mines called the Comstock Lode had put the state of California into the wildest speculation fever since '49, silver instead of gold luring the victims this time. Feeling lucky in having risen to the post of city editor of the *San Francisco Chronicle* within a year of his arrival in the city, and ascribing his success to his gambler's philosophy, William began trying his luck to increase his fortune. In gambling crazed 'Frisco, said one observer of the "terrible seventies," "rich man, poor man, servant, and master alike, all were playing the same deadly game. That anyone survived those years, particularly 1875 is a phenomenon that must be explained by the climate. Thousands did not. They either committed suicide or crawled away to hide themselves for the rest of their shattered lives. Only a few tremendous fortunes were made." Fortunes that were to change the city of Robert Frost's birthplace into a modern, industrial metropolis. The "silver kings" built carriage and watch factories, opened new theaters, and built for themselves houses against the hills to rival oriental palaces, staffing them with small armies of Chinese servants. To contrast this spectacular wealth, armies of poorly paid workers, only slightly better off than the unemployed poor, lived in squalor, and from time to time in the years Robert Frost roamed the streets as a boy, rioted, lighting up the night sky with fires as they sought vengeance for hunger, oppression, and broken dreams. William P. Frost, Jr., was not among the unemployed, would not have been among the poor except that his gambler's instinct put him into the ranks of the losers all along the way. In seven years of shifting fortune the Frost family was forced to move to seven different locations, each poorer than the one before. And now there were two children (Robert's sister Jeannie having been born in 1876) to share the poverty and heartbreak.

Belle Frost's tasks at home were not made easier by her young husband's moodiness in disappointment, his tendency to drown injured pride at bars with journalistic and political cronies. He had latched on to one Blind "Boss" Buckley, a politician described by historian Gertrude Atherton as one of "the most notorious, shameless of boss politicians, expert in every form of extortion, oppression, and demoralization of his army of human tools." True or not, politics in those days in California was a rough game to play, and Belle Frost had reason to be concerned, especially as winning at politics meant more to William even than winning at the gambling table or as a career journalist. Late and long despite poor health, he drove himself so that one day as a prominent

California politician he'd be in a position to see to it that the son he had named to honor his defeated hero, Robert E. Lee, could go to West Point or to any other military academy the boy might choose. Uncharacteristically Belle fled all the way to New England with Rob and Jeannie to consult the elder Frosts as to how to bring their young son to his senses. According to legend, she was treated coolly, informed that whatever troubles accrued for her or their son in California were her own doing. The rebuff was not altogether unexpected. Bundling up the two children for the long journey back to San Francisco, Mrs. Frost decided that whatever the dream driving her husband, her place was at his side, for she had, indeed, known from the beginning that life with him was not going to be easy.

At age seven Robert Lee Frost was out selling newspapers on the streets while the often ailing elder Frost lay at home with a tubercular cough. Mrs. Frost worked at reviewing books for the *Chronicle* or whatever other jobs she could find to help hold her impoverished family together. Born at Leith, seaport of Edinburg, Scotland, Robert's mother had a seafaring heritage and long-stored memory of ties between those who venture and those who patiently wait behind. An able, hard-working woman with enough romanticism in her nature to hold her to a dreamer like William, Belle Frost did her best to shield her two children from the impact of an often troubled marriage. But her young son saw more than she thought he saw, and through the years would carry memory of a family relationship fraught with all the human conflicts against which love has to struggle to survive.

Surviving on the streets of San Francisco was the problem of young Robert Lee Frost; he quickly learned that bravado was indispensable for getting along in a rough world. His sister Jeannie developed into a humorless, moody, dramatic-natured child less able to stand up to the trauma of a troubled home life. Playing foil to the little girl's persistent pessimism and tears, Robert's way with Jeannie was to pose as if the world was not as dark as she weakly made it out to be, striking up that posture all the more boldly whenever he saw his own fears mirrored in his sister's eyes. He was too young to know that constantly playing opposite to Jeannie's mood doomed her to live alone with her terrors, to feel outcast from the sympathy of the brother she adored. What he did learn, living among the poor in San Francisco, was that life and struggle were synonymous, that the strong took advantage of the weak unless the weak took courage to fight back. Boy or man, Robert Frost never would cater to whiners or easy despairers. By age ten he had seen enough of friction at home, and in the industrial city in which he lived —a city constantly torn by strikes and riots—to believe that conflict was part of life's daily business. As he grew older he would come to believe that only through dissension and struggle did issues become clearer and the world make progress. As a philosopher-poet he was to argue that in all people, all things, all times there is positive and negative constantly at war, and that obstacles that fall into a path make for learning something new, for forcing Man to go on from where he'd been bogged down in sameness.

> *The tree the tempest with a crash of wood*
> *Throws down in front of us is not to bar*
> *Our passage to our journey's end for good,*
> *But just to ask us who we think we are*
>
> *Insisting always on our own way so.*
> *She likes to halt us in our runner tracks,*
> *And make us get down in a foot of snow*
> *Debating what to do without an ax.*
>
> *And yet she knows obstruction is in vain:*
> *We will not be put off the final goal*
> *We have it hidden in us to attain,*
> *Not though we have to seize earth by the pole*
>
> *And, tired of aimless circling in one place,*
> *Steer straight off after something into space.*

In wars, in depressions, whenever anyone would say to Robert Frost the man, "We're all going to the dogs," he would reply, "Ah, rats," in much the same way he had responded to Jeannie in their stormy childhood. For he kept thinking back to the California of the 1870s and '80s, remembering times when San Francisco had been turned into an armed camp with unemployed Irish battling employed Chinese, with cavalry called out to patrol the manufacturing districts, and police the water district because a man named Dennis Kearney, heading the Working Man's party of California (the Sand Lot party San Franciscans called it), had issued a manifesto telling the poor, unemployed, ill-housed people of that city, "The rich have ruled us until they have ruined us. We will now take our own affairs into our own hands."

The world hadn't come to an end then despite all the violence.

Turmoil had made for change; change had brought progress. If he had learned anything living among the poor in California, among the poor in New England, from coming along with the old century into the new, it was that if trouble seemed on the ascendance today, good was just as likely to grow out of it tomorrow.

> *Its from their having stood contrasted*
> *That good and bad so long have lasted.*

This he learned directly from life itself. Education out of books came much more slowly.

Between household chores and the editorial work she did for a living, Belle Frost was only able to get in a few hours a week to teach her young son, but whatever knowledge she did manage to impart seemed to cling to him like burrs, which, as Robert Frost in later years liked to tell his own students, was the way poets had to get knowledge—"cavalierly, and as it happens, in and out of books." Poets, he would say, "stick to nothing deliberately, but let what will stick to them like burrs where they walk in the fields." The first book he clearly remembered seeing in one of the many parlors he had to get used to in the San Francisco years, was a volume of Robert Herrick's poems given to his literary mother to review for the *Chronicle*. That pleased his fancy, not then, at age seven, but years and years later when the memory of the little book in its place on the table under the lamp returned to him. In her Scottish brogue, his mother would read to him whatever to her at the moment seemed appropriate—Scottish tales, a smattering of history, poetry (she particularly liked Edgar Allan Poe, had Jeannie memorize "The Raven" and recite it before her husband's friends, among whom were Henry George, later to become famous for his book *Progress and Poverty*, and the Irish-American actor, James O'Neill, destined to become the father of Eugene O'Neill, the playwright). Sometimes, instead of reading, Mrs. Frost would tell stories of her life back in the old country, so stirring Robert's imagination that it became one of his ambitions to walk one day on those far away shores where his mother had lived as a girl.

Perhaps because it was her only guarantee that a boy as slippery as hers would get anything at all out of books, Belle Frost did not for many years compel Robert to learn to read, but always sat him down to listen. With sister Jeannie in the small circle under the lamp, Robert happily allowed the sound of his mother's emotion as she read to mark for him the corresponding language and tones associated with anger, love, joy, excitement, sadness. Later on, on the street, or in the saloon where often he was sent to fetch a beer for his sick father, he would identify drama in the factual world by those same familiar tones. It took only a word, or a clutch of phrases, as he was to say, without his having to see the faces of the men and women speaking them, to hold him listening with acute understanding to some human drama in which ordinary mortals were at war with one another over a trifle or for keeps. He never lost this "sound of sense" as he termed it, and made use of it for dramatic effect when he became a poet.

Another kind of education beneficial to young Robert Frost was obtained in the small kitchen-garden his mother kept behind whatever house she occupied. While seeding, weeding, or pulling, he acquired an affection for that "little farm" which was the place his "inclination to country occupations first began." As contrast to the rough contest of the streets, the country occupation was one in which newsboy Frost, at ages eight and nine could exercise the introspective side of his nature, dream and assess himself, learn to become as sharply tuned to inner as to outer weather. It was there he first felt a small boy's ego striving toward some wondrous, indefinable thing, something to give shape to the varying emotions he experienced at home where, between love and quarreling, no one seemed to know how to live together or apart; and the way he felt upon seeing his city wake at dawn, seeing the bay all bathed in fog, seeing and hearing the streets come alive with people vying with one another for position and trade. Sometimes the boy working the little farm would remember how, while camping once on the beach at Sausalito where his father was "taking the cure" for consumption, he had heard the sound of fear creeping into his bones when his mother, in low, anxious tones, scolded William P. Frost for swimming farther out in the Pacific than most men dared, coming back half alive to cough in frightening spasms as he lay shivering on the sand. At Sausalito there were cliffs, steep, out of reach to all but eagles, backed up as if nature intended them for a safeguard against the great waves. "The shore was lucky in being backed by cliff," Robert Lee Frost had thought then and later put it down in a poem, "The cliff in being backed by continent." But what could save his father? Darkness was closing round the little family on the shore. ". . . a night of dark intent/Was coming, and not only a night, an age./Someone had better be prepared for rage."

In 1884, William P. Frost, Jr., got up from a sickbed to campaign for Grover Cleveland for President of the United States, himself for tax collector of San Francisco. He took ten-year-old Robert along with him to help hang political posters in waterfront saloons, gambling halls, and stores. Talking votes, talking favors, talking politics, the boy got still another kind of education, a feel for campaigning that was never afterward to leave him. Politicking brought him closer to his father who seemed almost recovered in health and pride with this sudden surge of energy which he thought surely would result in his first political victory. But this dream like all others in William's life came to nought. Many years later his son wrote:

> How tragic it was for our family way back there in California in 1884 the year my father was defeated for tax collector of San Francisco. He didn't come home for days afterwards. He took it too hard. He was wrong about it, I can say that.

In the spring of 1885 William P. Frost, Jr., died, and rage began in earnest for two children forever losing their kingdom by the sea where dust was

> *. . . always blowing about the town,*
> *Except when sea fog laid it down,*
> *And I was one of the children told*
> *Some of the blowing dust was gold.*

As he accompanied his father's casket on the train moving slowly eastward, eleven-year-old Robert Lee Frost could not understand his father's request to be buried in New England in a dust that never blew gold at all. Carrying a chip on his shoulders for being fatherless, penniless, he had no enthusiasm for going to live among Yankee strangers who seemed to think all far Westerners barbarians. For once he wasn't scoffing at Jeannie's tears, but sat nursing unshed tears of his own for all the dreams that had flared and died in the childhood he was leaving behind. "A poem begins as a lump in the throat, a sense of wrong, a homesickness, a loneliness. It is never a thought to begin with. It is at its best when it is a tantalizing vagueness," he was to say in later years. The tantalizing vagueness was all the more an agony at age eleven not knowing then how and when it could be released. But memories and influences of the western experience remained. Many years later, he would be making connections and estimating contrasts, and, as childhood found its way into the landscape of his art, he would be surprised at "remembering something I didn't know I knew."

> "I am in a place, in a situation as if I had materialized from a cloud risen out of the ground. There is a glad recognition of the long lost and the rest follows. Step by step the wonder of unexpected supply keeps growing. The impressions most useful to my purpose seem always those I was unaware of and so made no note of at the time when taken, and the conclusion is come to that like giants we are always hurling experience ahead of us to pave the future with against the day when we may want to strike a line of purpose across it for somewhere."

And that was what was happening to the young boy who sat watching the West recede as the train pulled on taking him to an unknown future—he was "hurling experience ahead of him" against the day when he would see New England better for having known the street life of California; for the day when he would write his first "New England" poem. To measure the depth of snow not by inches but by the weight on the heart, the height of a tree not by its nearness to heaven but its closeness to earth—to find a meeting point in fire and ice takes having experienced a place where no snow fell, no trees were to climb, no ice formed to break so "you'd think the inner dome of heaven had fallen"—which was the way his father's death affected him before ever he saw how a birch could be bent under a New England ice storm. A child's first fear, first loss, first longing, first anger; his first knowledge of joy, love, disappointment—whatever the climate, whatever the time—is carried on to become linked with the mature poet's vision of the universe and the sound he makes when he finally speaks of himself and his world.

The New England years began for Robert Frost with half of his childhood behind him, with stubborn, fierce pride already deeply in-grained. After a brief try at living with her husband's parents, Mrs. Frost, whose pride was almost as raw as her son's, moved to Salem, New Hampshire, a rural hamlet where she soon found work as a teacher in a one-room schoolhouse; pay, nine dollars a week. Among the thirty-four pupils she singlehandedly educated were her own two children. At first Robert was one of her problem boys, as ornery as ever at being caught and pinned down for formal education. But his mother was firm this time. At age twelve he was finally being made to accept discipline, to learn to read, spell, and write.

I have got to read a composition after recess and I hate to offaly

was a note he passed on to young Sabra Peabody. Another, written soon afterward

> There are not many girls I like but when I like them I fall dead in love with them and when I get mad at you I feel mad at myself too

Sabra passed on to posterity.

Growing up was a painful process for this sensitive, fatherless boy. With braggadocio and feigned toughness he covered over his insecurity among Easterners, feeling a strong need to be on top in competitive sports and, gradually, as he awakened to his full intellectual potential, to be on top in his studies too. He discovered in himself a mania for perfection which, though in later years he would consider a fault, aided him in the strict discipline of creating a poem.

> In my school days I simply could not go on and do the best I could with a copy book I had once blotted. I began life wanting perfection and determined to have it.

In a year and a half he made up for eight missed years of formal schooling and went on to the Lawrence High School, no easy accomplishment for a boy forced to work after school, weekends, and summers. At age twelve Robert Frost was inserting nails into holes in the heels of shoes. At age thirteen he was working "behind a big machine run by a big man—a really dangerous process for a child" proud not to let his mother know *how* dangerous. But he liked a shop for its sturdy characters, and probably learned more there about the uninhibited expressiveness of the English language—what Emerson in "Monadnoc" called "that hearty English root"—than anywhere else. He was curious, too, about all mechanical and human processes; how men worked, why they worked, the beauty and dangers of a tool, the products it produced— something creative between man and his materials. Unlike Emerson, Robert Frost would never have to travel far from his own everyday experiences to find his language and ideas for a poem. Among all New England poets, he was to be unique in this respect: Hard physical labor and shoptalk were not only part of his education for life, but for literature too; he came to poetry wanting to sing the virtues of ordinary people and to use his supply of language to express what

he thought boy or man could make of letting his two hands count
for something. It was the years of hand-to-mouth struggle as a boy
that made Robert Frost say as a man:

> As gay for you to take your father's ax
> As take his gun—rod to go hunting—fishing.
> You nick my spruce until its fiber cracks,
> It gives up standing straight and goes down swishing.
> You link an arm in its arm and you lean
> Across the light snow homeward smelling green.
>
> I could have brought you just as good a tree
> To frizzle resin in a candle flame,
> And what a saving 'twould have meant to me.
> But tree by charity is not the same
> As tree by enterprise and expedition.

"That Rob can do most anything with his hands," he'd hear his mother
tell her friends in Salem when he was still in high school, and suddenly
his pride stirred to want to hear her boast about what he could do with
his mind too.

> Sometimes a person's real character is slow in blossoming. Until I
> was fourteen I had never read a book. I thought, and those who
> knew me thought, I was more mechanically minded than anything
> else. But after I had read my first book a new world opened up for
> me, and after that I devoured as many of them as I could lay my
> hands on. By the time I was fifteen I was already beginning to write
> verses.

Writing verses not too openly because of what other country boys might
say. He was being careful about his pride that way too.

> . . . you don't want to feel queer. You don't want to be too much
> like the others but you don't want to be clear out in nowhere . . .
> you like to mock 'em and to shock 'em but you really do care.

He cared enough to stay at the top of his class in Greek, Latin, and
mathematics while proving himself as good a man as any out where
it counted among the local boys. "I ran well, I played on town ballteams,
and on the High school football team. I had my share of fights." A rather
public fight in 1896 cost Robert Frost "the humiliation of going into
court and a ten dollar fine."

Proctor's *Our Place Among the Infinities* was one of the first books Robert read all the way through, "hovered over," as he said, and all his early verses could name the stars he thus came close to. He hovered over Prescott's *History of Mexico*, too, and wrote his first ballad "La Noche Triste," based on the wrongs done to Indians. In due time he discovered Shakespeare, Milton, Wordsworth, Homer, other giants of drama and poetry. Reading Shelley, Keats, Browning, he ached to be a giant for his own country. He had no idea then that the "terrible seventies" had spawned numerous other young hopefuls as anxious as he to do something about the state of literature in America—Edwin Arlington Robinson, born on the eve of the decade in 1869; Stephen Crane, 1871; Amy Lowell and Ellen Glasgow who came along in 1874; Sherwood Anderson, Willa Cather in 1876; Carl Sandburg, 1878; Vachel Lindsay, 1879. Isolated, restless, Robert Frost cared only about himself— a joshing schoolboy suddenly sobering down into the apprenticeship of an artist. It was rather awesome discovering all the things inside himself that had been lying fallow until now. He found the novels of Thomas Hardy and, in his words, "they struck the simple solemn," helping him to see more clearly how to celebrate the virtues of the poor. Shakespeare had made drama of tragedies of kings and princes. Hardy perceived in ordinary, rough-hewn folk on Wessex Down the tragedy and comedy that belonged not to kings alone. North of Boston, in New England, Robert Frost's subject now began to open up to him. He could see himself and his neighbors Hardy's way, just plain country folk living out "life's little ironies."

Using a young poet's eye, he now saw everything in his environment in a new way—isolated farms, winter silences, spring awakenings, woodshed, palings, singing streams, dark underbrush of forest, animals yoked, animals resisting the yoke, barns, farm machinery, weather, mountains, orchard, fields—not for nature's sake but as symbols of human strivings. A poor man laboring to overcome in isolation became a larger symbol for the meaning of all life. The more poetry he wrote the more he began to see how to use these symbols to make the kind of poetry that says more than it seems to say, to express the contradictions in life, to express his own individualistic philosophy. For him the definition of a poem became "saying one thing in terms of another." Writing like that wasn't easy, but something of prime importance in the making of Robert Frost had happened the moment he discovered that North of Boston could be both itself and more than itself. New England had, at last, become home.

As poetry quickened in Robert Frost, he saw that it was nothing if it had no connection to the human heart. "I like to hear it beating under the things I write," he said. He wondered if other people would hear it that way, too, understand what it was he trying to convey when he depicted for them what had to be done in country places to survive, what lay behind the eyes of a farmer standing in the doorway of his barn looking out toward the far end of the orchard and beyond, hungering for the freedom of a wild colt, or a doe, or a bear that came only for a sniff at civilization before thumping back to the forest. He decided that he wanted his poetry to be like a wild-game preserve, not pretty pictures of apple orchards or maples flaming in the fall, but people trapped inside the skin of civilization fighting back the need to howl when weather ruined crops, brought trees to the ground, when death or ruin struck. Death and ruin were things he knew well enough to tell. When he said of his poetry "It's where wild things live," would anybody understand?

His grandfather, for one, didn't understand about poetry at all. The old man was still overseeing the Pacific Cotton Mill (hiring his grandson to work there in summers) still resenting that William P. Frost, Jr., had struck out on his own to earn a living with the pen instead of reading for law or some other more respectable profession. William's son, he said, better get over the notion that he could make his way in life by writing verses. Any lad bright enough to be valedictorian of his high school class was surely bright enough to go to Harvard and become something more useful than a poet.

But not Harvard, nor any other college appealed to Robert Lee Frost. The only thing that had really excited him in high school had been being editor of the school newspaper; sometimes he'd write all the articles because he couldn't get the staff to fulfill assignments. Once or twice he had used the opportunity to put in a poem of his own, and seeing it in print seemed to him one of the grandest things in life. Not more education now—at least not in a formal sense—but more time to write poems was what he was looking forward to after graduation. His mother understood about poetry better than his grandfather, but she, too, argued for college, (Dartmouth, though; too much drinking at Harvard, she said); as did Elinor White, the girl he had fallen "dead in love" with at Lawrence High School. Elinor, that first summer after graduation, wouldn't agree to getting engaged on the slim promise that poetry no matter how good, would make a decent living for a family.

Robert Frost's lover's quarrel with Elinor—with the world—must have begun something like this:

> How will you make a living?
> *I'll write poetry.*
> How do you know anyone will want to read it?
> *They'll read it, they'll read it.*
> But maybe you aren't the poet you think you are.
> *If I know anything, I know that. I've got copy books full of poems, good ones, too. Conceit? When you can do a thing, you know it. The whole world will know it one of these days.*

Another New England poet, Amy Lowell, who one day was to play a part in helping Robert prove his boast to the world, said of her own boasting and engineering her way to fame: "I have to be my own impresario. There's no point in having a trumpet, or brass, if you don't blow it." A nineteen-year-old proudling named Frost found it an excruciating experience always to be having to blow his own brass to people when he was yet too young to be taken seriously. He didn't win his argument with Elinor. This girl, whom he loved to distraction (she had been his co-valedictorian at high school) left at the end of fall for four years of college in upstate New York, having exacted a promise of *him*—that he'd take up his grandfather's offer to send him to college.

In September 1892, eighteen-year-old Robert Frost entered Dartmouth. True to his mother's hope, Dartmouth was careful to see that there was "no drinking at all—if we wanted an orgy, we sat up all night with a box of Turkish paste [a jelly like candy],"—He found it difficult to adjust to college life, not because of the Turkish paste, but because he felt trapped; as trapped as he had felt that past summer working at various odd jobs, and earning money in a way that hadn't anything to do with what he was thinking and dreaming.

> I would work at almost anything rather well for a while but every once in so often I had to run off for a walk in the woods. I dreamed my way through all sorts of fortunes without any realizing sense of what I was enduring. Nothing seemed to come within a row of apple trees of where I really lived.

Where he really lived was in the world of poetry; at college, too, he kept thinking he ought to be able to convince someone besides himself that poetry was a way of "grappling with life." Meanwhile he was not grappling with academics. He was indifferent to the curriculum, scorned faternities, made only one intellectual friend with whom he had "high old talks" about religion, politics, history. He engaged in occasional escapades—"the more roughhouse the merrier"—and disgracefully allowed his room to pile up with ashes from the open coal stove until they reached the door. "My mother had to send up a friend to dig me out," he said. But she could not dig him out of his determination not to succeed at college. The moment the term came to an end he made a clean bolt for freedom.

On reaching Salem, he told his mother he'd rather help her manage the bigger, rougher boys she taught in her one-room school house than be a schoolboy himself. Belle Frost did not balk this time, seeing in her son his father's impatience and daring, but something to balance it too—her own ability to reason things out in a way that evidenced a care for life. Robert also had mirth going for him against self-pity, a quality she thought most beneficial of all in an uncertain and uncaring world. This time she believed him when he told her in prose what he was later to tell in poetry:

> My object in living is to unite
> My avocation and my vocation
> As my two eyes make one in sight.
> Only where love and need are one,
> And the work is play for mortal stakes,
> Is the deed ever really done
> For Heaven and the future's sakes.

Now it remained only to convince Elinor.

Selecting five of his poems, he had them printed and bound at his own expense under the title *Twilight*, two copies only, one for him, one for his love. Then, with the precious volumes under arm, he set out to woo Elinor White into taking a step in the dark. All the way to New York Robert Frost kept hoping that seeing his poems in print would turn Elinor's head a little as it did his a lot. But it proved folly, that October's journey. After putting *Twilight* into her hands, he stood below on the campus looking up to the window of the room which she shared with a number of other girls, and imagined her reading his poems to them while the whole covey sat laughing at him as if he were some poor, miscast troubadour. After a time he became convinced that Elinor was laughing too. His own humor draining entirely away, he impulsively destroyed his copy of *Twilight* and fled, not back to New England but "without address . . . out of time" tramping aimlessly through Maryland, Virginia, North Carolina, living a hobo existence, picking up an occasional job that barely paid enough to keep him alive. Running in defeat was something his father had done; somewhere along the way in this desolate journey Robert Frost remembered, and realized it was a devil in himself he had to conquer. Mirth and reason finally prevailed over self-pity sending him home again—just in time to celebrate his first success as a published poet.

While at Dartmouth he had come across a magazine called the *Independent* and had had his "very first revelation that a publication existed anywhere in my native land that was a vehicle for the publication of poetry." Subsequently he had decided to try his luck at the *Independent* with one of the poems he had chosen to include in *Twilight*. Thus it seemed to him as if destiny had all along been pulling him back from "experiences so absorbing that I am nothing morbid now" to see his name where he had always dreamed it would be: " 'My Butterfly,' An Elegy by Robert Frost" printed on the front page of an important periodical. His pride soared almost out of bounds when he saw how impressive the poem looked in print. He confronted Elinor with this proof that he was a man who could fulfill dreams, and was so earnest in his youthful ardor and determination that she yielded now to his proposal that they become engaged.

One year later, almost to a day, Robert Frost and Elinor White were married in Lawrence, Massachusetts, beginning a union that was to last until Elinor's death forty years later when her famous husband would say of her: "She has been the unspoken half of everything I ever wrote, and both halves of many a thing from "My November Guest" down to the last stanzas of "Two Tramps in Mud Time." During their marriage Elinor lovingly preserved her copy—the only one in existence—of *Twilight*. (There came a time, after her death when, as a collector's item, the romantic little book sold for $4000.) But for now, the poetic life was rich in everything but money.

Tying together meager fortunes and their fates against the best advice of both sets of parents, they settled into their "wayside nook" with Robert determined to repeat the miracle of "My Butterfly" and add up more sets of fifteen dollars to impress all doubters. But when rejection slips started coming in, he found himself to be one of the doubters. "I fear I am not a poet, or but a very incomprehensible one," he wrote in a bitter, "down" mood to the same editors he had earlier told of enthusiasm verging on egotism. He had stopped working as a millhand now; he and Elinor had joined his mother in teaching at her school. His restlessness even at that work was obvious, however. The only thing he could think about or say to his family was that he just wanted to "publish one more poem before I die."

In August 1896 the *Independent* caused a flurry of elation in the Frost household by accepting "The Birds Do Thus." But the poet's appetite for publishing persisted. The refrain: "Just one more poem . . . one more before I die," Elinor had to learn to live with.

The birth of a son, Eliot, in September 1896 was another great event. With his family growing, incentive became ever stronger for Robert to make a living by writing poetry. That winter the poet's lamp burned late into the night. By day, whenever he could get the time off from teaching he would sit so long at his lonely trade that he moaned he was "losing touch with mankind"—a statement Nathaniel Hawthorne would have understood. But for all his labors, the accumulated poems never found their mark, and the young father had to face up to the fact that he wasn't grappling with life by way of poetry after all. The editors of the *Independent* said he ought to get on with his education; Elinor argued for it, too, believing *that* was a factor in the rising of stars. So, in the fall of 1897, with sacrifices made on all sides, twenty-three-year-old Robert Frost reluctantly entered Harvard College as a special student. This time around he applied himself to his studies and won honors for his work. But, as he later put it, "I was restless and didn't seem to be liking things again." At the end of his sophomore year he once more disappointed his grandfather by bolting. Elinor, who was nursing daughter Leslie, born in the spring of 1899, agreed with him now that poets had to get their education cavalierly, and as it happens, in and out of books. She stopped trying to put her young husband into the ordinary mold and settled for winning or losing it all—his way. What he was asking for now was a farm on which to raise children, chickens, and crops of poems—and enough courage to get his grandfather to back him on *this* scheme.

> When I told Grandfather Frost I wanted to be a poet, he wasn't pleased. He was an old-line Democrat—here I was making good grades and wanting, he thought, to waste my life. "I give you one year to make it, Rob," he said. I put on an auctioneer's voice—"give me twenty, give me twenty"—My grandfather never brought up poetry again.

I had to find other means to make a living than poems—they didn't sell fast enough, and I didn't send poems out much. I had pride—I hated rejection slips. I had to be careful of my pride—

Living in Lawrence, a failure by that mill town's standards, he reached the ripe old age of twenty-six when the new century rang in. The year 1900 was a sad one for Frost. His mother was dying of cancer. But death had a blow for him that was not expected, striking suddenly at his baby son, Eliot, who succumbed within a day of cholera. The child was buried in Lawrence that grief-stricken July 5 and Elinor Frost had difficulty recovering from her loss. Robert took over her household chores despite his own heavy grief, doing his best to carry on with everyday realities. The distance between his child's grave and the front door of home was short, but a dialogue was set up by that distance in the lives of two for whom love now had another, deeper dimension. "Home Burial" written by Robert Frost many years past that dark July, rises beyond a statement of one family's personal tragedy to touch on the poignancy of emotion dividing any man and wife faced with individual ways of confronting the loss of a child. In the poem the man, after burying his child, comes back into the kitchen with mud stains fresh on his shoes and begins casually to talk of "everyday concerns." His distraught wife cries, "Think of it, talk like that at such a time!" accuses him of not caring. "You *couldn't* care," she says,

> *You can't because you don't know how to speak.*
> *If you had any feelings, you that dug*
> *With your own hand—how could you?—his little grave;*
> *I saw you from that very window there,*
> *Making the gravel leap and leap in air . . .*
>
> *I thought, Who is that man? I didn't know you.*

The depth of caring was beyond any words Robert Frost or any man might have used to tell. Speaking had to come later when art could transcend individual emotion. Of his theory of art, Robert Frost would say that the subject of any piece of creative work should be "common in experience and uncommon in books. It should have happened to everyone but it should have occurred to no one before as material." But he had a word of warning to himself as well as others—

> There is a danger of forgetting that poetry must include the mind as well as the emotions . . . The mind is dangerous and must be left in.

After Eliot's death, Frost moved his family to a small farm in Derry, New Hampshire (bought for him by his grandfather), and it was there his mother died in November. In the next few years, a hard time of struggle, his family grew in size. A son, Carol, was born in 1902, Irma in June of the following year, Marjorie in March 1905. Elinor Betina, born in 1907 lived but two days. Holding faith and family together while trying to write poetry and farm thirty acres of land was something Frost would never forget. People who didn't understand what he was about, called him a lazy farmer, but when a man tries to harvest two kinds of crops, something has to give a little. Hawthorne, in the *Blithedale Romance,* which he based on his experiences at Brook Farm, argued the case for the "lazy" poet-farmer. "Burns," he said, "never made a song in haying-time. He was no poet while a farmer and no farmer while a poet." Lazy or not, for Robert Frost a farm was the best place to work, and all his life when he wandered away from one to teach or speak, or live some other way, he'd tell people "I get a queer unhappiness when I don't have a land to farm." He'd say it even though farming had its problems for him the same as for more natural farmers who were his neighbors among the poor of New Hampshire.

> Our thermometer dropped to 25° night before last and thirty last night losing us all our seed and a month's growth where months are more precious than they are in your region. That worst night the larger farmers fought the cold with fire and water; the small farmers wrapped their gardens up in their own clothes and bedclothes and went without themselves. A lot of good it did. My favorite tomato froze right in my heavy winter overcoat.

Too many such lost seed and growth, too many rejection slips made Elinor and Robert Frost face up, finally, to need for a change. It was seventeen years now since a brash young poet, author of "My Butterfly," had told all and sundry he was a force to be reckoned with in literature. But few people beyond Derry or Plymouth (where he did some teaching now) had ever heard the name Robert Frost. "America! Pay attention to your authors!" Herman Melville had said; nobody had listened then—(Melville lived in impoverished obscurity the last years of his life) nobody was listening now to the sound Robert Frost was making, and the twenty years he had bargained for were almost gone. In the firelight of their farm parlor, Robert and Elinor decided it was time to seek elsewhere. England, Robert said, was a country that honored poets.

Friends in Derry and Plymouth thought him mad to uproot his family for the sake of finding in England what he couldn't find in America; behind his back they wondered how any man could keep faith in himself as a poet when so many reputable editors kept on hinting otherwise. Frost knew who the doubters were and kept their names in mind to spur him on to the goal he would not for anyone's sake abandon. "Writing is like anything else," he said, "it is a possession with some people, they can't let it alone and they forsake all else for it." This thing which possessed him and which he possessed, which he could not let alone, had his own family in a fever of excitement packing for a great adventure overseas. The thirty-eight-year-old poet fitted out a packing case with his favorite Morris chair and a plane of wood to fit across it for writing on—made certain Elinor packed plenty of five-cent copybooks—the only kind he would use to put down his poems—stuffed the bottom of his trunk with enough finished poems to make up two manuscripts, on top of which Elinor was then allowed to put all the household goods the trunk could carry, and they were off. "I never look behind me before I leap," Robert said, making his skeptical friends smile as they watched him board the S.S. *Parisian* September 8, 1912. To his old friends at the New York *Independent*, he wrote a note to explain his decision to leave the country. "My soul inclines to go apart by itself again and devise poetry. Heaven send that I go not too late in life for the emotions I expect to work in."

The Frost family spent its first morning abroad in Glasgow, then traveled all day across Scotland (a dream fulfilled for Robert) arriving in London at the first glow of evening lights, "greatly excited at being all alone, without a single friend in the biggest city in the world." Within a few days the poet located a cottage in the town of Beaconsfield where, he wrote friends back home, "it is my plan to stay for a year if our courage holds out." He settled down to work almost at once, while Elinor with her children scattering all directions in front of her went out into the field to listen to another kind of singing. Said the wife of Robert Frost.

> I can understand now why the lark is the subject of so much English poetry. Every few minutes one will rise from the ground as if overcome by emotion and soar straight up in the air until one can scarcely see him, singing all the while such a sweet, rapturous song and then let himself straight down again, singing until he reached the ground.

In such a land, might not someone hear the singing of her husband?

That winter, for the first time in years, Robert's mood sparkled with expectancy, and mirth too. "We have had ice (a few times) on the rain barrel—if that constitutes winter," he wryly commented to a friend living out the New England winter, "and one morning early in December the papers were out with scare heads like this:

ENGLAND IN THE GRIP OF FROST

I accept the omen, says I, I accept the omen."

From the Beaconsfield cottage which stood between high hedges of laurel and red-osier dogwood—barely a mile or two from where Milton finished *Paradise Lost*—it was not far to London. Sometimes while out walking, the poet could see its "not very distinct lights . . . flaring like a dreary dawn." They beckoned him as if he were another shabby Dick Whittington bound to succeed if only he'd "come down to London town." One morning, on impulse, he answered the call, unobtrusively slipping a manuscript of poems onto the editorial desk of David Nutt & Co. (a firm chosen at random) and without having spoken to anyone, he slipped himself out just as unobtrusively. That day the wheel of fortune turned for Robert Frost. David Nutt & Co. read, liked, sent word to the unknown Beaconsfield poet they'd be happy to publish the volumes he called *A Boy's Will*.

"A boy's will is the wind's will and the thoughts of youth are long, long, thoughts. From this line made famous by Henry Wadsworth Long-fellow* had come the book's title; its content, the long, long thoughts of Robert Frost going back to the first bittersweet days of an ambitious youth. When he saw the book in print that April 1913, pride welled up in him with an I-told-you-so kind of feeling that at first made him want to shout it into the ear of every doubting colleague back home, every editor who had ever turned a poem down—some of the same poems now inside the covers of a book. But the all-too-human first wave of gloating passed and uncertainty took over. "My divinity shaping my ends had been building better than I knew," he said in one breath, and in the other "won't it be traitorous, unAmerican to have all my first work come out over here?"

English critics heaped praise upon *A Boy's Will*, extolling Frost's "ear for silences" his ability to "quickly relate an object with its correlated emotion." They liked the spontaneity of his poems, his subtlety in evoking mood, his perceptions of "the intimate places in the heart

* Longfellow had taken it from a Lapland folksong which he translated.

and life of a man." On the eve of his fortieth birthday, Robert Frost's long, long dream had finally come true. Doors began opening almost immediately, first among American expatriates in London, T. S. Eliot and Ezra Pound; then William Butler Yeats, king of poets in London's literary circles, invited Frost to one of his famous Monday Nights. There, for the first time he met fellow New Englander Amy Lowell, who immediately wanted to take his future into her hands, and to his amusement treated him somewhat as if he were a rustic country farmer flung confused into the world of the elite. She and Ezra Pound belonged to the *Imagist* school of poetry, had as their purpose the restoration of poetry to "common speech, evocation of hard and clear images, concentration of effect, freedom of form and subject matter." Both poets tried to win Frost over as convert during the exciting discussions they had with him in the weeks that followed publication of his book, but he smiled inwardly thinking how long before imagists appeared on the scene Emerson had written essays appealing for common speech and freedom of form and subject matter. Emily Dickinson had followed, so had Whitman, and by now he, too, was following in his own, original way.

He listened with greater excitement when Amy Lowell informed him that ironically, almost at the precise moment he had deserted the United States, a new magazine called *Poetry* had been launched in Chicago by Harriet Monroe, which by now was influential enough to make the reputation of any American poet. Frost jovially allowed Ezra Pound to send *Poetry* "a fierce article denouncing a country that neglects fellows like me. I am afraid he overdid it." Amy Lowell also sent Harriet Monroe notice to be on the lookout for the genius of Robert Frost. With his name going strong now in two countries, the beaming poet gathered old and new poems together to shape a second book which his English publishers brought out on May 15, 1914. Significantly enough he had titled it *North of Boston.*

Sending friends in New England word of the glory he was reaping in old England, he set them to work writing advance publicity about him for American magazines. "A little of the success I have waited for so long won't hurt me," he said. "I rather think I deserve it." Like Amy Lowell, he was out to engineer his own way to fame. A *Boy's Will,* which he described as being a study in a certain kind of waywardness, "the story of five years of my life in which I went away

from people and college," contained among other poems one called
"Storm Fear":

> *When the wind works against us in the dark,*
> *And pelts with snow*
> *The lower-chamber window on the east,*
> *And whispers with a sort of stifled bark,*
> *The beast,*
> *"Come out! Come out!"—*
> *It costs no inward struggle not to go,*
> *Ah, no!*
> *I count our strength,*
> *Two and a child,*
> *Those of us not asleep subdued to mark*
> *How the cold creeps as the fire dies at length—*
> *How drifts are piled,*
> *Dooryard and road ungraded,*
> *Till even the comforting barn grows far away,*
> *And my heart owns a doubt*
> *Whether 'tis in us to arise with day*
> *And save ourselves unaided.*

North of Boston, Frost told his friends, was filled with poems about
the New Hampshire people he came back to in his curved line of flight.
Besides "Home Burial," the book included two poems now among his
most famous: "The Hired Man" and "Mending Wall":

> *Something there is that doesn't love a wall,*
> *That sends the frozen-ground-swell under it*
> *And spills the upper boulders in the sun,*
> *And makes gaps even two can pass abreast.*
> *The work of hunters is another thing:*
> *I have come after them and made repair*
> *Where they have left not one stone on a stone,*
> *But they would have the rabbit out of hiding,*
> *To please the yelping dogs. The gaps I mean,*
> *No one has seen them made or heard them made,*
> *But at spring mending-time we find them there.*
> *I let my neighbor know beyond the hill;*
> *And on a day we meet to walk the line*

And set the wall between us once again.
We keep the wall between us as we go.
To each the boulders that have fallen to each.
And some are loaves and some so nearly balls
We have to use a spell to make them balance:
"Stay where you are until our backs are turned!"
We wear our fingers rough with handling them.
Oh, just another kind of outdoor game,
One on a side. It comes to little more:
There where it is we do not need the wall:
He is all pine and I am apple orchard.
My apple trees will never get across
And eat the cones under his pines, I tell him.
He only says, "Good fences make good neighbors."
Spring is the mischief in me, and I wonder
If I could put a notion in his head:
"Why do they make good neighbors? Isn't it
Where there are cows? But here there are no cows.
Before I built a wall I'd ask to know
What I was walling in or walling out,
And to whom I was like to give offense.
Something there is that doesn't love a wall,
That wants it down." I could say "Elves" to him,
But it's not elves exactly, and I'd rather
He said it for himself. I see him there,
Bringing a stone grasped firmly by the top
In each hand, like an old-stone savage armed.
He moves in darkness as it seems to me,
Not of woods only and the shade of trees.
He will not go behind his father's saying,
And he likes having thought of it so well
He says again, "Good fences make good neighbors."

Reading Frost for the first time, many American critics tended to mistake him for a nature poet. Edward Garnett, an English critic got close to all but the western influence in Frost's thinking. "Mr. Frost is really representative," he said, "carrying on those literary traditions of New England which are associated with talents as diverse as Hawthorne, Thoreau and Sarah Orne Jewett . . . since Whitman's death, no Ameri-

can poet has appeared of so unique a quality as Mr. Frost." (The last
reference was one the poet had been waiting for since 1892). In *Poetry*
magazine Harriet Monroe said of *North of Boston*, "His New England is
the same old New England of the pilgrim fathers—a harsh, austere, velvet-
coated granite earth . . . To present this earth, these people, the poet
employs usually a blank verse as massive as they, as stript of all apologies
and adornments. His poetry is sparing, austere, even a bit crabbed at
times; but now and then it lights up with a sudden and intimate beauty;
a beauty springing from life-long love and intuition."

On the thirteenth of February, 1915, Robert Frost, now age forty-
one sailed from the dangers of war in Europe into the dangers of fame
in the United States. "There is a kind of success called 'of esteem' and it
butters no parsnips," he said, thinking about his future, "That means a
success with the critical few who are supposed to know. But really to
arrive where I can stand on my legs as a poet and nothing else, I must
get outside that circle to the general reader who buy books in their
thousands. . . . I want to be a poet for all sorts and kinds." He decided
not to worry about popular poets being downgraded with critics; he decided not worry about those critics who couldn't make up their minds
if the poetry he wrote was of the lasting sort. "It is absurd to think
that the only way to tell if a poem is lasting is to wait and see if
it lasts. The right reader of a good poem can tell the moment it strikes
him that he has taken an immortal wound—that he will never get over
it." He decided to pay attention only to right readers.

From the moment Frost stepped off the boat he was being feted and
dined by editors, critics, educators—so dizzily that Elinor went on to New
Hampshire with the children, leaving him to face alone in Boston and
New York interviews and contract talks with publishers. With wit and
pride Frost played the game of celebrity in a swift-paced life that was
not to let up until his name was on the lips of all his countrymen from
the President on down.

Even he was astonished at how fast it all happened now, how well
he had laid the ground while abroad for what was due him at home.
Within three months of his arrival from London, Tufts College, Boston,
named him Phi Beta Kappa poet. A year later Harvard College offered
the same honor. For a single poem, "Snow" *Poetry* magazine awarded him
its top prize—"So much wealth and glory," he exclaimed, wealth being
one hundred dollars. Not many years later when he got elected to the
National Institute of Arts and Letters and was given the sum of a

thousand dollars, it marked the difference on the ladder rung from which he could look back to his modest beginnings.

Mountain Interval was published in 1916; *Selected Poems* in 1923; *New Hampshire*, also published in 1923, won him the Pulitzer Prize. (He was to take that prize three more times—for *Collected Poems* in 1931, for *A Further Range* in 1937; *A Witness Tree* in 1943.) By 1924, at age fifty, his hair already white, he felt he had a right to speak of himself as a witness tree. From a farm where he kept busy writing poems "between milking one cow and another," he said he thought it time for an old man like himself to rest. "All I ask in this age of speed is to be allowed to go slow," he pleaded. "An oxcart on a soft dirt road, cost what it will, is my idea of a self-indulged old age." But no one, not even the poet himself, seriously intended to let him go slow. The roaring twenties surprised everyone by flaunting not only flappers, the Charleston, big money, and booze—Culture, too, was "in." Poet Malcolm Cowley who returned to New York in the mid 1920s to get caught up in the literary life of a group centered in the Algonquin Hotel said, "The literary business was booming like General Motors." There were still, of course, plenty of artists starving merrily or tragically, but Robert Frost wasn't one of them. The books in which he was using "a language appropriate for the values I celebrate" were selling by the thousands. Poems like "Birches," "Stopping by Woods on a Snowy Evening," "Mowing," and "Mending Wall" were being widely quoted by "all sorts and kinds." Fame took him to campuses to lecture and to teach because he liked the young and wanted them to like him for poetry's sake.

Belief. Belief. You've got to augment my belief in life and people.

he told his students when the 1930s rolled in, putting an end to the boom, when the depression, the rise of fascism, the threat of war seemed to have stopped belief among most Americans. Sounding off against "whiners and easy despairers" in his own jovial kind of way in speech-prose, in poetry he kept to the Emersonian philosophy which now to most "moderns" seemed corney and out of date, but which had for so long bolstered and inspired him. *We have it hidden in us to attain.* No matter what else Robert Frost was saying, he was saying *that*, ringing it into almost every poem he wrote, the sound it gave off being sometimes faint, sometimes stark and compelling, as if when the bell of belief stopped, the stillness would be death.

Meanwhile, in the back of his head, a new dream stirred. Poets, he thought, ought to get mixed up more with politics not for politics' sake but poetry's and people's; governments ought to raise poets to positions of honor not for the poet's sake but for philosophy. Poetry in the White House seemed to Robert Frost the power the United States needed in order to lick a lot of things, including the "image" problem his country had to face as being materialistic and big-business-minded. He went politicking for that dream, had fun doing it, and became the first lobbyist for artists Washington ever caught in its legislative corridors. He was soon swinging some deals for poets inside and outside of Congress. He helped initiate the idea of writer-in-residence in American colleges and universities; he helped establish the famed Bread-Loaf Writers' Conference in Vermont; in the fifties he had the satisfaction of seeing government take a chance on the wisdom of poets by sending them (himself at least three times before he died) on good-will missions abroad. A poet by the name of Robert Frost even got a Congressional Medal of Honor for mixing into politics.

But politics got him into trouble on all sides, radicals damning him for being too conservative, conservatives for being too liberal. He thrived on having his name the center of controversy, won a reputation for being a kind of crusty old cracker-barrel philosopher who could disarm his enemies as well as his friends by saying such things as, "Ain't politics a funny thing to be so serious about?" and "I never dared be radical when young/For fear it would make me conservative when old." He got into trouble in the world of poetry, too, by ignoring "schools" such as *modernism* and *new criticism*, by staying his own man and letting no side pin him down for or against anything but belief in life.

Behind the scenes he was having troubles of another kind, troubles that sometimes came dangerously close to cutting off even *his* belief. Tragedy hit at him again and again during his years of peak fame: he lost three of his children, one, his son Carol, dying a suicide; lost his sister Jeannie who drifted off into a perpetual world of fantasy; and was robbed of Elinor at a time when it seemed almost easier to go Jeannie's way than face reality without the wife who had made so much possible for him.

But of all this the world at large knew little. The ranges of his fame extended far beyond his own country to "right readers" in all parts of the globe. As Dean of American Poets, he was claimed by all the New England states, for he had lived some part of his life in all of them, mostly on farms. "I always thought if I were a king," he once said, "and if there were a row of buttons in front of me to press, I'd press the one which would strengthen farming. Farming has languished. It's the kind of life you'd hate to see a country lose." Frost didn't mind getting "claimed" (he wished California would speak up as loudly as New England) but he couldn't resist quoting a line he had heard in school when he was a boy: "The seven cities claimed the Homer, dead, through which the living Homer begged his bread." Asking where *he'd* say he belonged as a native son, he once responded: "I've about decided I am an American—U.S.A."

But New England he remained in the minds of all who read or wrote about him, right up to his last books: A *Masque of Reason*, A *Masque of Mercy, In the Clearing*. He looked fixed in old age, with his glistening white hair, his thickset, weathered face, his slow, remembering kind of speech—as if time before and after were going to forget, going to let him stay forever this one way in the vision of wishful thinkers. "He *is* New England," Amy Lowell had said, and no one would have it any other way. He was also America's own claim to greatness in something besides power and money, something to show off to the rest of the world when people said commercialism was all the United States stood for. Nobody wanted to see Robert Frost go. Nobody knew quite who could replace him.

That thought must have been in the minds of many who saw the oldest of poets standing next to the youngest of Presidents on the climactic January day in 1961 when John F. Kennedy was inaugurated President of the United States. Kennedy was looking far into the future, Frost far into the past, and there was a symbol there the poet liked, a line that went back and forth in time like the cross currents of a stream. The young President made a hopeful speech, the old poet read a hopeful poem. There in the icy weather, itself a kind of personal symbol as far as the poet was concerned (he had filled his early poems with words like snow, ice, frost), standing before millions of television viewers, a man like Robert Frost who seldom forgot his beginning must have also had his thoughts, wondering how many remembered or knew he'd been born when Indians were still skirmishing in the western hills for land rightfully theirs; that he'd grown up poor in a turbulent century when no one ever dreamed of splitting atoms or sending pictures out across the waves by way of Telstar. On this triumphant day, an eighty-seven-year-old poet was surely stirred, too, by thoughts of feeling lucky in how his life had been charted, lucky for having been able to cross the line from one century into another, from west to east, and another line, more important than either of the others which had made him come to believe that no matter how lonely the human figure against any given landscape, no matter what a man's trial or intensity of pain, someone before him had walked the same ground, prayed the same prayer, come to the same end or the same beginning. It was a law of life that each man in his journey through experience be alone, but it was also a law of life that those who survive are those who recognize that they are not alone. The revelation had come to him at a time when, as an obscure poet, he walked lonely one afternoon onto a vast open field, obsessed with choked thoughts against the world for paying no attention to his work. Then, suddenly, he became aware of another lonely man's unappreciated labors—the early morning "mower in the dew" who because he had seen the beauty of a tall tuft of flowers growing by the brookside had spared it out of "sheer morning gladness at the brim." It was then a poet could

> . . . *feel a spirit kindred to my own;*
> *So that henceforth I worked no more alone;*

then the moment he had crossed the most critical line of all—the one carrying him from youth to maturity, from the ranks of the losers into the ranks of the winners. Reversing his tracks across the field, a young poet had gone back to people, taking with him the strengthened philosophy that formed the basis of the poems he wanted to share with the world.

The year of dying for a young President and an old poet turned out to be the same—Robert Lee Frost, age eighty-nine, on January 12, 1963; John Fitzgerald Kennedy, age forty-six, November 22, 1963. The irony of their coming in and going out together was one even this dealer in ironies might not have been able to bear had he been the last to go. "How can we be just in a world that needs mercy and merciful in a world that needs justice?" were the last words he spoke to his daughter before going further along than she could see in the clearing.

Frost, who had been categorized by varying critics as a moralist, as "a Job in our times," as "a dealer in whimsies" had lived long enough to know that there were millions of readers who had taken an "immortal wound" upon meeting his poems, that there were some scholars, at least, who considered him "a major poet not only in regard to this age, but in regard to our whole literature, a great American poet." But, like John F. Kennedy, he had wanted to live long enough for something else too—the landing of a man on the moon:

> "And where will I be? With my toes turned up, my hands composed."

But being Robert Frost, he had had a compensating thought:

> *. . . I may return*
> *If dissatisfied*
> *With what I learn*
> *From having died.*

Frost's humor was called by one of his critics "a Greek cheerfulness," while another saw him as wearing the "comic mask of a whittling rustic designed for gazing without dizziness into the tragic abyss of desperation." Louis Untermeyer, who compiled the best of Frost's poems into an annotated book, said that the poet was most profound when he was most playful. "No other poet," he said, "has been so successful in combining an outer lightness and an inner gravity." If Frost had had to choose a few lines which came closest to understanding what he was all about, the likelihood is that he would have taken these from a biography titled *A Swinger of Birches* written by his friend Sidney Cox:

> Mirth has always been attendant on his moral. He will not for earnest half-truths stay completely reverent. He has to keep the door ajar for the other half of the truth. Even in his caperings . . . wisdom is usually implicit. . . . Even with God, the fear of not pleasing whom is the beginning of wisdom, Robert Frost sets his soft hat on one side of his head and looks Him in the eye.

"And were an epitaph to be my story," wrote the poet himself,

> *I'd have a short one ready for my own.*
> *I would have written of me on my stone:*
> *I had a lover's quarrel with the world.*

BIBLIOGRAPHY

A *Library of Literary Criticism:* Modern American Literature, Compiled and Edited by Dorothy Nyren, Frederick Ungar Publishing Co., New York, 1960.

American Poets From the Puritans to the Present, Hyatt H. Waggoner, Boston, Houghton Mifflin Company, 1968.

American Renaissance, F. O. Matthiessen, London, New York, Oxford University Press, 1941.

Cavalcade of the American Novel From the Birth of the Nation to the Middle of the Twentieth Century, Edward Wagenknecht, New York, Holt, Rinehart and Winston, 1952, 1964.

The Continuity of American Poetry, Roy Harvey Pearce, Princeton, New Jersey, Princeton University Press, 1961.

Dreamers of the American Dream, Stewart H. Holbrook, New York, Doubleday & Company, Inc., 1957.

Interpretations of American Literature, Edited by Charles Feidelson, Jr., and Paul Brodtkorb, Jr., New York, Oxford University Press, 1959.

The Life of the Mind in America from the Revolution to the Civil War, Perry Miller (Books one through three), New York, Harcourt, Brace & World, Inc., 1965.

Literary History of the United States, Third Edition: Revised, Editors: Robert E. Spiller, Willard Thorp; Thomas H. Johnson, Henry Seidel Canby, Richard M. Ludwig; New York, The Macmillan Company, 1963.

Making the American Mind, Social and Moral Ideas in the McGuffey Readers, Richard D. Mosier, New York, Russell & Russell, Inc., 1965.

New England Discovery, A Personal View, Nancy Hale, New York, Coward-McCann, Inc., 1963.

The Shock of Recognition, Edmund Wilson, New York, Farrar, Straus and Cudahy, 1955.

The Shores of Light: A Literary Chronicle of the Twenties and Thirties, Edmund Wilson, New York, Farrar, Straus & Young, 1952.

Nathaniel Hawthorne, An Introduction and Interpretation, Arlin Turner, American Authors and Critics Series, Barnes & Noble, 1961.

The Life of Ralph Waldo Emerson, Ralph L. Rusk, New York, Charles Scribner's Sons, 1949.

Selected Writings of Ralph Waldo Emerson: Edited and with a foreword by William H. Gilman, New York, The New American Library, 1965.

A Week on the Concord and Merrimack Rivers, Henry David Thoreau, Sentry Edition, Boston, Houghton Mifflin Company, 1961.

The Days of Henry Thoreau, Walter Harding, New York, Alfred A. Knopf, 1965.

Walden, Henry David Thoreau, Edited with Notes and Introduction by Gordon S. Haight, New York, Walter J. Black, Inc., 1942.

Trumpets of Jubilee, Constance M. Rourke, New York, Harcourt, Brace, Inc., 1927.

The Complete Poems of Emily Dickinson, Edited by Thomas H. Johnson, Boston, Little, Brown and Company, 1960.

Emily Dickinson, An Interpretive Biography, Thomas H. Johnson, Cambridge, Mass., Harvard University Press, 1955.

The Letters of Emily Dickinson, Vols. 1, 2, and 3, Edited by Thomas H. Johnson, Assoc. Editor, Theodora Ward, Cambridge, Mass., Harvard University Press, 1958.

This Was a Poet, A Critical Biography of Emily Dickinson, George Frisbie Whicher, New York, Charles Scribner's Sons, 1938, Ann Arbor Paperback, University of Michigan Press, 1957.

The Years and Hours of Emily Dickinson, Vols. 1 and 2., Jay Leyda, New Haven, Yale University Press, 1960.

Collected Poems of Edwin Arlington Robinson, New York, The Macmillan Company, 1954.

E. A. Robinson, Selected Early Poems and Letters, Edited by Charles T. Davis, New York, Holt, Rinehart and Winston, 1960.

Edwin Arlington Robinson, A Biography, Hermann Hagedorn, New York, The Macmillan Company, 1938.

Untriangulated Stars: Letters of Edwin Arlington Robinson to Harry de Forest Smith, 1890–1905, Edited by Denham Sutcliffe, Cambridge, Mass., Harvard University Press, 1947.

Where the Light Falls, A Portrait of Edwin Arlington Robinson, Chard Powers Smith, New York, The Macmillan Company, 1965.

Collected Poems, Edna St. Vincent Millay, New York, Harper & Brothers, 1956.

The Indigo Bunting, A Memoir of Edna St. Vincent Millay, Vincent Sheean, New York, Harper & Brothers, 1951.

Letters of Edna St. Vincent Millay, Edited by Allan Ross MacDougall, The Universal Library, New York, Grosset & Dunlap, by arrangement with Harper & Brothers, 1952.

The Poet and Her Book, A Biography of Edna St. Vincent Millay, Jean Gould, New York, Dodd, Mead & Company, 1969.

Restless Spirit: The Life of Edna St. Vincent Millay, Miriam Gurko, New York, Thomas Y. Crowell, 1962.

A Swinger of Birches, A Portrait of Robert Frost, Sidney Cox, New York, New York University Press, 1957.

Complete Poems of Robert Frost, Holt, Rinehart and Winston, Inc., 1968 edition.

Interviews with Robert Frost, Edited by Edward Connery Lathem, New York, Holt, Rinehart and Winston, Inc., 1966.

The Letters of Robert Frost to Louis Untermeyer, with commentary by Louis Untermeyer, New York, Holt, Rinehart and Winston, Inc., 1963.

The Poetry of Robert Frost, Edited by Edward Connery Lathem, New York, Holt, Rinehart and Winston, Inc., 1969.

Robert Frost: Trial by Existence, Elizabeth Shepley Sergeant, New York, Holt, Rinehart and Winston, Inc., 1960.

Selected Letters of Robert Frost, Edited by Lawrance Thompson, New York, Holt, Rinehart and Winston, Inc., 1964.

INDEX

Adams, Henry, on the New England mind, and the divine system, 136

Agnes of Sorrento (Stowe), 128

Aids to Reflection (Coleridge), 44

Alcott, Bronson, 26, 54, 86n; on Thoreau, 65

Alcott, Louisa May, 65

Aldrich, T. B., 200

Algonquin Hotel, literary group centered in, in mid 1920s, 269

Alice Doane's Appeal (Hawthorne), 9

"Amaryllis" (Robinson), 192

Ambitious Guest, The (Hawthorne), 8

American character, Hawthorne as first major author to interpret in psychological terms, 11

"American Scholar, The" (Emerson), 51

Anderson, Sherwood, 255

Aria da Capo (Millay), 222, 224–25

Atherton, Gertrude, 246

Atlantic Monthly, and Harriet Beecher Stowe, 127, 128

"Bean Stalk" (Millay), 223

Beecher, Catherine (sister Katy), 103, 105, 107–8, 110–11, 115, 121

Beecher, Harriet. *See* Stowe, Harriet Beecher

Beecher, Harriet Porter (Mrs. Lyman), 103–4, 105

Beecher, Henry Ward, 115, 118, 121, 128, 154n

Beecher, Rev. Lyman, 41–42, 101–5, 115; as minister in Boston, 106; and the slavery issue, 107, 109, 112, 113 125; as head of Lane Theological Seminary in Cincinnati, 109–10, 112–13, 114, 117–18, 125; heresy trial of, 114; joined in Ohio by Samuel Fowler Dickinson, 136–37

Beecher, Roxanna (Mrs. Lyman), 102

Benes, Dr. Eduard, and Edna St. Vincent Millay, 231

Bhagavad Gita, Hindu poem, and Thoreau, 90

"Birches" (Frost), 269

"Birds Do Thus, The" (Frost), 260

Blithedale Romance, The (Hawthorne), 9, 17, 20, 22–23, 262

Boissevain, Eugen Jan, 228–29, 232

Boston, Emerson on organizations and cults springing up in, 54–55

Bowdoin College, 6, 117, 118, 202

Bowles, Sam, and Emily Dickinson, 164, 169

Boy's Will, A (Frost), 264, 265

Bradstreet, Anne, 180

Bread-Loaf Writers' Conference in Vermont, 270

Bridge, Horatio, and Hawthorne, 6, 7, 10, 11, 17, 25

Bridges, Robert, on Emily Dickinson's love poems, 175

Bronte, Emily, 166n, 174

Brook, Van Wyck: on Margaret Fuller, 14; on Hawthorne, 27

Brook Farm, 13–15, 55; and Hawthorne's *The Blithedale Romance*, 17, 20, 22–23, 262

Brown, John: Thoreau on, 65–66; Thoreau's aid to, 96–97

Brown, Lucy Jackson, 75

Browning, Robert and Elizabeth, 24

Bryant, William Cullen, 1, 24

Buck in the Snow, The (Millay), 227

Buckley, Blind "Boss," of California, 246

Byron, Lady, and Harriet Beecher Stowe, 126, 128

Captain Craig (Robinson), 186, 198, 201

Carlyle, Jane, 46

Carlyle, Thomas, and Emerson, 44, 46–47, 53, 61

Cather, Willa, 201, 203, 255

Channing, Edward, 72

Channing, Ellery, 26, 86n

Chapman, John Jay, as Emerson biographer, 47

Children of the Night, The (Robinson), 201, 202

"Circles" (Emerson), 40
"Civil Disobedience" (Thoreau), 87, 90–91
Clarke, James Freeman, 15, 26
Coleridge, Hartley, 178
Coleridge, Samuel: and Emerson, 44, 46, 54; and Thoreau, 72
Collected Poems (Frost), 269
"Compensation" (Emerson), 40
Concord Academy, of the two Thoreau brothers, 76–77, 78
"Concord Sage," Emerson dubbed as, 51
"Conversations" conducted by Margaret Fuller, 54
Cooper, James Fenimore, 1, 24
Country of the Pointed Firs, The (Jewett), 200, 201
Cowley, Malcolm: on Edwin Arlington Robinson, 205; on the literary business of the mid 1920s, 269
Cox, Sidney, on Robert Frost, 273
Crane, Edwin, 255
Cummings, E. E., 234
Curtis, George William, on Brook Farm, 14

Dana, Charles Anderson, and Brook Farm, 14
Darwin, Charles, 135
Deephaven (Jewett), 200
Dell, Floyd, on Edna St. Vincent Millay, 222–23
Dial magazine, of Emerson and Margaret Fuller, 13, 14, 54, 84
Dickinson, Austin, 134, 135, 138, 142, 143, 146, 148, 149, 151, 159
Dickinson, Edward, 131, 137, 141–42, 143, 148, 160; tyrannical attitude of, toward his daughters, 154, 157
Dickinson, Mrs. Edward, 141–43
Dickinson, Emily, 53, 66, 83, 85, 88, 131–76, 227, 265; interest in her personality, as causing her work to be neglected, 131; mystery of her life as elusive spinster recluse, 131; as legendary figure to her Amherst neighbors, 131–32; poems of, found after her death, 131, 132, 134, 174; identity of "him" in her posthumously published poems, sleuthing for, 132; and

Thomas Wentworth Higginson, 132–33, 140, 153, 161, 165–69, 173, 174; and Mabel Loomis Todd, 133–34, 174; as "the myth" to citizens of Amherst, 134; tragedy of, as isolated artist in environment not comprehending her genius, 135; the world into which she was born (1830), 135; the Amherst village into which she was born, 135; family background and childhood of, 137–43; and growing up with her brother, Austin, 138–42; and family home on North Pleasant Street (Eden), 143, 157; as student at Amherst Academy, 143–44, 145; words as playthings for, 144; her writing in early schooldays, 144–45; schoolgirl letters of, to Abiah Root, 145, 146, 147–49; nervous collapse of, after death of dear friend, 145–46; loneliness as motivation in schoolday friendships of, 146; early interest of, in self-denial, 146; religious dilemma confronted in her teens by, 147–48; as student at South Hadley Seminary for Females, 148–50; depressing home atmosphere, and its effect on spirits of, 150–51; friendship of, with Ben Newton, 152–53, 166n, 169; and mutual enjoyment of association with Austin's college friends, 152–53; becoming increasingly rebellious against her tyrannical father, 154; discarding of church-going by, 155; on life inside the Dickinson mansion, 156; determination of, to "live in truth," in spite of loneliness and isolation, 156–57; traumatic break in her relationship with her father, 157; similarities between Thoreau and, 158, 159; on madness, 158; on ability to make her own company in solitude, 158–59; on her own ecstatic type of religion, 159; beginning of neighbors' gossip about recluse habits of, 150–60; first and last trip of, outside of New England, 160; and Rev. Charles Wadsworth ("My Philadelphia"), 160–61, 166n, 169; and her capacity to love, 161; nature of "love" poems of, 161; visual handicap of, 162–63, 165; philosophy of, about poetry, 164; attitude of, toward publishing her poetry, 164–65, 167, 173; and her poetry, 168–73; last years of, 173–74; funeral of, 174; posthumous publishing of her poetry, 174; critical reception of her *Poems*, 175

Dickinson, Samuel Fowler, 135–37

Dickinson, Susan Gilbert (Mrs. Austin), 164, 165

Dickinson, Vinnie, 132, 137, 143, 146, 150, 153, 154, 156, 160, 174

Dow, Caroline B., and Edna St. Vincent Millay, 216

Dred: A Tale of the Great Dismal Swamp (Stowe), 126

"Dry periods" in a poet's life, 227–28

Dudley, Thomas, 180

Earle, Ferdinard, 215

Eliot, T. S., 214, 234, 265

Ellis, Charles, 224–25

Emerson, Ellen Tucker (Mrs. Ralph Waldo), 43, 45

Emerson, Lydia Jackson (Mrs. Ralph Waldo), 48–49, 50, 55, 83, 85

Emerson, Mary Moody, 32–33, 35, 38, 41, 44, 45, 70

Emerson, Ralph Waldo, 12, 13, 29–62, 135, 265; transcendentalism and, 13, 54; and Hawthorne, 14, 15–16, 17, 20, 26; family background and boyhood of, 29–35; as student at Harvard, 35–38; as teacher in girls' school in Boston, 38–39; as student at Harvard Divinity School, 39–40; as young minister of Second Church (Unitarian) in Boston, 40–42; central thought in sermons of, 42; resignation of, from the ministry, 42–43, 44; aroused over slavery, and attitude of the church toward, 43; happiness of, in brief marriage to Ellen Tucker, 43; European trip of (1833), 44–47; and his enthusiasm for America, 47, 52; on essence of his religious faith, 47–48; in role of itinerant philosopher-poet, 48; as lecturer, 48, 51–52; marriage of, to Lydia Jackson, 48–49; and

appearance of his first book *Nature*, 50–51, 135; "The American Scholar" address of, 51; impact of Emersonianism, 53–54; and Brook Farm, 55; attitudes of many conservative Americans toward philosophy of, 55; as a father, 55–56; grief of, over loss of his son, Waldo, 56–57; active participation of, in anti-slavery struggle, 57–58; in the Civil War years, 59; closing years of life, 60–61; influence of, upon his times, continuing on into the present, 61–62; funeral oration for Thoreau by, 97–98

Emerson, Ruth Haskins (Mrs. William), 29, 33–34, 41

Emerson, Waldo (son), 55–57, 62, 83, 84; and Emerson's poem "Threnody," 56–57

Emerson, Rev. William, 29, 30, 32, 33, 34

Endicott of the Red Cross (Hawthorne), 9

Epitaph for the Race of Man (Millay), 233

Essays, First and Second Series (Emerson), 53

Essays on Various Subjects Principally Designed for Young Ladies (Hannah More), 140

Ethan Brand (Hawthorne), 8

Fanshawe (Hawthorne), 9

Feminist movement, and Harriet Beecher Stowe, 128

Few Figs from Thistles, A (Millay), 223

Ficke, Arthur Davison, 217, 218

Fields, James T., and Hawthorne, 19, 25

Fiske, D. T., on Emily Dickinson as student, 144

"Forest Trees" (Millay), 210

"Friendship" (Emerson), 85

Frost, Belle Moodie (Mrs. William P.), 242, 244–45, 246, 247, 249, 250, 252, 256, 258, 262

Frost, Elinor White (Mrs. Robert), 259, 260, 261, 262, 263, 268, 270; Robert Frost, on her life with, 259. *See also* White, Elinor

Frost, Eliot, 260, 261

Frost, Jeannie, 246, 247, 248, 249, 270
Frost, Robert, 203, 211, 214, 234, 237–73; "My Butterfly," as first published poem of, 237, 238, 259; ambition of, for life lived by and for poetry, 238–39; reaction of, to rejection of some early poems, 239; attitude of, on relationship of a poem to personal life of the poet, 240; image projected to the world by, as contrasted with the real Robert Frost, 240–41; family background of, 241–52; childhood of, in California, 242–43, 246–52; and his "sound of sense," 250; and his affection for his "little farm" as a boy, 250; reaction of, as an eleven year old, to death of his father, 251–52; last years of childhood of, in New England, 252–54; and development of his desire "to be on top," 253, 254; and his mania for perfection, 253; as a reader, in his youth, 255; and other young literary hopefuls spawned in the "terrible seventies," 255; and seeing of his environment with a young poet's eye, 255; and the definition of a poem for, 255; the quickening of poetry in, and its connection to the human heart, 256; and his grandfather, 256, 260, 261; and his high school sweetheart, Elinor White, 256–57; as student at Dartmouth, 257; rebels against more college after one term, 258; and Twilight, 258, 259; tramping tour of, 259; and first success as published poet, 259; marriage of, to Elinor White, 259; and rejection slips, 259–60, 262; as teacher in his mother's school, 260; as special student at Harvard at twenty-three, 260; children born to Elinor and, 260, 262; and death of his baby son, Eliot, 261; as farmer in New Hampshire, 262; and writing poetry on the farm, 262; and transplanting of family to England, 262–63; Beaconsfield cottage of, in England, 263–64; and success of A Boy's Will in England, 264–65; recognition achieved by, in England, 265; return of, from England to U.S.

as a celebrity, 268; honors heaped on, 268; Pulitzer prizes awarded to, 269; and poets in politics, 270; personal tragedies of, during years of peak fame, 270; as Dean of American Poets, 270–71; and the 1961 Kennedy presidential inauguration, 271; his own epitaph for himself, 273
Frost, William P., Jr., 241–42, 243–47, 249, 250, 251, 256
Fuller, Margaret, 13, 54, 84; and Hawthorne, 14
Further Range, A (Frost), 269

Gardiner, Maine: as home of the Edward Robinsons, 181; loneliness of Edwin Robinson in, as young man, 189; Edwin Arlington Robinson as most famous son of, 202
Garnett, Edward, English critic, on Robert Frost, 267–68
Garrison, William Lloyd, 43, 58, 73, 106–7, 109, 113, 123, 124, 135
Geography for Children (Stowe), 111
George, Henry, 249
Gilbert, Susan, 143, 150, 159. See also Dickinson, Susan Gilbert
Glasgow, Ellen, 255
Godey's Lady's Book, 18
"God's World" (Millay), 218
Grandfather's Tales (Hawthorne), 14
Great Stone Face, The (Hawthorne), 8
Greeley, Horace, and Thoreau, 93
Guthrie's Geographical Grammar, 2

Hall, Judge James, and Harriet Beecher Stowe, 111–12, 113
"Hangman's Oak" (Millay), 230
Hardy, Thomas, 190; on Edna St. Vincent Millay, 228; impact of novels of, on the young Robert Frost, 255
Harp-Weaver and Other Poems, The (Millay), 223
Harte, Bret, 190
Hawthorne, Elizabeth Clarke Manning, 1, 2–3, 7–8, 20–21
Hawthorne, Julian, 19, 21
Hawthorne, Nathaniel, 1–27, 267; determination of, to become a writer, 1–2, 7; recluse mother of, 1, 2–3, 7–8, 20–

21; background and childhood of, 2–5; Puritan ancestors of, 3–4; and his private key to tradition, 4; aversion of, to organized study as a youth, 5; boyhood newspaper issued by, 5–6; as student at Bowdoin College, 6; appraisal of, as young man, by his Salem neighbors, 7–8; as the Watchman, observing and recording, 8; years of apprenticeship of, to his writing, 8–9, 12; source material used by, 8–9; and failure of first attempt in print, 9; style and theme, as Hawthorne stamp on his stories, 9, 11; and his merciless driving of himself in writing and rewriting, 10; and a sense of separateness from his fellows, 10–11; success of *Twice-Told Tales*, 11–12; drawn into social group of the Peabodys of Salem, 12–13; and Brook Farm, 13–15, 262; happiness of, in his marriage to Sophia Peabody, 15, 16; financial worries of, 16, 17; as surveyor in Salem Custom House, 17, 18, 19; success of *The Scarlet Letter*, 20; *The House of the Seven Gables*, popularity of, 22; and choice of names for his characters, 23; and politics, 23–24; as Consul in Liverpool, 24; in Italy, and writing of *The Marble Faun*, 24–25; death and funeral of, 26; and the critics, 26–27

Hawthorne, Rose, 17, 21

Hawthorne, Sophia Peabody (Mrs. Nathaniel), 15–16, 19, 20, 21, 25–26; on characteristics of her husband, 17

Hawthorne, Una, 16, 21

Hawthornes (Hathornes) of Salem, 3–4

Herrick, Robert, and Frost's memory of a volume of his poems, 249

Higginson, Thomas Wentworth: as revolutionary abolitionist, 58, 165; and Emily Dickinson, 132–33, 140, 153, 161, 165–69, 173, 174; on first interview with Emily Dickinson, 133; and posthumous publishing of Emily Dickinson's poetry, 174, 175

Hillyer, Robert, on Millay's *Mine the Harvest*, 235

"Hired Man, The" (Frost), 266

History of Mexico (Prescott), 255

Holland, Josiah Gilbert, and Emily Dickinson, 164, 169

Holmes, Oliver Wendell, and Hawthorne, 20, 26

"Home Burial" (Frost), 261, 266

Hopkins, Gerard Manley, 208

House of the Seven Gables, The (Hawthorne), 9, 20, 21, 22, 23

"House on the Hill, The" (Robinson), 198, 200

Housman, A. E., 228

Howells, William Dean: on Emily Dickinson's *Poems*, 175; and literary realism of early 1900s, 199; and *Deephaven* of Sarah Orne Jewett, 200

Humphries, Rolfe, on Edna St. Vincent Millay, 234

Huntsman, What Quarry? (Millay), 230

Imagist school of poetry, 265

"Immortality" (Emily Brontë), 166n, 174

Independent magazine: and Frost's first published poem, 237, 259; and acceptance of Frost's "The Birds Do Thus," 250; Frost's message to friends at, on leaving for England, 263

Ingersoll, Robert, on Lyman Beecher, 103

In the Clearing (Frost), 271

Irving, Washington, 1, 24; on Hawthorne's *The Scarlet Letter*, 20

Italian Notebooks (Hawthorne), 25

Jackson, Helen Hunt, and Emily Dickinson, 173

James, Henry, on Hawthorne, 10, 26

Jewett, Sarah Orne, 200–1, 267

Jewett and Company of Boston, as publishers of *Uncle Tom's Cabin*, 122

Johns, Orrick, 215

Jude the Obscure (Hardy), 190

Kennerley, Mitchell, 214, 222

King Jasper (Robinson), 203

King's Henchman, The (Taylor), 229

Lady Byron Vindicated (Stowe), 128

Lady Eleanor's Mantle (Hawthorne), 9

"La Joie de Vivre" (Millay), 210, 211

Lamp and the Bell, The (Millay), 224

"Land of Romance, The" (Millay), 210
Landor, Walter Savage, and Emerson, 44, 46
"La Noche Triste," first ballad of Robert Frost, 255
Lawrence, D. H., on Hawthorne, 26–27
Leaves of Grass (Whitman), 53
Letters and Social Aims (Emerson), 60
Liberator, of William Lloyd Garrison, 73, 113, 135
Lincoln, Abraham, 52, 58, 124, 127; on Harriet Beecher Stowe, 99
Lindsay, Vachel, 214, 255
Longfellow, Henry Wadsworth: and Hawthorne, 7, 10, 11, 17, 26; and Emerson, 58, 61; and title of Frost's A Boy's Will, 264
Lowell, Amy, 205, 214, 255, 257; and Robert Frost, 265, 271
Lowell, James Russell: on Hawthorne's The House of the Seven Gables, 22; on Emerson as lecturer, 51, 52; on Thoreau, 65; on Thoreau's A Week on the Concord and Merrimack Rivers, 92
Lyman, Joseph, and Emily Dickinson, 144, 153, 156, 162, 169
Lyon, Mary, of South Hadley Seminary for Females, and Emily Dickinson, 149–50
Lyric Year, The, 214, 215, 217

MacDowell Colony in Peterborough, N.H., 203
McGuffey Eclectic Readers, and the Beechers, 111
Make Bright the Arrows (Millay), 230
Manning, Robert, and Hawthorne, 5, 6
Mansfield, Katherine, 131
Man Who Died Twice, The (Robinson), 202
Marble Faun, The (Hawthorne), 9, 24–25
Markham, Edwin, 199
Masque of Mercy, A (Frost), 271
Masque of Reason, A (Frost), 271
"Mattias at the Door" (Robinson), 191
May, Georgiana, 108, 110, 114, 116, 117, 118
May Day and Other Pieces (Emerson), 60

Mayflower, The: or Sketches of Scenes and Characters among the Descendants of the Pilgrims (Stowe), 114
Mayor of Casterbridge, The (Hardy), 190
Maypole of Merry Mount, The (Hawthorne), 9
Melville, Herman: on Hawthorne, 11, 16–17; on Hawthorne's Mosses from an Old Manse, 18; and Hawthorne, 21–22; on America and her authors, 262
Memories of Hawthorne (Rose Hawthorne), 17
"Mending Wall" (Frost), 266–67, 269
"Merlin" (Emerson), 62
Mill, John Stuart, and Emerson, 44, 46
Millay, Cora, 209, 210, 214, 225, 226, 231; three daughters of, 209
Millay, Edna St. Vincent, 207–35; and nostalgia for childhood, 207–8; adoption of, by a whole generation of American youth, 208; family background and childhood of, 209–10; composing of poems by, at age of ten, 210; publication of childhood poems of, in St. Nicholas Magazine, 210; as adolescent, 210; teen-age notebooks of, with unpublished poems, 211–12; as pianist, 213, 219; Renascence of, 213–15, 218, 222, 223; as student at Barnard, 217–18; relationship of, with mother and sisters, 218–19, 225; as student at Vassar College, 219–20, 233; as Greenwich Villager in the 1920s, 221, 222; with firmly established reputation as fine lyric poet, 223; as perfectionist, 223–24, 231; first trip abroad (1921), 224; in Paris, 224–25; writing of articles and short stories under "prose-name" of Nancy Boyd, 224; and arguing with herself on pros and cons of marriage, 225–26; in England, 226–28; as Pulitzer prize winner, 228; marriage of, to Eugen Jan Boissevain, 228–29; efforts of, in behalf of Sacco and Vanzetti, 228, 229–30; "Steepletop" home of the Boissevains, 229, 231, 232; at peak of her fame, 229; writes libretto for Deems Taylor's The King's Henchman, 229; political orientation and

controversial nature of later poems of, 230–31, 233; on involvement of her reputation in writing of propaganda, 231; at end of World War II, 231; reminiscences of, about her childhood, 231–32; and death of Eugen Jan Boissevain, 232–33; last words of, 233–34; and the critics, 234–35; epitaph for, 235

Millay, Kathleen, 209, 211, 213, 222

Millay, Norma, 209, 211, 212–13, 222, 224, 235

Mine the Harvest (Millay), 235

Minister's Wooing (Stowe), 101, 128

Moby Dick (Melville), 21–22

Monroe, Harriet: and Poetry, a Magazine of Verse, 214, 265; on Edna St. Vincent Millay, 220; on Frost's North of Boston, 268

Moody, William Vaughn, 199

Moore, Marianne, 214

More, Hannah, 140

Mosses from an Old Manse (Hawthorne), 16, 17–18, 19, 21

Mountain Interval (Frost), 269

"Mowing" (Frost), 269

Murder of Lidice, The (Millay), 231

"My Butterfly" (Frost), 237, 238, 259

My Wife and I (Stowe), 128

National Institute of Arts and Letters, 268

Nature (Emerson), 15, 49, 50, 53, 74, 135

New Hampshire (Frost), 269

Newton, Ben and Emily Dickinson, 152–53, 166n, 169

Nightingale, Florence, 24

North of Boston (Frost), 265, 266, 268

Noyes, Alfred, 218

Nutt, David, & Co. of London, acceptance of Frost's A Boy's Will by, 264

Old Manse, The: Emerson's Concord home, 15, 35, 49; as home of the Nathaniel Hawthornes, 15; and Hawthorne's Mosses from an Old Manse, 16, 17

Old Town Folks (Stowe), 101, 128

Oliver, Benjamin L., and Hawthorne, 5

O'Neill, James, 249

"On First Having Heard the Skylark" (Millay), 227

Our Old Home (Hawthorne), 24

Our Place Among the Infinities (Proctor), 255

"Outcasts of Poker Flat" (Harte), 190

Parker, Dorothy, 221

Parker, Theodore, 58

Peabody, Elizabeth, 12–14

Peabody, Mary, 12

Peabody, Sabra, and Robert Frost, 253

Peabody, Sophia, 12, 14, 15. See also Hawthorne, Sophia Peabody

Pearl of Orr's Island, The (Stowe), 101, 128

Phillips, Wendell, 58, 109, 123; reaction of, to Uncle Tom's Cabin, 124–25

Pierce, Franklin, and Hawthorne, 6, 7, 11, 17, 23–24, 26

Pink and White Tyranny (Stowe), 128

Poe, Edgar Allan: review of Hawthorne's Mosses by, 17–18, 19; on Hawthorne's Twice-Told Tales, 18; response of the young Edwin Arlington Robinson to "The Raven" of, 183

Poems (Dickinson), 175

Poems (Emerson), 53, 152

Poetry, a Magazine of Verse, 214, 265, 268

Poets in politics, 270

Poganuc People (Stowe), 101, 128

Porter, Katherine, on Katherine Mansfield, 131

Pound, Ezra, 214, 234, 265

Provincetown Players, and Edna St. Vincent Millay, 222, 224

"Raven, The" (Poe), 183, 249

Renascence (Millay), 213–15, 218, 222, 223

Representative Men (Emerson), 53

Richards, Laura E., and Edwin Arlington Robinson, 196–97

Riley, James Whitcomb, 199

Ripley, George, and Brook Farm, 13

Ripley, Rev. Ezra, 35, 49

Robinson, Dean, 179, 182, 183, 184, 185, 187, 188, 197, 202

Robinson, Edward, 179, 180–81, 184, 185, 188, 197

Robinson, Edwin Arlington, 177–205, 211, 234, 255; awkwardness of, 177; as a man born out of season, 177; and his sense of humor, 178; avoidance of "society" by, 178; growing up as "puzzlement" to his elders, 178; and his sense of destiny, 178, 189; motto of, 178; on accepting himself for what he was, 178–79; family background and boyhood of, 179–84; naming of, 179–80; and his ambition to write poetry, 183, 184, 185; and his appreciation of effectiveness of language, 183; and the tragedy of his older brother, Dean, 184; high school years of, 185, 186; determination of, not to go into business, 185; friendship of, with Dr. Alanson Tucker Schumann, 185–86, 189, 203; as youngest member of Gardiner Poetry Society, 186; writing ambitions formulating during his high school days, 186; and loss of Emma Shepherd to his brother Herman, 187–88; as a lonely outsider, committed only to becoming a poet, 188; and the Robinson household of his young manhood, 188; publication of his sonnet "Thalia," 188–89; loneliness of, as young man in Gardiner, 189; extensive and intensive reading of, 190; fierce pride of, 190–91, 195; as general handyman for his family, 191; and finding his method for presenting his characters in his poems, 191–92, 193; two years as special student at Harvard, 194; years of hard apprenticeship of, 194–95; refusal of, to become discouraged or to give up, 195; and publishing of his *The Torrent and The Night Before,* 195–96; at thirty, moves to New York, still with his ingenuous self-confidence, 198; and tough years in New York, 198; beginnings of turn in fortune for, 201; and a flurry of favorable notices by critics, 201; and Kermit Roosevelt's enthusiasm for *The Children of the Night,* 201; appointment of, by President Theodore Roosevelt

to New York Custom House, 201; and end of his long night of neglect, 201–2; honors poured out before him, continuing until day of his death, 202; as Gardiner's most famous son, 202; honorary degrees conferred on, 202; Pulitzer prizes received by, 202; on the "central message" of his poetry, 203; MacDowell Colony in Peterborough, New Hampshire, as second home of, 203; last years of, 203; assessment of, as an artist, 203–5; points of praise of critics for, 205

Robinson, Emma Shepherd (Mrs. Herman), 187–88, 197, 198, 202

Robinson, Herman, 179, 183, 185, 187, 188, 197

Robinson, Mary Elizabeth (Mrs. Edward), 179, 180, 181–82, 188, 194; death of, 196

Roller coaster: Edna St. Vincent Millay's account of ride on, 211; and world's downhill ride in 1950, 233

Roosevelt, Kermit, enthusiasm of, for Robinson's *The Children of the Night,* 201

Roosevelt, Theodore, Edwin Arlington Robinson as protégé of, 201–2

Root, Abiah, schoolgirl letters of Emily Dickinson to, 145, 146, 147–49

Sacco and Vanzetti, efforts of Edna St. Vincent Millay in behalf of, 228, 229–30

St. Nicholas Magazine, publication of youthful Edna St. Vincent Millay's poetry in, 210

Salem, of Hawthorne's youth, historical background of, 2

Sandburg, Carl, 214, 255

Sartor Resartus (Carlyle), 47, 190

Scarlet Letter, The (Hawthorne), 9, 18, 20, 23

Schumann, Dr. Alanson Tucker, and young Edwin Robinson, 185–86, 189, 203

Second April (Millay), 223

"Second Avenue" (Johns), 215

Selected Poems (Emerson), 60

Selected Poems (Frost), 269

Sewall, Ellen, and the Thoreau brothers, 77–78

Seward, Henry, 127

Sheean, Vincent, 227

Slavery: attitude of organized churchdom of New England on abolition of, 43; and *Uncle Tom's Cabin*, 99–100; increasing acuteness of issue of, in politics, 108–9; the Beecher sisters and the anti-slavery movement, 108–9; mounting clouds over issue of, 119–20

"Snow" (Frost), 268

Snow Image and Other Twice-Told Tales, The (Hawthorne), 23

"Snow-Storm, The" (Emerson), 59

Society and Solitude (Emerson), 60

Stedman, Edmund Clarence, 200

"Steepletop" home of Eugen and Edna Millay Boissevain, 229, 231, 232

Stevens, Wallace, 214, 234

"Stopping by Woods on a Snowy Evening" (Frost), 269

"Storm Fear" (Frost), 266

Stowe, Calvin, 114, 115–17; Harriet Beecher's marriage to, 116; as husband and "housefather" to Harriet, 117; transfer of, to Bowdoin College in Maine, 118; pride of, in his wife's literary ability, 119, 121, 129

Stowe, Charles, 127

Stowe, Eliza (Mrs. Calvin), 114, 115; death of, 115

Stowe, Fred, 127

Stowe, Harriet Beecher, 99–129, 200; as author of *Uncle Tom's Cabin*, 99–101, 107, 121–26; appraisal of, by literary historians and critics, 100–1; some important books by, and quality of her writing, 101; family background and childhood of, 101–5; early interest of, in religion, 104–5, 106; adolescent fantasies of, against realities to be faced, 105; writing as driving passion of, 106, 107, 108; as teacher of religion in sister Katy's school in Hartford, 107; and entering of new life on move to Cincinnati, 110; teaching in Cincinnati, 110–11; earns first money as writer with *Geography for Children*, 111; and Semi Colon Club in Cincinnati, 111–12, 116; wins first prize in magazine contest with "A New England Tale," 112; growing confidence of, in her capability as a writer, 112; visit of, to southern plantation to observe slavery firsthand, 113–14, 121; and the Cincinnati "underground," 114; friendship of, with Eliza Stowe, 114–15; marriage of, to Calvin Stowe, 116; little tales of, published in *Western Monthly*, 117; and motherhood, 117, 118; grief of, at loss of a baby, 118; happiness of, on the Stowes move to Maine and Bowdoin College, 118–19; and plans of Harper and Brothers to bring out collection of her New England stories, 119; urged by her family to "write something about slavery," 121; as most talked about woman in America after appearance of *Uncle Tom's Cabin*, 122; as an activist in anti-slavery movement, 123; literary skill and insight of, revealed in *Uncle Tom's Cabin*, 123; tumultuous reception given to, in England, 126; labeled as "fanatical agitator," 127; fame and wealth of, 127; sorrow in personal life of, 127–28; and driving force within her, 128–29; infantilism of, in her old age, 129; as the "infamous," or as the "great," little lady who "started this big war," 129

Stowe, Isabella, 127

"Success" (Dickinson), 173

Swinger of Birches, A (Cox), 273

"Sympathy" (Thoreau), 84

Taylor, Bayard, 200

Taylor, Deems, 229; on Edna St. Vincent Millay, 234–35

Teasdale, Sara, 217

Theater-going, and nineteenth-century morality, 154

Thompson, Maurice, and Frost's youthful poem "My Butterfly," 237

Thoreau, Cynthia (Mrs. John, Sr.), 66, 67, 69–70

Thoreau, Henry David, 15, 54, 57, 63–98, 169, 173, 267; and Hawthorne, 15–16, 18–19, 25–26, 65; and Emerson, 50, 53, 56, 61, 65, 74, 75–76, 79, 80, 81, 83, 94; purist habits of, 65; family background and boyhood of, 66–73; and his flute, 70; working in his father's pencil factory, 71; as student at Harvard, 71–74; and Emerson's *Nature*, 74; as school teacher, 76–78; end of his attempts at "respectable" professions, 78; on his "unsuccessfulness," 78–79; and his profession of naturalist-poet, 79; river journey of, with brother John, 79–82; as a village character defying established custom, 82; and Lydia Emerson, friendship of, 83, 85; and year spent in Emerson's home, 83–84; as tutor to children of William Emerson, 85; and the two years spent in hut built on Walden Pond, 85–92; writing done by, in Walden Pond hut, 87; and India's philosophers and poets, 90; night spent in jail, and "Civil Disobedience" essay of, 90–91; as professional surveyor, 92; and publication of *Walden*, 93–96; death of, 97; Emerson's funeral oration for, 97–98; ringing of the bells of Concord for, 98

Thoreau, John, Jr., 66, 67–68, 69, 71, 76, 77–78, 79, 84

Thoreau, John, Sr., 66, 67

"Threnody" (Emerson), 56–57

"To a Young Poet" (Millay), 235

Todd, Mabel Loomis, 133, 134; on Emily Dickinson, 134; role of, in bringing Emily Dickinson's genius before the public, 134; on funeral of Emily Dickinson, 174; and posthumous publishing of Emily Dickinson's poetry, 174

Torrent, The, and The Night Before (Robinson), 195–96

Transcendental Club, The, and Emerson, 54, 79

Transcendentalism: New England brand of, 13, 53–54; and Emerson, 13, 54; and Thoreau, 72

Transformation (Hawthorne), 24

Tristram (Robinson), 202

Trollope, Anthony, 24

Twice-Told Tales (Hawthorne), 11–12, 16, 18, 19

Uncle Tom's Cabin (Stowe), 99–101, 107, 121–26

Unitarianism: of Emerson, 41–42; Lyman Beecher's fight against, 106, 107

Untermeyer, Louis, on Robert Frost, 273

"Very Little Sphinx, A" (Millay), 226

Village Uncle, The (Hawthorne), 8

Wadsworth, Rev. Charles, and Emily Dickinson, 160–61, 166n, 169

Wagenknecht, Edward, as biographer of Harriet Beecher Stowe, 100

Wakefield (Hawthorne), 9, 21

Walden (Thoreau), 68, 70, 72, 78, 83, 84, 87, 88, 92, 93–96

"Walking" (Thoreau), 97

Ward, William Hayes, of *Independent* magazine, 237; young Robert Frost's reaction to advice from, on his plans to become a poet, 239

Wayside, home of Hawthorne, 25

We and Our Neighbors (Stowe), 128

Webster, Daniel: and Emerson, 57–58; and the slavery issue, 109, 120–21

Webster, Noah, 136

Week on the Concord and Merrimack Rivers, A (Thoreau), 19, 77, 81, 82, 87, 92–93

Weld, Theodore, and slavery issue, 112–13, 117–18, 123, 125

White, Elinor: as Robert Frost's high school sweetheart, 256–57; and Robert Frost's *Twilight*, 258, 259; marriage of, to Frost, 259. See also Frost, Elinor White

Whitman, Walt: and Emerson, 53; and young Robert Frost's dreaming himself into position of, 238, 267–68

Williams, William Carlos, 214

Wilson, Edmund, on Edna St. Vincent Millay, 235

Wine from These Grapes (Millay), 230

Witness Tree, A (Frost), 269
Wonder Book for Boys and Girls, A (Haw-
    thorne), 23
Wordsworth, William, and Emerson, 44,
    46

Writer-in-residence in American colleges
    and universities, 270

Yeats, William Butler, 265
Young Goodman Brown (Hawthorne), 9

About the Author

HILDA WHITE, author of two previous biographies for young people, does most of her writing—poetry, adult fiction, non-fiction, and book reviews—in "a cabin much like Thoreau's at Walden" near her home in upper Westchester County, New York.

Mrs. White was born in Oklahoma City, Oklahoma, and attended schools in New Orleans and in Chattanooga, Tennessee. She studied at New York University, City College of New York, and Columbia University, where she took a course in Children's Literature under Ellen Buell. In 1957, her first book, *Wild Decembers: A Biographical Portrait of the Brontës*, was published, followed by *Song Without End: The Love Story of Clara and Robert Schumann*.

Mrs. White lives in Shrub Oak, New York, with her husband, Arthur. The Whites have two married daughters, Cathy and Laurie, and a daughter in college, Julie.